All across America, on the small town Main Streets and the rural country roads, discovery awaits. It hides in the most unlikely places, behind the most unlikely ordinary facades, patiently waiting. Waiting for those that tire of the endless concrete interstates. Waiting for those truly in search of America. Waiting for those who take the time to venture off the beaten path; for those who take the time to look... to listen... to learn. To those... the true joy of discovery is there!

Mom and Pop Stores

A Country Store Compendium of Merchandising Tools for Display and Value Guide

Richard A. Penn

Pennyfield's Publishing
Box 1355 Waterloo, IA 50704-1355

ISBN-0-9664576-0-9
Library of Congress Catalog Card Number: 98-96452

Production, design and coordination; Melissa Lynch
Editorial support; Nancy Schipper

Printed in the U.S.A. by Image Graphics, Paducah, KY

Designed, produced and printed in the United States of America.

CONTENTS

General Merchandise Store interior with a wide assortment of display items. Can you find the partially hidden Gold Box gum display as seen on page 110?

A Drug Store interior with a variety of cigar display material and candy and gum jars. See if you can spot the Beechnut gum display.

About the Author

Author Rich Penn drops back in time, about 90 years, in search of Soda Fountain treasures.

Author Rich Penn brings a diverse and varied set of interests and talents to "Mom and Pop Stores." He's been an avid Country Store collector for over 25 years. But in his words, Rich calls himself an "accumulator"....which he defines as "... a collector that's run amuck and likes everything."

His collection includes country store and country store photographs, advertising, chewing gum, vending machines, slot machines, trade stimulators, Coca-Cola, juke boxes, fountain pens, pocket mirrors and among other things, "architectural building parts"! Rich also has an interest in old buildings and is restoring an historic property for inclusion on the National Register.

His educational background includes a BA in marketing and business management, from the University of Northern Iowa. He later spent nearly ten years there on the faculty in the School of Business. He also holds an MSJ in journalism from Northwestern University.

Rich spent ten years in Chicago. While there he was Vice President at J. Walter Thompson, a leading advertising agency. After leaving there, he returned to Iowa to teach at Northern Iowa and launch his own advertising agency. Rich and his wife Sharon still live in Iowa, where they both grew up. All this time he has eagerly pursued his interests in collecting and gathering material that has ended up being the basis for this book.

Feel free to contact Rich at:

R.S. Pennyfield's
Box 1355
Waterloo, IA 50704
1-319-291-6688 or 319-233-9928
WWW.MOMANDPOPSTORES.COM
E-mail: PNYFLDS@AOL.COM

Here's another Drug and Candy Store interior. This photo has a number of collectable display items. Look for the Toledo candy scale, Columbus peanut machine and the Zips Cherri-o and Grape Julep syrup dispensers.

This Drug Store interior has several elusive display items, including a rare trade stimulator; The Drobisch Star. Also look for the Primley's gum display as seen on page 110, and the sponge case, seen on page 288. Here it's actually being used for sponges!!

DEDICATION

....

As we navigate through this adventure called life, we oftentimes run into people, and events that will forever impact the course of our journey.

There have been times in my life I've had the good fortune to encounter several of those. One was meeting an exceptional man named Dick Bueschel. Reflecting on the twenty five years I knew him, I can't help but marvel at all he did and the vigor with which he did it. The years I knew him were interesting and exciting ones. And I can't look back without warm feelings about all we shared over those years.

Dick was beyond the realm of being a prolific and creative writer. He was an energetic, enthusiastic, inspiring and an always optimistic human being: even during the most difficult of times. His contagious passion for gathering, recording and organizing bits and pieces of information about wonderful "artifacts" has been one of the primary points of inspiration for me completing this book.

It was a "work in progress" for a number of years. Dick's gentle prodding and encouragement brought it to completion.

For that I will be forever grateful.

My work is dedicated to my exceptional friend Dick Bueschel. The world lost him too soon.

....

Acknowledgements

No project like this could ever be completed without the help of a
number of generous people; collectors, dealers, auctioneers and friends
in the hobby. And I've had help from all. This project has been a joy
to produce and the end product is as much a result of the extensive
help from others as it is from my own efforts.

I couldn't have begun this project without the jump start from
two people. Special thanks to **Roy Arrington** at Victorian Casino Antiques,
for allowing me to pillage his photo archives. Also special thanks to
James Julia for access to his extensive auction archives as well.
And thanks to his staff members **Irene Bolduc** and **Pam Bowman**
for their polite and professional help.

I must also thank a number of people for allowing me to photograph
their wonderful collections, or for providing me photographs;
Gary and Shirley Allen for many of the spool cabinets,
DuWayne and Pat Bakke for the superb cigar cutters and lighters,
John and Jessie Chance for magnificent dye cabinets,
Joe Cohen for his impressive assortment of clock photos,
Charlie Cook for his great ice cream dippers and......
his brother **Gordon** for the super photography,
Dr. Tom and Jackie Dupree for many unusual display cases,
Sam Elardo for fountain pen and other store displays,
Bill Enes for gum displays, but most importantly......
his well seasoned sage advice,
Jerry and Judy Fiola for all the syrup bottles,
Bill Gasperino for all kinds of country store things,
Norwood Jones at the Casey Jones Old Country Store,
Jim and Connie Leete for their cigar cutters,
Don Mangels for a super variety of just neat cases,
Norman Rubenstein for his dye cabinets
(special thanks to his dog *Rambo* for help with photography),
and
Jeff Storck, for many of the unusual scales.

Dozens of other photos and information came from a wide variety of helpful people. My thanks to them also;
Alvin and **Judy Barr**, **Dave Beck**, **Dale Bliss**,
Bill Bobbitt, **Trisha** & **Gus Brown**, **Robert Callen**,
Bart & **Deanne Charon**, **David** & **Cathy Clark**,
James Cornelius, **Dwight Craft** & **Ed Wilson**, **Rick Davis**,
Otto & **Lore Davis**, **Wilma Eyermann**, **Joe** & **Sue Ferriola**,
Marc Fortin, **Leonard** & **Charlotte Goedken**, **Dr. William Graves**,
Joe & **Sharon Happle**, **Bob Harpe**, **Dave Harris**,
Dennis & **Gloria Healzer**, **Bob Helton** & **Debra Daniels**,
Dave Hirsch, **Susan Ingram**, **Allan Katz**, **Leslie** & **Marian Kirby**,
Terry Lefler, **Ernest Lueder**, **Denny Mager**, **Andy Maravelas**,
Terry McMurray, **Doug Moore**, **Glen** & **Violet Moore**,
Wm. Morford Auctions, **Dale** & **Patsy Moran**,
Steve Mumma, **Gerald** & **Carol Newman**, **Dan Rosinski**,
Don & **Sandy Stuart**, **Skip Urich**, **Patrick Ursomano**,
Ronald VanAnda, **Amy** & **Bill Vehling**,
Marcia & **Bob Weissman**, **Terry Wright**,
and **Mark Zarkos**.

All these people were wonderfully helpful and accommodating.
To all of them I am grateful. To anyone I might
have inadvertently missed, my apologies.

And finally, to that one enthusiastic, kind and hospitable *anonymous*
collector, you know who you are......my sincere thanks!

Standing Alone

They're skeletons...ghosts...empty shells of what used to be the bustling centers of commercial and social energy. You can see what's left of them, sprinkled across America, mostly on roads less traveled. They hide in the valleys and rolling hills of Eastern America. They stand alone in the heartland—weathered and barren—in stark contrast to the plush richness that surrounds them. The American Country Store, you can see their remains, mostly where two important travel routes crossed. Where lives, commerce and culture all intersected, where the genesis of American retailing began. Where a unique part of American culture ended. The American rural country store was the helix.

No more.

A former Country Store in West Central Illinois as it looked in the summer of 1997.

The Beatty Hardware Store, Beardstown, IL. In business since the late 1800's.
The night before the selling out auction, December 1997.

Progress??

Trampled by the juggernaut of progress and the interstate highway system, they've been lost to the growth of cities and urban sprawl. Consumed by retail giants with voracious appetites for even the most remote consumers. Country stores have been swallowed, one at a time, by mass merchandisers with never ending growth objectives.

What used to be bright whitewash on clear pine clapboard siding has aged from years of inattention and turned a soft weathered gray. Narrow, tall, stately windows no longer reflect the summer sun. Instead, their cracked and broken panels reflect generations of youthful target practice. Many with tattered lace curtains waving gently in the wind at passers by. Others, covered with plywood and galvanized metal.

Ornate Victorian porch pillars and columns have vanished over the years, replaced by simple pine posts...bent from years of a burden never intended. Rooflines once supported by those long since gone columns, now sag where their simpler cousins were removed to serve a more important purpose.

Those front porches, once furnished with long pine communal benches, now sit vacant. The chatter and whispers of community news and gossip that moved down the bench line have vanished. Now replaced by the sounds of bustling communities of sparrows and starlings.

An important way of life—an institution that helped fuel 200 years of our nation's growth and development—has largely vanished. All that's left to chronicle this important piece of our history are the handful

Ziegler Store in Kimmswick, MO c.1913.

of remaining country stores and museums scattered about our nation. They give us a glimpse of this colorful period in our past. A period when—in many respects—life was much simpler. But, at the same time, it was much more challenging. That's part of the magic of country store collecting.

Much that's being collected today represents examples of how things were done in times when it wasn't so simple. Coffee grinders. Spool cabinets. Bulk grain bins. All are examples of ways to buy components that consumers then used to make other things on their own. Much of this is returning to "vogue" today. Starbucks coffee......and organic food stores, where you can buy bulk "natural" grains and fresh vegetables, both are appropriate examples. We see other examples where the country store has been "recycled" and renovated to serve a retailing purpose more in keeping with current consumer interests. This is not only true in specialty retailing.....but

in theme restaurants as well. It's also spreading to entire communities. National Main Street... the organization that helps revitalize small city downtowns has made major headway in reviving—at least the look—of old store buildings.

These photos show a small country store that still exists in a more contemporary style and use. It's in Kimmswick, MO, a tiny town where the residents have gone a long way toward retaining some of the wonderful history of the community. This store, which was the "Ziegler Store," c.1913, has been kept in nearly the same condition as it was in the early part of this century. It was a true "general merchandise" store then....and now it houses a gift shop.

Restaurateurs have also re-captured some of the magic of the early country store. All across America we see Cracker Barrels scattered along the interstates. They do a wonderful job of translating much

Ziegler Store as it looked in the summer of 1997.

of the feeling of the early country store, but in a more "contemporary" style. But perhaps one of the best examples of a country store... more in keeping with what a real store was like, is in Jackson, Tennessee. Here you can find a superb meal.....set in what feels like a very authentic country store. As the photos on the following pages illustrate, much of what this book is about is found at places like the Old Country Store at Casey Jones Village.

All of this has gone a long way toward maintaining and adding interest to country stores as a unique part of our American history. But there is one other important asset in the field of country store collecting that can't be overlooked. That asset is the network of country store collectors. These men and women passionately search out, preserve and cherish the remnants of the country store institution.

This book is a tribute to those wonderful collectors and their passion. As we talk about country stores, keep one thing in mind. The term "country store" is used rather broadly. It has become generic for anything that is "store" or commerce related. That's fine, since that's the broad view covered in this book. Country store could mean a traditional rural country general merchandise store. It could also mean a drug store, a hardware store, a jewelry store or anything commerce or store related. It also could cover a broad period of time. Most of what's in this book might have been used in stores between 1850 and the end of the first half of the twentieth century. So, when this writer uses the term, "country store," it's generic. But there are purists that believe true country stores were found only in the country. As such....the merchandise found there was much broader in nature, especially when compared to early stores in small towns, which had begun to become more specialized. To those purists...please forgive me.

Exterior and interior shots
of the Old Country Store in
Casey Jones Village
Jackson, Tennessee.

Ornate walnut, onyx and marble
soda fountain back bar, still in use.

View of soda fountain area, showing
leaded glass hanging drug store
mortar trade sign.

Interior shots of the
Old Country Store in
Casey Jones Village
Jackson, Tennessee.

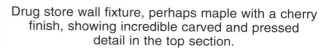

Drug store wall fixture, perhaps maple with a cherry finish, showing incredible carved and pressed detail in the top section.

Lower left shows German silver jewelry case (see page 119) on top of oak, curved glass cigar case. Below, oak seed counter serves as check out.

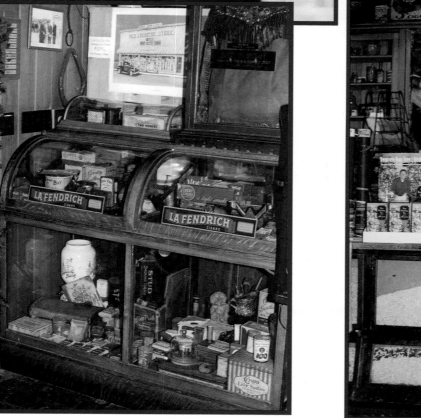

Evolution

To better appreciate the unique charm of the country store...and associated collectibles, it's important to have some understanding of the evolution of the country store as an institution. To do that, it's interesting to look to scholarly works on retailing. One of the academic theories that helps to explain why country stores were such treasure troves of a wide variety of interesting artifacts is the "Wheel of Retailing."

This theory examines retailing and purports to explain how stores evolve from low-status, low-margin, low-price stores with limited goods, into more elaborate stores. These more elaborate stores offered more extensive lines, with more service, in nicer surroundings....and of course, at higher prices. What this did, was present opportunities... again.... at the lower end of the circle. This evolution was nothing more than a reflection of the efforts by retailers to compete. And... they did compete. As communities grew and prospered, the retailer was looked to as a source for more than just life's essentials.

The country store was selling virtually everything; textile goods, food goods, hardware goods, feed, seed, firearms, toys, watches, clocks and jewelry. You name it, the country store was the source!

If you look carefully at the store photo from Kimmswick, (page 12) you see a typical example. It's a "General Merchandise Store," selling Dry-Goods,

Specialty Store selling hard goods.

Groceries, Watch Repairing, and Engraving. If you study the windows, you can see it must be near Christmas time. Both windows faintly show a sign with Santa Claus. On the left, a nice selection of dolls and children's toys. On the right, neckties, clocks and glassware. A true general merchandise store!

Then...as this evolution continued, and consumers sought more choices, specialty stores evolved. Specialty stores took many of these lines and focused on just them. The hardware store, the drug store and the jewelry store are common examples.

You can see this in picture form as you look at some of the interior photos of very early country stores. They show merchandise lines that cover not much more than the bare essentials. Other stores show a wide range and depth of merchandise. Then, finally came the stores that offered single or a very narrow group of product lines.

Because of this slow evolution...country stores were, and are, a source for an incredible variety of display vehicles, cases, counters and containers. From chewing gum to chewing tobacco. From watches to wringers. From ribbon racks to rope racks...you could find all of them...and more, in the country store!

And the search for these treasures can take you interesting places. If you're serious about collecting, there are a number of places to find country store collectibles. Antique shops, some of the better malls and

Specialty Store selling soft goods.

the bigger shows, especially the advertising shows, all are good places to begin your search. But by far, the most fun is the closing out auctions of old stores. If you watch the trade papers—several times each year you'll see auctions like these. For me, they've always been worth the time and travel.

In the last several years, this author has been to store auctions all over the midwest. Each time, I've come home with a treasure. Not always a bargain, but a treasure just the same.

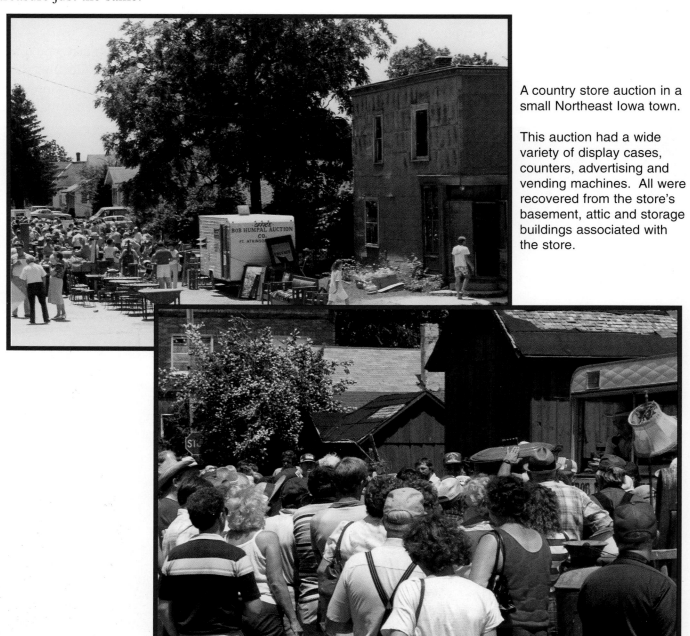

A country store auction in a small Northeast Iowa town.

This auction had a wide variety of display cases, counters, advertising and vending machines. All were recovered from the store's basement, attic and storage buildings associated with the store.

This shows the interior, and some of the contents of the Beatty Hardware Store, in Beardstown, IL. The closing out auction, in the fall of 1997, included considerable new old stock from the store's beginning in the late 1800's. There was also a wide variety of cabinets, display cases, advertising and even, still in their original wooden cases, panels and trim for tin ceilings.

The "Garner" Country Store, c.1920, Western Mississippi, Spring of 1998.

In this General Merchandise Store, notice the fresh pies. They were probably exchanged by a customer for goods or credit. To the right of the pies sits a wooden Zeno gum vender. On the opposite counter is a Dayton scale.

Cigar Store with social area in back, showing both a floor card gambling machine and a counter machine.

Because the country store sold everything...everyone went to the country store. In addition to providing staple merchandise, many country stores served other uses. Some were also the post office. They also served as a marketplace for local farmers to exchange produce, eggs and baked goods for credit, cash or other merchandise. From the stockmen to the prairie farmer to the small town banker, they all were visitors or shoppers at the country store. It was the only game in town. And in many cases it served that purpose literally. The country store also functioned as a social center of sorts.

The potbelly stove sat at the rear of the store. Often times standing on a firebrick platform. It provided the focus and warmth for all the neighborly games of checkers and local gossip. In later years...with the advent of many of the gambling devices offered by the cigar and candy salesman...the rear of the store also offered more sophisticated forms of entertainment! This photo is an interesting example. Here's a store, probably a tobacco or cigar store, that offered not only merchandise, but a game of billiards, or you could even try your luck at the slot machine! Many an old slot machine has been uncovered in the back room of an old country store!

If there *was* a central place of commerce or recreation in many rural communities in America, it was the country store. But as communities grew, the country store continued to evolve.

The social center is at the rear, with an early Mills slot machine.

Town vs. Country

That evolution was indeed a function of competition. It caused the country store to either broaden product line offerings, to compete with specialty stores in town, or suffer the risk of losing the business of customers willing to wait for the weekly trip to town. Again...growth caused country stores to continue to add product lines and all the wonderful merchandising tools that went along with them.

Mass Merchandise

That begins to explain why you would see things in country stores as diverse as cigar counters and cases next to clock and jewelry counters. Today's retailers think they've discovered new retailing strategies, when they talk about "scrambled" merchandising; stocking anything a consumer might buy fairly often. But that kind of retailing has been around for a long time. And for a number of good reasons.

Not only were manufacturers of goods constantly trying to add points of distribution, but just like today, the retailers of 1900 were always on the look out for new products to sell their customers! And many of the stocking offers from nationally branded products were too good for the merchant to pass up. Many of the distribution strategies that are in wide use today, have their beginnings in early country store selling methods. More about this later.

Specialty Stores

After the Civil War, as the industrial growth of America continued to boom, communities were growing and bursting at their seams. As Americans continued to move west, towns sprang up throughout the heartland. As those towns grew and prospered, specialty retailing began to flourish. Now, instead of the country store providing everything, separate stores were offering specialty lines of goods. The drug store, the millinery store, the hardware store, the

Mass Merchandise type General Store. Kluckhone Bros. Store in Klemme, IA c.1905.

cigar store...and others, all offered a wider line of merchandise and more depth in the lines they offered. Instead of one brand in a product category...now there might be two...or even three. This really marked the beginning of the "Brand Wars." Many brands of merchandise we have in our cupboards today have their roots in this time period. In the first part of the 20th century, names like Coats' & Clark's, Gillette, Nabisco, Parker Pens, Aunt Jemima, and Wrigley's Gum were fierce and aggressive competitors in their respective categories.

These specialty stores not only had special lines of merchandise, that merchandise required specialized display material. As you look at some of the old trade catalogues from fixture companies, you can see the different varieties.

Drug store floor fixtures had their own look, as did jewelry store floor fixtures. Wall fixtures from each were different as well. Drug store wall fixtures weren't required to be as deep as the fixtures in a jewelry store, where they displayed larger merchandise. Drug store wall fixtures were for displaying packaged goods and bottles. Because of that, to use those fixtures today requires special smaller item display use. Store keepers today, who value shelf space, prefer the deeper shelves.

The product display materials had their own personalities as well. For example, fountain pen display cases, usually found in jewelry stores, were much more "reserved" in design. They were designed to make a quality presentation of the product for view and little else. The store keeper did the selling. The display materials for drugstores, on the other hand, were often times intended to merchandise product. Display material for personal care items, especially, helped sell the product with colorful graphic selling messages.

Specialty Store selling textiles and soft goods.

Branding

Many of these companies were new and so were their brands. To compete, branding became an important activity for many of these relatively new companies. They were trying to sell their goods in a newly "National" market. But the use of the tools for branding were vastly different then.

These brands (Nabisco, Campbell's Soups, Wrigley's, Aunt Jemima, etc.) were all in their Introductory Life Cycle stage. They were not well known. Many were in new industries. The fountain pen industry... spool thread... chewing gum...all were fairly new in the late 1800's. Because of that, these companies needed to reach a broad consumer market. They had to get as much product exposure as they could. And they didn't have the luxury of reaching 50 or 60 million Americans through network television. The selling effort was almost one customer at a time!

Advertising

In the late 1800's there were national media, but not like we know them today. It was all print, newspaper and magazine, and all relatively low circulation. Radio didn't become a practical medium until well into the 20th century. Television didn't really become useful as an advertising vehicle until the 1950's. All that remained was print and outdoor advertising. Outdoor advertising was primarily a local medium. You could see large sheet posters in some of the bigger cities, and in the late 1800's trolley cards even became an advertising medium.

So how did this impact country store collectibles? You can see the answer if you have looked closely at photographs of the interiors of country stores.

Distribution

Because national companies wanted to grow and be successful, the most effective way to do that was to dominate distribution at the store level. The tools used were not a lot different than they are today. Display material was offered free, or at very low cost. There were all kinds of stocking promotions. This was especially true for the candy and gum companies. Wrigley's Gum is a classic example. They offered all kinds of merchandise to retailers, free with orders. Candy scales, freight carts, even gambling machines.

Wrigley's trade stimulator card front and back offered free with eight boxes of 5c packs of gum.

Wrigley, like the Coca-Cola company, used very sophisticated methods to build distribution....and at the same time, pull the product through the distribution channels. The result? Today, there are all kinds of wonderful things that are carryovers from these promotions. Much of the material was for point of sale. And collectors aggressively hunt for these.

Drug or Cigar Store filled with point of sale display items.

Point of Sale

Because there were few tools for competing at the national level, these companies were masters at using point of sale material: the final point of decision making for the consumer. So point of sale was not only used to display and protect product...but also to help in the product branding. Much of what is most desirable today is so because of the wonderful point of sale graphics. Graphics incorporated the extensive use of early color lithography, die-cut metal and cardboard, embossing on metal, wood and composition, and high quality construction.

Not only was this period point of sale material beautiful, it was highly functional! One reason was much of the merchandise was high value and needed security. We don't think much about having a pack of gum displayed openly. But a 5 cent pack of gum in 1900 was expensive. So, much of the merchandise

needed protection, for security and also from the elements! Many of these stores were heated by coal or wood burning stoves. They produced heat, and soot. That didn't add to the flavor of candy or chewing gum, and it didn't add to the color of spool silk!

Because much of this display material used quality materials and was well built, it survived. It also found secondary uses. Many display cabinets have been found with the original etched glass, that showed brand names, replaced with plain glass. Then it could be used for other merchandise. Many a wonderful gum case has been found without the original marquee. Many a spool cabinet has been found converted to a file cabinet or a miscellaneous hardware depository, losing its wonderful lettering and artwork in the process. But....at least these alternative uses helped much of this early display material survive. As a result, it's collected, treasured and restored by those of us that have hunted it out!

Understanding Value

The most challenging part of this book was developing a method that would be both equitable and useful for addressing price or value. Unfortunately, it was quickly determined that methodology in setting value isn't a perfect science. In fact it's not methodology at all. Instead it's much closer to an art than science. Because of that, I suspect there will be some that will respond to the values on certain things in this book as being too high. Others might respond just the opposite: the values on those same things are too low. When there's not a true market, in the economic sense, both points of view could be correct. Each point of view can reflect the individual circumstances of the person holding that view. Therefore, their individual assessments of value could be vastly different and correct in both instances.

That might also suggest that books that say a given item is worth "x" amount are oversimplifying the dynamics of the antique market. If an item is worth "x," does it always sell for that amount? It's not likely. In fact, that's one of the elements that makes the antique market such an exciting one. It's truly dynamic and so are values. In fact many times, perhaps most times, selling price is set by negotiation between the seller and the buyer. So there are no absolute values. They're a function of a wide range of considerations that affect both the buyer and the seller. But before we discuss those factors, we must recognize there are two levels of value, retail and wholesale.

This book deals with estimating retail values and it discusses some of the factors affecting those values. But there is another equally important level of price and/or value: the wholesale level. If you're selling—and there's urgency to sell—you may have to sell in the wholesale market, to a dealer. This market can reflect a different set of considerations and different prices. To sell to a dealer, you must expect to sell at something below top retail values. The only incentive for a dealer to buy something is because he or she has a potential profit margin. So, if you're selling in the wholesale market, expect to get less than top retail. Many times wholesale prices are half of retail, and sometimes, for items that may require considerable time and effort to find a retail buyer, wholesale prices might be even less than half of retail. These margins are required to make the marketplace work.

With that as a baseline, we'll try to discuss some of the factors that affect value.

First, to better understand value, you must begin from a very simple premise: *things are without value until someone wants to buy them.* Then value becomes a function of a number of variables. Those variables could be divided into at least four major areas; Market Factors, Product—or item—Factors, Buyer Factors, and Seller Factors.

Market Factors

These are factors we can't control as a buyer or a seller, but they can impact our assessment of value.

 * *Cost of capital* impacts both the buyers ability to buy and the sellers need to sell.

 * *Geography* can affect the number of buyers and sellers. Certain things have stronger demand in certain areas. Some things have greater supply in certain areas.

 * *Seasonality* can affect both the buyers willingness to buy.....and the sellers willingness to sell.

 * *Publicity* can also affect the buyers and sellers interests in certain antique and collectible categories.

 * *Decorator trends* can quickly stimulate interest and demand in certain antique categories, they can also direct interest away.

 * *What's happening* in films and the "Arts".

Product Factors

These factors are discussed in more detail a bit later. but first, here's a summary:

 * *Condition* can have a major difference in what something is worth.

 * *Rarity* can influence value upward, if there's sufficient demand.

 * *Quality* of an item also has a great influence on value.

 * *Location*, geographically, also influences value. Demand can vary regionally.

Buyer Factors

As a buyer, these are the elements in your domain. You can have a direct impact on them. You can control them.

* *Ability to buy*: Not all buyers have the financial ability to buy what they want.

* *Authority to buy*: Sometimes purchases are joint decisions.

* *Willingness to buy*: Even though buyers might have both ability and authority, they must then be willing to buy something. These three previous factors can translate into economic demand.

* *Experience*: A buyer's experience with the market, the category and his or her experience as a negotiator can influence selling price.

* *Knowledge:* Knowledge within a category can impact both willingness and buying urgency. The more you know......the more likely you are to act on intuition, or qualified judgement.

* *Urgency to fill a collection*, or to get a piece in particularly good condition can effect the need to act now!

Seller Factors

* *Economic Issues*;

-Cost of Goods: Often times, when a dealer has a generous margin, he/she has more pricing flexibility.

-Inventory Carrying Costs: The amount of revenue tied up in inventory can influence sellers need to sell, discounting merchandise may cost less than borrowing operating capital.

-Cash Flow Circumstances: There are times when cash flow circumstances require selling, even below merchandise cost.

* *Ability to Replace Inventory*: When it comes time to sell, dealers always worry about their ability to replace quality merchandise.

* *Knowledge*: A dealers level of knowledge, just like the buyers, can influence willingness to negotiate prices....up or down.

* *The "Like" Factor*: This can be one of the most illusive factors in the market. A seller sometimes likes something at a level much higher than it might realistically be worth. That makes price more firm.

Most of these factors are beyond the buyers control. But all have an impact on both value and buying dynamics. In fact, the **Buyer Factors** are the only variables here that can be controlled by the buyer. And one could argue those aren't completely controllable. So when you examine all these variables and how their levels of influence can impact each other, you could likely have hundreds of different combinations of active influencers on every purchase. So, it would seem naive to say any given item has a specific value at all times in all circumstances. That simply isn't possible in a free market system. That's why most things float within ranges in value. That's why all good price guides try to say prices are only a guide. This one is no different in that sense. It is different, in that this discussion has tried to offer a better understanding of why that situation exists.

So, as you can see, value is a complex issue and it involves a wide variety of factors. We'll try to discuss the most significant factors. But to understand value, you must first begin from the premise we defined earlier. ***Things are without value, until someone wants to buy them.*** How much they want to buy it is the true measure of something's worth. How much they want to buy it (the strength of demand) is also a function of a number of other factors. Some are quantitative....some are qualitative.

We'll discuss quantitative first. Essentially, these factors include the *rarity* of something and the *condition* of the particular piece. Even though there are some that would suggest condition is qualitative, much has been done in recent years, in several categories, to try to quantify condition in a manner similar to coins. Petretti's work in Coca-Cola collectibles is one good example. We also see quantitative scales for condition of soda pop machines and juke boxes.

So, we'll try to at least give an idea of the variances in value that are a result of the condition of a piece. But let's discuss rarity first.

Rarity

I'm sure we've all seen something marked in an antique shop with a little sticker proclaiming "Very Rare." Because something is rare doesn't necessarily mean it has any value at all.

I can recall seeing an old hornet's nest in an interesting country antique shop I visited in Western Ohio. It was an unusual looking piece and it had one of those signs on it; "Rare Hornet's Nest." And I must admit, although I don't see a lot of these, just because they're rare doesn't mean they have great value! I'm sure there are those that find this kind of primitive piece interesting and even decorate with them! But that kind of "rare" item doesn't have the same collector interest as a rare coffee tin or a rare syrup dispenser. Rarity is only a valid consideration for value, when there is significant enough demand to drive the price up.

If there are more people collecting the item, than there are items, then rarity adds value.

One of the things that makes collecting country store things so exciting, is most things *are* relatively rare. Additionally, they have fairly strong collector interest. So, when you find something that's a bargain, it's especially exciting. Consider all the things about stores that are collected.....and then think about the number of stores there were. You begin to appreciate the relative consideration of rarity. In many communities, there was only one store. That store may have had only one advertising regulator clock, one floor coffee grinder, one spool cabinet, and one or two candy display cases. When you compare that to household antiques, you can better understand the interest in country store pieces. In a small town with one store and two hundred homes, there were likely two hundred kitchen clocks for every store regulator clock. So, rarity can be a factor. But it only adds value if it's coupled with demand.

Condition

Condition is another factor that effects value. As you look at the things pictured in this book, you'll see that most are in quite nice condition. Many are in excellent condition. And some are in near mint original condition. You'll also find a few examples of things that are in below average condition and in need of restoration.

Some things can be restored to enhance the value. But....as a general rule, the more desirable piece is something that is complete, and in wonderful original condition.

When you start to look at the value of things in poor condition—especially with missing parts or pieces, value can drop off sharply. Many times I've overheard comments at shows, where someone is looking at a piece and they're saying to their friend,

> *".....Oh my.....look at the price on that!! I have one JUST like it at home. I had no idea it was worth that much. The only thing ...... mine doesn't have those handles.....and it doesn't have that writing all over it!!!"*

Unfortunately then......the "at home" piece in question, isn't just like the one being examined.

And....the piece in question is likely not worth as much as the one examined. Interestingly, when you look at auction prices on some things in this book, there are price differentials as much as 200-300% on some of the same things. That differential is many times, although not always, a function of condition. Things that are in excellent original condition vary substantially in value, when compared to things that are in average....or below average condition. And that's an unexplained factor in many of the current price guides: those that just list items. In one guide there will be a listing that might be half of—or twice as much as—the same listing in another guide. Without knowing condition and other factors, it's difficult to determine which is the more appropriate price. When, in reality, both might be.

When trying to assess the effect condition might have on value, it's helpful to try and determine where the condition might fall, in quintiles.

Mint condition items carry the highest premium. Again, this is a subjective determination. But to help support value determination, here's a "rule of thumb" method using indexes and five levels of condition.

Condition	Value Index
Mint	200+
Excellent	150+
Good	100
Fair	50
Poor	25

Indexes are a simple way of comparing things to a base value. The base value has an index of 100. All comparisons are against that base. We're going to assume things in "Good" condition are our base. But keep in mind, most of what you will see in this book is in better than good condition. So values are set accordingly.

Here's how this might work. If something is in good condition (which we'll define shortly) it might be worth—as an example—$200. That same thing, in mint condition, with an index of 200, would be worth twice that, or $400. In contrast, the same piece in poor condition might be worth only $50. (An index of 25—or 25% of the base value where the index is 100.)

Here's how we've tried to define levels of quality.

1. **Mint**. This means a piece is in perfect or near perfect original condition. This should not be a restored piece. The mint piece may have minor scratches or blemishes. But artwork or lithography should be bright and crisp and clean. On wooden pieces, the finish should be original. But it can be professionally cleaned. Mint pieces command the highest prices.

2. **Excellent**. Much of what we find that is restored probably falls in the excellent condition category. Still, the piece should be complete. It should have all original parts, but exact replacement parts can be ok, if used sparingly. If wood, it may be refinished. If the piece has artwork, some may be restored or inpainted. Or, if the art is in great original condition, even with a few flaws, it's better to leave the flaws. Remember, if you have a piece that is in great original condition, evaluate carefully how much restoration you want to put into it.

3. **Good**. This probably represents "average." Good condition can show the wear and tear of the years. Most of the artwork would still be there and legible. This may—or may not—be a refinished piece. Some of the original parts may be missing or replaced. But the piece would show well as it is and make a useful addition to anyone's home or collection.

4. **Fair**. This level of condition means the piece needs attention. If refinishable, that probably is worth considering. It might have missing or damaged pieces. Artwork is probably incomplete or discolored. Metal might show some rust and pitting. Wood might have the finish worn through or show aging and some dry rot. Surfaces might show scratches or gouging. This level of condition can often times be brought to "good" with appropriate care.

5. **Poor**. This level of condition usually means a basket case or a parts piece. It's substantially incomplete, meaning, it's missing key components: the kind of components that can't be replaced or remanufactured at reasonable costs. Many times, a piece that looks to be in fair condition, is bought as such. Then after close inspection, is determined to be in poor condition and works its way to the back of the project list. There it sits until another one like it

comes along. Then, many times, the two are made into one. Assess purchases in this condition carefully.

When looking at the pieces in this book, keep in mind most things are in at least excellent condition. Many things would fall into the mint classification.

Remember, the values are set accordingly. So if you see something in this book that's in excellent condition—and it's valued at $500, that value reflects the condition you see. If you're considering buying, or selling, a piece you'd grade as *good*, there's a difference in value. Excellent indexes at 150. Good is 100. So the excellent piece would be worth 50% more than the good piece. In this example, where the excellent piece is valued at $500, the same piece in good condition might be worth around $335.

Here's another way to look at that. If the piece was in good condition, valued at $335 with an index of 100, it would increase to around $500 (index of 150) in excellent condition, and around $670 (index of 200) in mint condition.

Economics

There is another important issue to keep in mind, especially as you consider values on highly sought after, very rare items. In the last several years there have been a number of rare advertising items that have come up for auction, with stunning results. In November of 1997, a rare 1903 Coca-Cola tray/sign was auctioned. The pre sale estimate was $10-15M. It sold for over $80,000, plus commission.

Rare 1903 Coca-Cola tray/sign.

In the fall of 1997, there was a significant collection of soda fountain items that were sold at auction in Colorado Springs. Much

Rear view of a J. & P. Coats' cherry spool cabinet in near mint condition. The pressed composition panel is in perfect condition.

Front view of a J. & P. Coats' cherry spool cabinet in near mint condition. This cabinet has all original drawer pulls and perfect drawer panels. This cabinet is in excellent condition and would have a value index between 150 and 200.

of the collection was Hires Root Beer, including a very rare ceramic syrup dispenser. A similar dispenser sold the previous year in the mid thirty thousand dollar range. The dispenser sold in 1997 went for well over a hundred thousand dollars. So how do you explain this variance? Perhaps it's "situational economics." Let's talk about economics. Simple economics accounts for much of the baseline value of antiques. But not all of it. And... the more there are of any given commodity... the more stability there is in price. But the inverse of that can be true as well.

Rear view of a J. & P. Coats' painted walnut spool cabinet in fair to good condition. The pressed panel has repaired damage.

Front view of a J. & P. Coats' walnut spool cabinet in fair to good condition. This cabinet is missing drawer pulls and drawer trim. This cabinet would have a value index between 50 and 100.

Assuming, of course, demand is fairly constant.

For example, if you look at tobacco tins, you see a good illustration. There are literally hundreds—perhaps thousands—of different kinds of tobacco tins. And, there are likely thousands of different examples of some of the more common tins; the Lucky Strike Flat Fifty for example. It's not likely that you would

Common Lucky Strike tin.

expect to see dramatic changes in the value of that tin, since there are so many. Most collectors should be able to find a very good example, at quite reasonable prices. The Orcico tobacco tin is a different case. It's uncommon, very attractive and highly sought after. When one comes up for auction, its selling price is more a function of nuances of condition and who will spend the most, rather than someone's—even an expert's—opinion on what it's worth.

You see this proven over and over again as the rarity and quality of items come into play. On excellent examples of rare and sought after items, there are different factors at work in the market place. Price seems to be highly inelastic and is a function of the buyers ability and willingness to pay, more so than anything else!! Estimates of value often times evaporate in the heat generated by spirited bidding. As the rarity of an item increases, and

Rare Orcico tin.

the number of collectors pursuing the item also increases, so does the volatility of change in selling price. Especially at auction. Price becomes much less rational and much more emotional!

As you look through this book, keep in mind that the prices are a guide. They reflect the estimated value of things that are like the items pictured, and are in like condition, under reasonable and normal market circumstances.

There are also qualitative factors that affect value.

These factors are even more difficult to account for. But, they're an equally important area to consider when assessing value. The first area we'll consider is the overall desirability of something.

Desirability

Desirability is a very personal factor. But it's also made up of a number of very reasonable considerations. For example, what artistic value does a piece have? Very simply, is it attractive to look at? Is it well proportioned? Is it well designed? Does it have interesting detail? If a piece has all these characteristics, it's probably going to be much more desirable than one that doesn't. And these factors are irrespective of whether or not it might be rare. A beautiful piece has value because of its beauty.

Country store collectibles also have value because of decorator appeal. That appeal is a function of not only beauty, but how a piece can be used. That's an issue that needs to be plugged into the value equation as well. Decorator appeal can be a very important factor. And many times, things that a serious collector wouldn't find appealing, work just the opposite for decorators.

That's especially true when it comes to painted things. Many people that decorate with antiques, love early pieces that have been painted. Not necessarily originally, but have been painted with some of the attractive early country colors, especially blue. A "purist" collector would be offended at paint, if it weren't part of the

"Excelsior" showcase in use at the Casey Jones Country Store in Jackson, TN.

original piece. So paint isn't always bad. It depends on how the collector wants to use the piece.

Utility is another factor that falls under decorator value. Many country store pieces have wonderful contemporary uses. This dramatically enhances value. You see that in categories like spool cabinets. They make splendid end tables. They also make great filing cabinets. And seed counters make wonderful kitchen counters. All these additional decorator uses bring additional demand to the marketplace. That helps push value upward. If a piece has beauty and some functional use, it is likely to be more valuable than if it just had beauty.

Quality

Quality is another issue that always effects value.

When it comes to a clear definition, defining quality can be illusive. Yet we all know it when we see it. It's reflected in construction methods, detail, material, color..... and the amount of color.

In general, country store items were well built because they were intended for commercial use. Many of these pieces were factory

Joint construction shown in the J.W. Storandt Mfg. Co., Rochester N.Y., fixture catalogue.

No 56 A

No 52 A

built and mass produced, with excellent grade clear lumber. Cabinets and cases were constructed with mitered or dovetailed joints and have survived their working life to be appreciated by today's collectors.

The value of a piece is enhanced when it reflects quality construction.

Much of this display material was built and designed to incorporate considerable flourish and detail. Both of which were quite typical design goals of the Victorian era. If you look closely at much of the detail on spool cabinets especially, you see this well illustrated. Look at the back plates for the drawer pulls on the Brainerd & Armstrong spool cabinets pictured on pages 55 & 56. You see the kind of detail that can dramatically enhance the value of a piece.

Brainerd & Armstrong spool cabinet pull.

When display material incorporates graphics, you see some of the Victorian craftsman's finest work. Medicine and dye cabinets are brilliant examples.

Not only is much of the artwork produced on embossed tin panels, it's lithographed in multiple colors, sometimes as many as ten. Even with today's technology, maintaining accurate color registration when printing multiple colors is extremely difficult.

That makes some of these earlier pieces even more magnificent.

As you can see, quality is made up of many variables. And it can be very difficult to compare across similar pieces, each displaying different elements of quality. But there is always one good rule of thumb. The importance of quality is something that is fairly constant. And it's an attribute that has value over time. So when you're looking at two similar pieces...

with varying levels of quality, it's usually the wiser decision to buy all the quality you can afford.

Location

Where something is located can also effect its value. Much like "basis" in the commodity market, the value of something must reflect the cost of getting it to the geographic market with the strongest demand.

Jacob's ice-cooled candy case in use at Casey Jones Country Store.

We see that in country store collectibles as well. Additionally, interest in certain kinds of country store collectibles varies as you move through the country.

This author observed a perfect example of that at an auction in the fall of 1997. There was a store cabinet at the auction that stimulated considerable interest, in spite of its condition and the fact that it was well anchored to several other large fixtures. The cabinet was primitive and painted. It needed considerable work to remove it and to get it in saleable condition. The bidding stopped somewhere around $400, which seemed to be appropriate, given the condition and other factors.

About three months later I saw the piece at a major show in Nashville. It looked much nicer, having been cleaned and put in very "showable" condition.

It was priced around $1,100 and sold quickly to another dealer. That dealer then priced the piece at $1,800. In each circumstance, the price seemed reasonable. Each dealer added value, whether through improving the condition, or by adding logistical value by taking it to a stronger market. So location does change value.

In the Midwest and areas where there's a strong agricultural base, you see that reflected in strong prices for country store items that relate to agriculture. Veterinarian medicine and supply cabinets, cream separator parts cabinets, feed and seed cabinets and hardware and supply cabinets, all have a strong demand in the agricultural Midwest.

Shot cabinet displayed in Casey Jones Country Store, see page 86.

As you move North or West, you can see stronger demand for sporting goods material. Ammunition display material, shot cabinets, fishing equipment displays, trapping and hunting supplies... all seem to have demand that varies with geography. As a shopper, there are two ways to look at this. Because of these regional differences, as a collector you would expect to find more of this type of collectible, in the appropriate geographic area. And...likely...you will. You might also expect to find higher prices.

There are also geographic differences that are a result of the way our nation grew.....from East to West. You would expect to find earlier country store pieces

As found, very good Humphreys' Vet cabinet.

in the East.......and more of them. That makes sense simply because the Eastern country store had at least a fifty year jump start on the Midwest country store.

Because of that.....you could expect to find earlier examples of country store items at many of the larger Eastern markets....and the Eastern auctions. And you do! So, that's always something to keep in mind when you're planning your next shopping vacation.

Display Manufacturers were also regional. Once you start to examine who the manufacturers were of some of this display material, you see they were equally diverse as well. This also explains much of what are the subtle differences in commercial display cases.

There were hundreds of manufacturers, all over the country; Denver, CO; Saginaw, MI; Quincy, IL; St Louis, MO; Buffalo, NY; San Francisco, CA... just to name a few. They all made quite similar display cases and counters. Some fixtured entire stores, like the J.W. Storandt Mfg. Co., in Rochester, NY.

It's also interesting to note the materials used in these display fixtures. Cabinets and cases that were made in

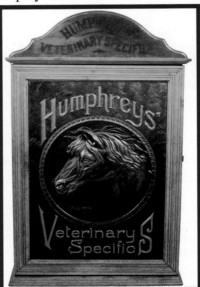
Mint quality Humphreys' Vet cabinet.

the Midwest, especially the upper Midwest, were often found in oak. That was a wood plentiful to the Michigan furniture industry, and it was equally common to the fixture industry. Finer woods, walnut and cherry, were often found in fixtures intended for stores other than the typical small country "general" store. The drug store or the jewelry store often had these fixtures made of more higher quality woods.

As part of collecting, it's always interesting to explore these differences. What was this piece used for? What kind of a store might it have served? When was it made? Who made it? When you examine the manufacturers name plate on a display piece, you often times wonder, "how did that piece get all the way to here, from there?" That's one more interesting way to collect, by cabinet manufacturer.

All of these elements make collecting country store things interesting and fun. They also have a major impact on how the value of a piece is established. That makes collecting much more complex than it might seem on the surface.

So, how do we determine value?

Given the extensive bundle of considerations.... you can see that arriving at the value of something can be a difficult project. All of these factors affect a sellers willingness to sell and they also affect the buyers willingness to buy. Price is ultimately determined, when the two of those meet, in an unencumbered marketplace.

What we've tried to do in this book, is to look at prices at which these items have been offered for sale. Then we've compared that to what things have actually sold for, both at auction and on the open market. On top of all that, we've put the good judgement of a number of advanced collectors to work. What we've ended up with is a subjective evaluation, using fairly objective information. But, this is still just a guide. And that's all it's intended to be. There are dozens of factors....many we've already pointed out....that can affect what something might be worth. Use this guide as a tool. What something is worth to you is, simply, all that you're willing to pay for it.

Jewelry Store designed and fitted in solid mahogany and rosewood by the J.W. Storandt Mfg. Co., Rochester N.Y. for F.S. Thompson, Gloucester, Mass.

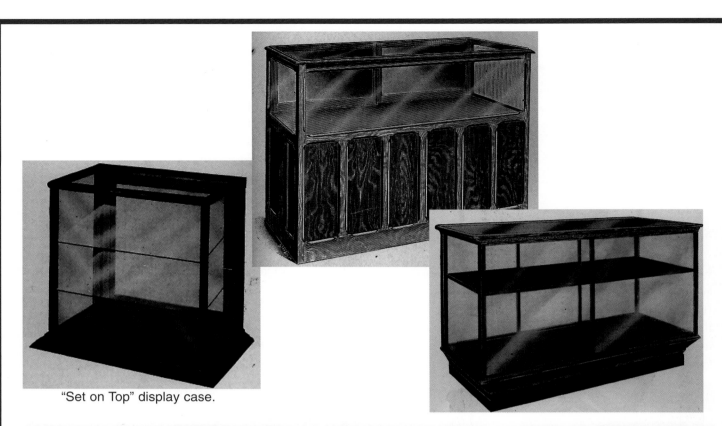

"Set on Top" display case.

Drug Store designed and fitted in solid Mahogany by the J.W. Storandt Mfg. Co.,
Rochester N.Y., for Blau & Co., Rochester, N.Y.

Barber fixtures from the Hatch Barbers' Supply Co., Cedar Rapids, IA, and Kraut & Dohnal, Chicago, IL, catalogues.

Self-locking showcase, cash register and money drawer. See page 142.

This store keeper stands vigil with his German Shepard dog, guarding the Mother's Bread case. Look at the interesting die-cut cardboard signs, on the right, for Butternut Bread and Pinch Hitter Tobacco.

This photo, c.1930, shows a smiling store keeper. He is no doubt pleased with the 75 cent broom special. Look closely in the rear, at the right. A life size die-cut cardboard figure stands offering Hills Bro's coffee.

These men are standing near a cigar case that has an early Griswold cigar trade stimulator on top.
Can you see it? Look directly next to the shoulder of the clerk standing on the left.

This store interior, probably Midwestern, c.1910, shows a complete Independent Baking Company
Biscuit rack. A Selz Shoe chair sits in front. Can you find the "Whites Yucatan Gum" sign?

This drug store interior shows a number of interesting things. But you have to look close. Can you see the Diamond Dye "Governess" and the large Sanford's Inks display? Both in the very rear.

This long narrow Drug Store displays a variety of perfumes and personal care items. The young clerk, on the left, stands in front of a baker's rack being used as a book display.

Section 1

Spool Thread
•
Spool Silk
•
Dyes & Coloring
•
Ribbon

DISPLAY CABINETS

Seed
•
Nuts & Bolts
•
Shot Powder
•
Separator & Parts
•
Tobacco
•
Needle
•
Medicine

A. **Chadwick's**; Spool cabinet; 9-drawer, oak, reversed lettering is silver foil under black glass, c.1910, 25"W x 18"D x 22"H. $1600-1900

B. **Clark's**; Mile-End spool cabinet; 6-drawer, cherry, carved and pressed drawer fronts, brass pulls with pressed spool design and brass bales, ornate trim on front corners, paneled on two sides, flat back, c.1900, 25"W x 18"D x 22"H. $1100-1300

C. **Clark's**; O.N.T. spool cabinet; 2-drawer, walnut, ruby glass front, c.1910, 21-1/2"W x 14-1/2"D x 7"H. $350-450

A.   **Clark's**; Mile-End spool cabinet; 6-drawer, oak, carved drawer fronts, brass pulls, ornate turned spindles on front corners, paneled on three sides, each panel different: one with flowers, one with birds, one with Clark's Trade Mark, c.1900, 26"W x 19"D x 21"H. $1200-1600

B.   **Clark's**; Mile-End spool cabinet; left side of cabinet with pressed bird design.

C.   **Clark's**; Mile-End spool cabinet; rear of cabinet with raised letters.

D.   **Clark's**; Mile-End spool cabinet; right side of cabinet with pressed flower design.

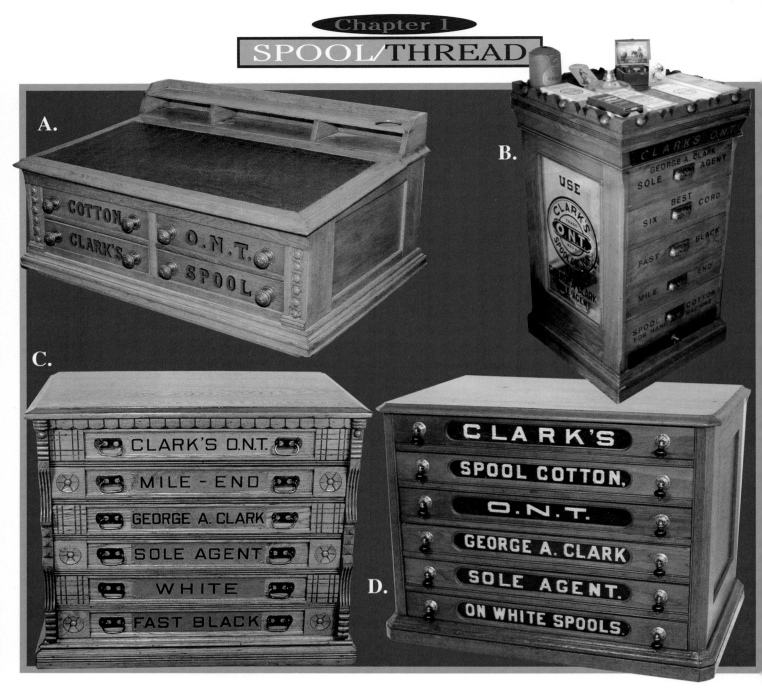

A. **Clark's**; O.N.T. spool desk; 4-drawer, oak, lift top, brass pulls, c.1910, 29-1/2"W x 21-1/2"D x 15"H. $450-650

B. **Clark's**; O.N.T. thread cabinet; 6-drawer, ash, c.1910, (this cabinet was originally a Belding's with glass front drawers.) 19-1/2"W x 19-3/4"D x 36-1/2"H. $700-900

C. **Clark's**; Mile-End spool cabinet; 6-drawer, ash, draped top, stamped Mile-End brass spool pulls, c.1910, 25-1/2"W x 19"D x 22"H. $900-1300

D. **Clark's**; O.N.T. spool cabinet; 6-drawer, walnut, red ruby glass door fronts, tear-drop brass and wood pulls, c.1910, 29"W x 19"D x 22"H. $1600-1900

A.   **Clark's**; Mile-End spool cabinet; 6-drawer, oak, Mile-End brass spool pulls, raised lettering and flower/leaf on drawer ends, c.1900, 25-1/2"W x 18"D x 22"H. $1400-1800

B.   **George A. Clark**; O.N.T. spool cabinet; 7-drawer, walnut, reverse etched ruby glass fronts, brass and wood pulls, paneled on three sides, c.1910, 29"W x 18-1/2"D x 22-1/2"H. $1500-2000

C.   **George A. Clark**; O.N.T. spool cabinet; 6-drawer, oak and ash, reverse painted glass panels in drawers, brass pulls, paneled on three sides, c.1910, 27"W x 20-1/2"D x 23"H. $900-1300

D.   **Coats' & Clark's**; Spool cabinet; slant front, birch, c.1915, 21"W x 11"D x 20"H. $550-650

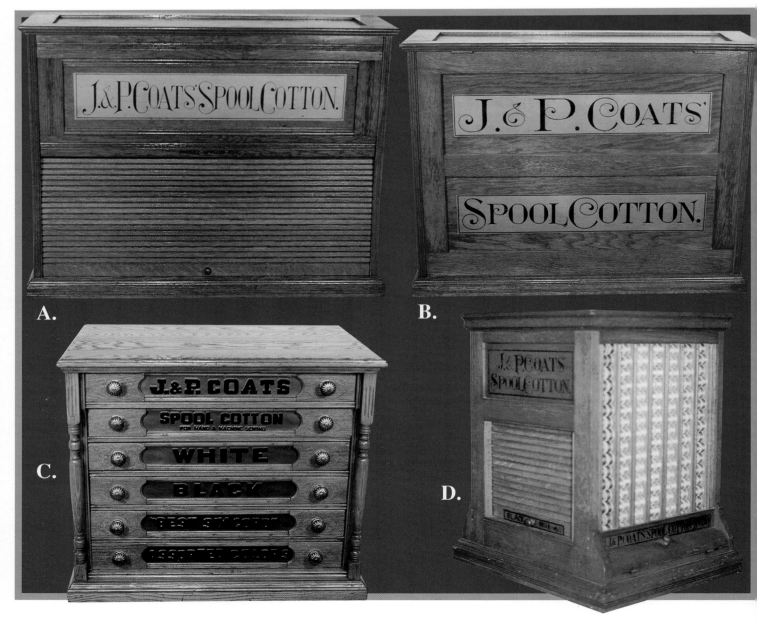

A.

B.

C.

D.

A. **J. & P. Coats'**; Spool cabinet; roll front, oak, load thread at lift-up top, c.1900, 31"W x 11"D x 24"H. $1600-2200

B. **J. & P. Coats'**; Spool cabinet; reverse side of A, black letters applied on gold background.

C. **J. & P. Coats'**; Spool cabinet; 6-drawer, ash, raised spool of thread (large) on back, raised lettering on front drawers, full

turned pillars on corners, c.1900, 26"W x 19"D x 22"H. $1200-1600

D. **J. & P. Coats'**; Spool cabinet; oak, used on all four sides, columns of spool thread on two sides, other two sides have slide-up door panels, c.1890, 16"W x 17"D x 22-1/2"H. $900-1400

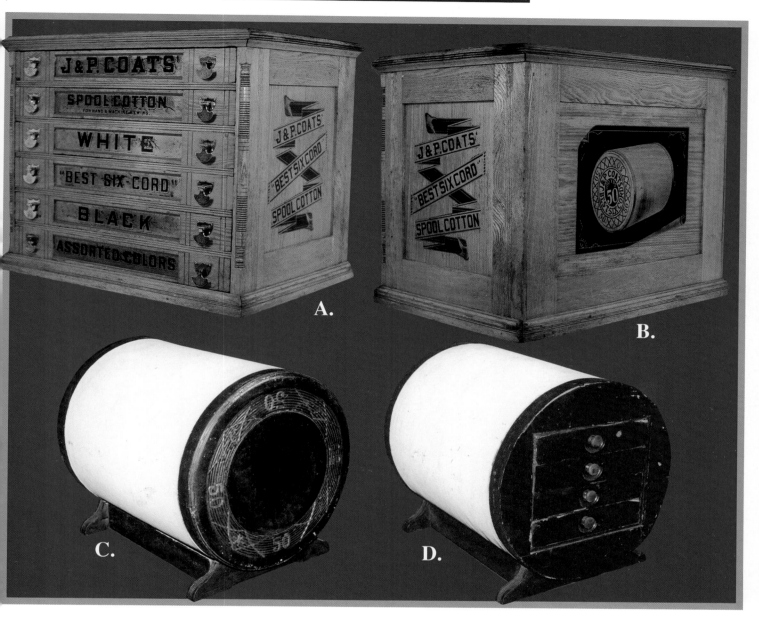

A. J. & P. Coats'; Spool cabinet; 6-drawer, ash, J.P. Co. brass anchor pulls, black lettering on tin inserts, c.1890, 25"W x 18"D x 21"H. $900-1500

B. J. & P. Coats'; Spool cabinet; side and back of A.

C. J. & P. Coats'; Spool cabinet; figural spool with composition thread around body, four drawers in end, holds the

"Best Six Cord Spools", end panel embossed, c.1900, 18"W x 22-1/2"D. $550-700

D. J. & P. Coats'; Spool cabinet; figural, opposite end of C, shows four drawers for thread.

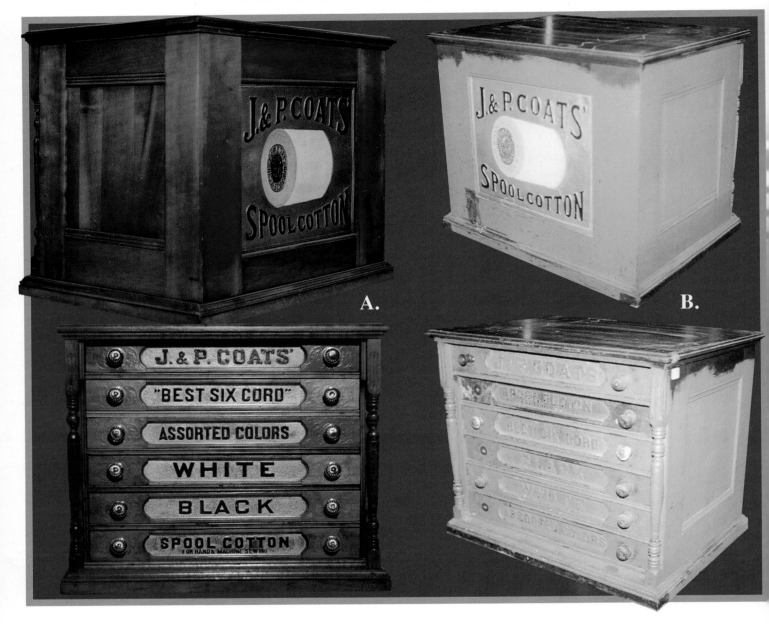

A.

B.

A. **J. & P. Coats'**; Spool cabinet; 6-drawer, cherry, turned spindles on front and pressed drawer fronts, brass pulls, paneled on two sides, pressed panel in back with spool, c.1900, 26"W x 19"D x 22"H. $1400-1800

B. **J. & P. Coats'**; Spool cabinet; 6-drawer, walnut with paint, turned spindles on front and pressed drawer fronts, brass pulls, paneled on two sides, pressed panel in back with spool, (this cabinet has some damage), c.1900, 26"W x 19"D x 22"H. $650-900.

These two cabinets are the same cabinet, except for the wood. The difference in value is a function of the difference in condition.

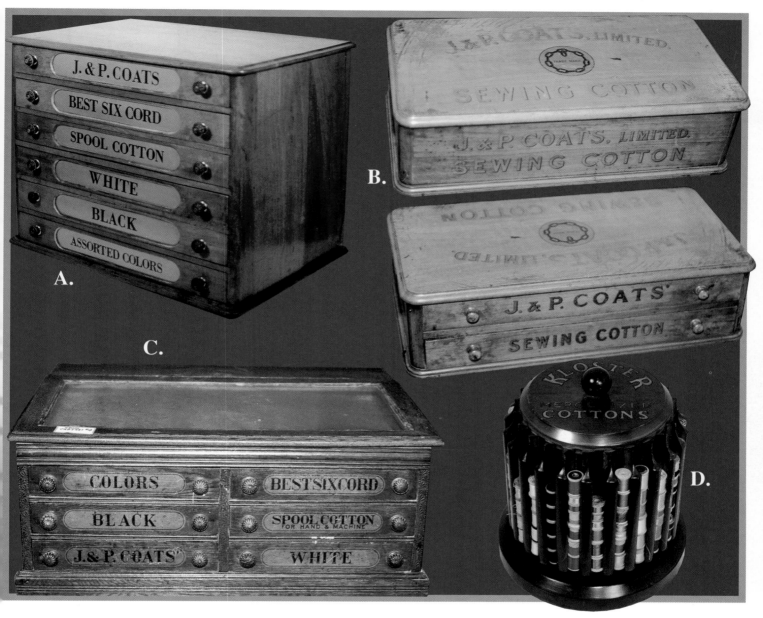

A. **J. & P. Coats'**; Spool cabinet; walnut, 6-drawer, tin inserts in drawer fronts replaced with contemporary panels, c.1910, 24"W x 16-1/2"D x 18-1/2"H. $400-750

B. **J. & P. Coats'**; Spool cabinet; walnut, 2-drawer, applied lettering, top, front and back, unusual, c.1890, 22"W x 11-1/2"D x 6-1/2"H. $600-850

C. **J. & P. Coats'**; Spool cabinet desk; oak, 6-drawer, glass top — as found, original pulls with applied decal lettering on drawers, c.1915, 30"W x 22"D x 15"H. $500-800

D. **Kloster**; Circular spool; stained poplar wood, c.1910, 12"W x 14"H. $900-1400

A. **Merrick's**; Double spool cabinet; unusual panels of horseshoe glass on ends, oak with two revolving interior spools, mirrored center on front and back, Pat. 1897, 32"W x 17"D x 24"H. $2500-3000

B. **Merrick's**; Spool cabinet; 6-drawer, ash wood with walnut burl, ring pulls, c.1900, 30"W x 18"D x 17"H. $800-1400

C. **Merrick's**; Single spool cabinet; circular, oak and curved glass with revolving interior, original glass advertising panels promoting Merrick's spool cotton, open door on bottom to select thread, c.1900, 18"Dia. x 23"H. $900-1500

A.

B.

C.

A. **Merrick's**; Double spool cabinet; two revolving interior spools, gold stenciling on four panels of curved glass, "Merrick's Six Cord Soft Finish Spool Cotton", open drawer on bottom to select thread, c.1900, 31"W x 17"D x 23"H. $1900-2400

B. **Merrick's**; Spool cabinet; mirror, oak, front drops down to make desk, load thread from top, unload where numbers are at bottom of thread, c.1890, 36"W x 18"D x 31"H. $1500-1800

C. **Royal Society**; Embroidery floss cabinet; oak, 12 drawers, brass pull handles and glass fronts, applied lettering, c.1900, 19"W x 19"D x 36"H. $800-1000

A.

B.

C.

A. **Willimantic**; Spool cabinet; 6-drawer, cherry, raised lettering on drawers and sides with raised flying spool on back, clear glass knobs, c.1890, 26"W x 20"D x 21"H. $1400-1900

B. **Willimantic**; Spool cabinet; 6-drawer, ash, pulls say "Willimantic Spool Cotton", diagonal owl transfer on back, c.1890, 26"W x 19"D x 20"H. $1200-1600

C. **Willimantic**; Spool cabinet; this is nearly the same cabinet as B, but made in walnut, with vertical owl transfer on back, c.1890, 26"W x 19"D x 20"H. $1200-1600

A. Belding; Silk spool cabinet; clock, walnut, 30-drawer, glass drawers have curved front, mirrored door in center, c.1890, 35"W x 17"D x 45"H. $2400-2800

B. Belding's; Silk spool cabinet; 26-drawer; two drawers with wood fronts, 24 glass fronts, ash and oak, mirrored sides, c.1900, 36"W x 19"D x 32-1/2"H. $1100-1400

C. Belding's; Silk spool cabinet; glass, oak, with revolving interior spool, three drawers on bottom, Pat. 1911-13-14, 16"W x 16"D x 33"H. $1500-1800

D. Belding's; Decal close up; reverse transfer on glass door of C.

A. **Belding**; Silk spool cabinet; oak, 26 glass front drawers with two wood front drawers, 31"W x 17"D x 40"H. $2200-2500

B. **Belding Bro's & Co.**; Silk spool cabinet; ash, 13-drawer, 10 glass, three wood, mirrored sides, gallery top, "The Belding Bro's & Co." carved panel is carved "Corticelli" on the reverse side, c.1890, 19-1/2"W x 19-1/2"D x 36"H. $1400-1800

C. **Belding, Paul & Co. Ltd.**; Silk spool cabinet; 6-drawer, mirrored door, clock gallery, oak, c.1890, 21"W x 14"D x 29"H. $900-1400

D. **Belding's**; Double silk spool cabinet; glass doors, two revolving interior spools, oak, c.1890, 31"W x 18"D x 27" H. $2500-2800

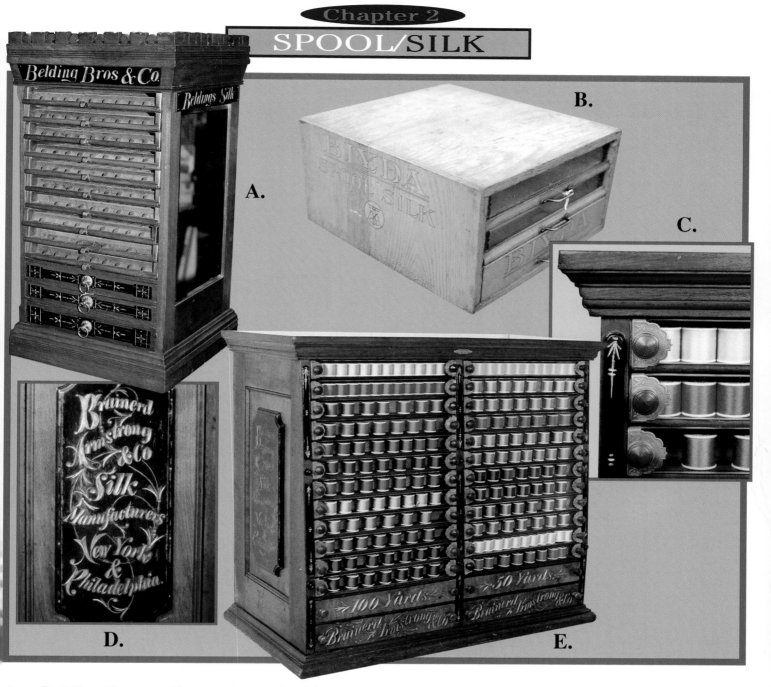

A. **Belding Bros & Co.**; Silk spool cabinet; 13-drawer, walnut, c.1910, 19-1/2"W x 18-1/2"D x 36"H. $1600-2200

B. **Blyda**; Silk spool cabinet; oak, 3-drawer, two glass front, one oak front, c.1910, 14"W x 18"D x 7"H. $200-350

C. **Brainerd Armstrong & Co.**; Close up of wood pulls, brass backplate says "Brainerd Armstrong & Co., Pat. 1-24-1877".

D. **Brainerd Armstrong & Co.**; Close up of spoon carved wood side panel of E.

E. **Brainerd Armstrong & Co.**; Silk spool cabinet; 28-drawer glass front, walnut, bottom drawers have spoon carved lettering, c.1880, 37"W x 19"D x 32"H. $2900-3200

A.

B.

C.

A.   **Brainerd & Armstrong Co.**; Silk spool cabinet; front and side view, 20 drawers with glass fronts, with four bottom drawers having wood fronts with applied letters, sides also have applied letters, hardware at ends of glass drawers has silkworm moth and "Brainerd Armstrong Company" stamped in brass, manufactured by *Guggisberg Bros., Preston, Ont.*, c.1880, 36-1/2"W x 17"D x 25"H. $1600-1900

B.   **Brainerd & Armstrong Co.**; Silk spool cabinet; 10-drawer, glass fronts, walnut, carved lettering, c.1880, 23-1/2"W x 18"D x 27"H. $1500-1800

C.   **Brainerd & Armstrong Co.**; Close up of drawer ends of cabinet B; brass hardware on each end shows, "Brainerd & Armstrong Co." with horn of plenty.

A.   **Corticelli**; Silk spool cabinet; 14-drawer, oak, mirrored sides, spoon carved lettering, c.1890, 21"W x 20"D x 41"H. $2000-2200

B.   **Corticelli**; Silk spool cabinet; oak, 3-drawer, glass fronts, litho decal showing logo of cat, c.1910, 21"W x 18"D x 9-1/2"H. $300-550

C.   **Corticelli**; Silk spool cabinet; 10-drawer, walnut, c.1890, 23"W x 17"D x 24"H. $1200-1900

D.   **Corticelli**; Silk spool cabinet; 10 glass front drawers, oak, carved lettering, applied transfer of cat on sides, c.1890, 21-1/2"W x 18"D x 33"H. $1600-1900

A. **Corticelli**; Silk spool cabinet; quarter-sawn oak with glue chip reverse gold leaf under silver glass, door slides up, c.1890-1900, 31"W x 16"D x 50-1/2"H. $4000-5000

B. **Corticelli**; Inside view of A; 60 drawers with glass fronts, five columns across, 12 drawers down.

C. **Corticelli**; Silk spool rack; bird's-eye maple, logo of cat on front, c.1900, 9"Dia. x 4"H. $325-425

D. **Corticelli**; Silk spool cabinet; 11-drawer, cherry, spoon carved letters on sides and front at top, stenciled lettering at bottom, mirrored sides, c.1890, 23"W x 17"D x 30"H. $1500-1800

A.   **Cutter's**; Silk spool cabinet; oak, 16 beveled glass front drawers, three oak drawers, c.1890, 18"W x 19"D x 44"H. $1500-2200

B.   **Eureka**; Silk spool cabinet; 10-drawer, walnut, burled front, eight beveled glass drawers, c.1890, 18"W x 19"D x 31"H. $900-1500

C.   **Eureka**; Silk spool cabinet; walnut, seven glass front drawers, six wood drawers, applied lettering on sides and gallery with clock in gallery, c.1900, 22"W x 17"D x 40"H. $1500-1800

A. **M. Heminway & Sons**; Silk spool cabinet; 3-drawer, walnut, cash register style, drawers at top and bottom are ruby red, five interior slide-out shelves are under curved glass, c.1890, 21"W x 16"D x 18"H. $1900-2500

B. **M. Heminway & Sons**; Silk spool cabinet; eight glass front drawers, one wood front, oak, c.1890, 17"W x 18"D x 22"H. $1400-1900

C. **M. Heminway & Sons**; Silk spool cabinet; 9-drawer, eight with glass fronts, ash and/or butternut, painted trim and lettering, c.1900, 18"W x 18"D x 18"H. $900-1200

D. **J. & P. Coats**; Silk spool cabinet; oak, revolves, applied vertical lettering on four corners, c.1900, 13"W x 13"D x 14"H. $1100-1600

A. **Klostersilk**; Silk spool display case; metal with green paint, applied lettering, c.1920, 18"W x 9"D x 13"H. $275-575

B. **J.N. Leonard's**; Silk spool cabinet; 15 glass front drawers, basswood/pine and walnut, probably had mirrored sides, painted trim and lettering, North Hampton, Mass., c.1890, 22-1/4"W x 24"D x 41-1/4"H. $1300-1700

C. **J.N. Leonard's**; Side and rear of Leonard's silk cabinet B.

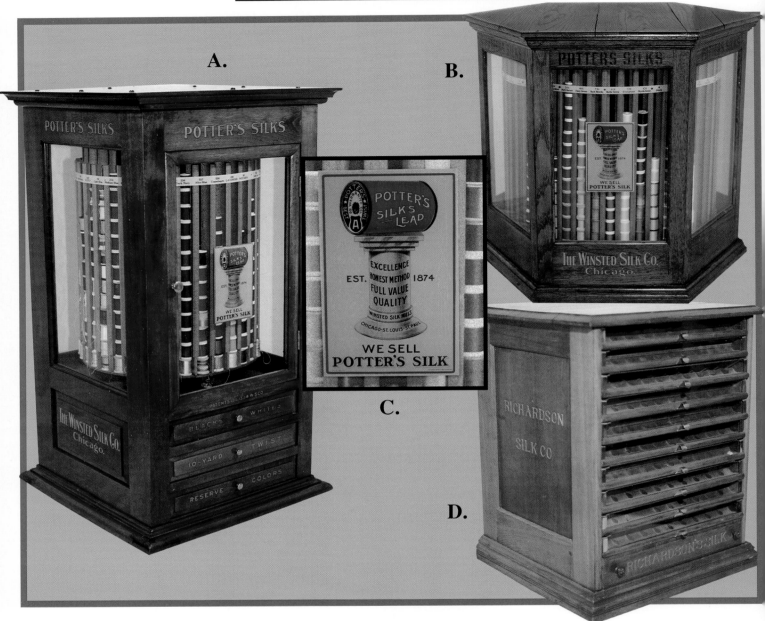

A.

B.

C.

D.

A.   **Potter's**; Silk spool cabinet; with interior revolving spool, three drawers, cherry, Pat. 1911-13-14 W.S.Co., 18"W x 18"D x 33"H. $1200-1800

B.   **Potter's**; Silk spool cabinet; 6-sided, door on back side to get to revolving spool, (this comes in a coin-operated version), c.1890, 24"W x 24"D x 25"H. $2800-3500

C.   **Potter's**; Decal on front of A & B.

D.   **Richardson Silk Co.**; Spool cabinet; 10 glass front drawers, one wood drawer, ash, name spoon carved in both sides, c.1900, 19"W x 18"D x 25"H. $700-900

A. **Ampollina**; Dye cabinet; basswood case with glass door, Quebec, Canada, French Canadian and English, c.1920, 15"W x 5"D x 24"H. $425-550

B. **Diamond Dyes**; Dye cabinet; oak, embossed tin litho shows "Children with the Balloon",*Wells & Richardson Co.*, c.1910, 15"W x 9"D x 24"H. VG to excellent, $1100-1400

C. **Diamond Dyes**; Dye cabinet; oak, embossed tin litho shows "Children with the Balloon", *Wells & Richardson Co.*, c.1908, 15"W x 9"D x 24"H. Excellent to mint, $1300-2500

D. **Diamond Dyes**; Back of cabinet B.

E. **Diamond Dyes**; Alternate back.

F. **Diamond Dyes**; Back of cabinet C.

1887 Druggist supply catalogue ad for Diamond Dye Cabinet.

A. **Diamond Dyes**; Dye cabinet; shows "Mansion" or "Children Skipping Rope", *Wells & Richardson Co.*, c.1910-1914, 15"W x 9"D x 24-1/4"H. VG to excellent, $1100-1400

B. **Diamond Dyes**; Dye cabinet; birch, tin litho front panel shows "Baby", known as the "Presentation" cabinet, *Wells & Hope Co., 918-922 Vine St., Philadelphia, PA*, c.1887, 16-1/2"W x 9-1/2"D x 20"H. VG, $1400-1600

C. **Diamond Dyes**; Dye cabinet; birch, tin litho front panel shows "Baby", known as the "Presentation" cabinet, *Wells & Hope Co., 918-922 Vine St., Philadelphia, PA*, c.1887, 16-1/2"W x 9-1/2"D x 20"H. Excellent to mint, $2200-3400

D. **Diamond Dyes**; Back of cabinet C.

A.

B.

C.

A. **Diamond Dyes**; Dye cabinet; birch, tin litho front panel shows "Court Jester", c.1890, 21"W x 10-1/4"D x 27-1/4"H. Good to VG, $1100-1400

B. **Diamond Dyes**; Back of cabinet A; both doors open to access compartments that hold dye packets.

C. **Diamond Dyes**; Dye cabinet; birch, tin litho front panel shows "Court Jester", c.1890, 21"W x 10-1/4"D x 27-1/4"H. Excellent to mint, $2800-3600

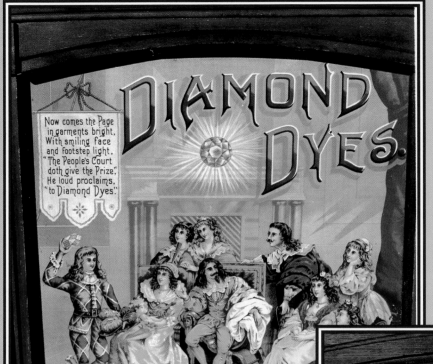

Close up of "Court Jester" tin insert. This tin would classify as mint condition.

Close up of "Evolution of Woman" tin insert. This tin would classify as mint condition.

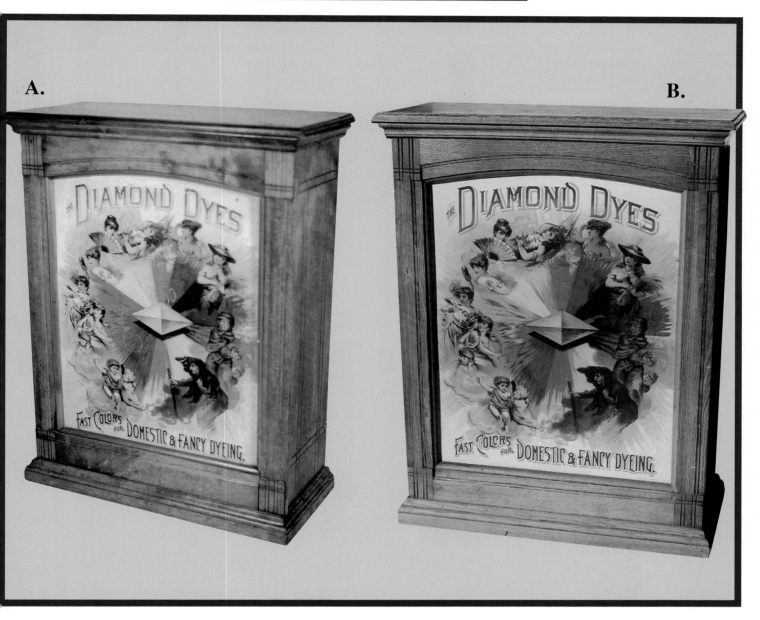

A. **Diamond Dyes**; Dye cabinet; tin litho front panel shows "Evolution of Woman", c.1890, 22-1/4"W x 9-3/4"D x 29-3/4"H. Good to VG, $1400-1800

B. **Diamond Dyes**; Dye cabinet; tin litho front panel shows "Evolution of Woman", c.1890, 22-1/4"W x 9-3/4"D x 29-3/4"H. Excellent to mint, $2400-3100

A. **Diamond Dyes**; Dye cabinet; birch, tin litho front panel shows "Blonde Flowing Hair Fairy with Wand", *Wells & Hope Co., 918-922 Vine St., Phila, PA,* c.1890, 23"W x 10"D x 31"H. VG+, $1600-1800

B. **Diamond Dyes**; Dye cabinet; birch, tin litho front panel shows "Blonde Flowing Hair Fairy with Wand", *Wells & Hope Co., 918-922 Vine St., Phila, PA,* c.1890, 23"W x 10"D x 31"H. Excellent to mint, $2600-3400

C. **Diamond Dyes**; Back of cabinet A.

D. **Diamond Dyes**; Dye cabinet; shows "Red-Headed Fairy with Wand" version, (more difficult to find), 24"W x 10"D x 30-5/8"H. Excellent to mint, $2900-3600

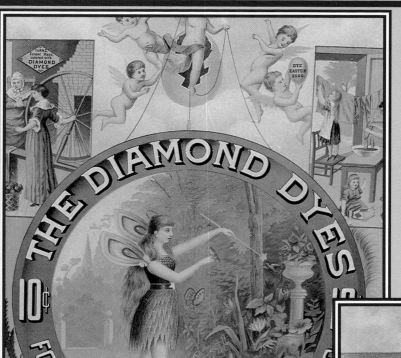

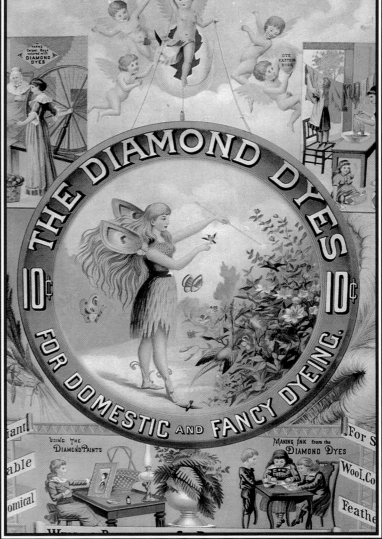

Close up of "Red-Headed Fairy with Wand" tin insert. This tin would classify as mint condition.

Close up of "Blonde Flowing Hair Fairy with Wand" tin insert. This tin would classify as mint condition.

Close up of "May Pole" tin insert. This tin would classify as mint condition.

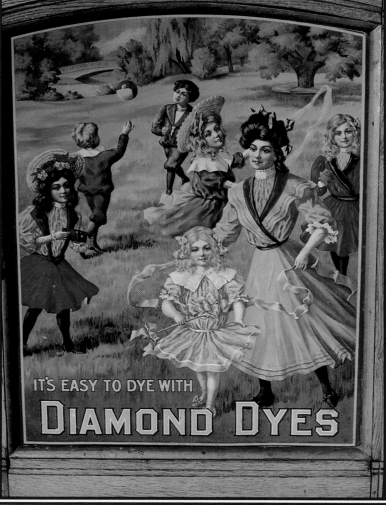

Close up of "Governess" tin insert. This tin would classify as mint condition.

A. **Diamond Dyes**; Dye cabinet; embossed tin litho front panel shows "Governess", *Wells & Richardson Co., Copyright U.S. and Canada*, c.1906, 22"W x 10"D x 30"H. VG to excellent, $1600-1800

B. **Diamond Dyes**; Dye cabinet; shows "Governess", c.1906, 22-1/4"W x 10"D x 30"H. Excellent to mint. $2400-3200

C. **Diamond Dyes**; Dye cabinet; embossed tin front showing "May Pole", c.1906, 22"W x 10"D x 30"H. VG to excellent, $1600-1800

D. **Diamond Dyes**; Dye cabinet; embossed tin front showing "May Pole", c.1906, 22"W x 10"D x 30"H. Excellent to mint, $2400-3200

A.   **Diamond Dyes**; Dye cabinet; ash and birch, embossed tin litho front panel shows "Washerwoman", green background, c.1910, 22"W x 10"D x 30"H. VG to excellent, $1400-1600

B.   **Diamond Dyes**; Dye cabinet; ash and birch, embossed tin litho front panel shows "Washerwoman", green background, c.1910, 22"W x 10"D x 30"H. Excellent to mint, $2800-3200

C.   **Diamond Dyes**; Dye cabinet; shows "Washerwoman", blue background, (more difficult to find), 22"W x 10"D x 30"H. Excellent to mint, $2900-3400

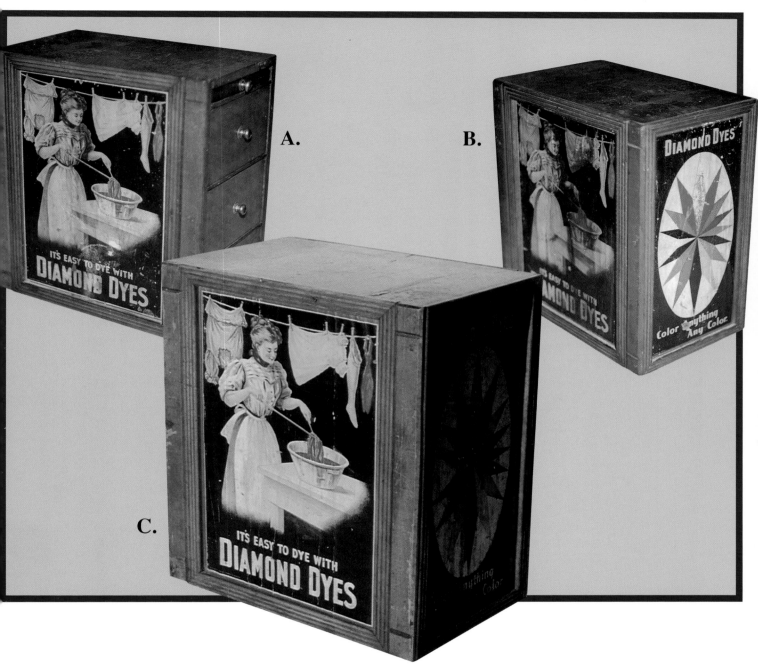

A.   **Diamond Dyes**; Dye cabinet; paper on wood, three sides, shows "Washerwoman" on two sides, four drawers on one end, mahogany and ash, *Forbes Co.*, *Boston*, c.1898, 13"W x 8"D x 14"H. Good to VG, $1400-1800

B.   **Diamond Dyes**; Back of cabinet A.

C.   **Diamond Dyes**; Dye cabinet; shows "Blue Washerwoman", paper litho on two sides, 12-5/8"W x 8"D x 14"H. Excellent to mint, $1800-2400

A.

D.

B.

C.

E.

A. **DY-O-LA**; Dye cabinet; birch with walnut finish, lithographed tin panel in door, same panel in rear, c.1920, 14"W x 9"D x 17"H. $300-425

B. **Electric Dyes**; Dye cabinet; pine with embossed lithographed tin panel, French Canadian and English, *The Dr. Ed Morin Medicine Co., Quebec, Canada*, c.1915, 21"W x 10"D x 30"H. $700-950

C. **German Household Dyes**; Dye cabinet; ash/oak with paper insert in door, fox graphic, *Paul Oppermann, sole importer, Milwaukee*, c.1900, 15"W x 8"D x 24"H. $675-800

D. **German Household Dyes**; Dye cabinet; oak or ash, large paper label, *Mfgr. Paul Oppermann Sole Importer, Milwaukee*, c.1890, 24"W x 8"D x 32"H. $500-650

E. **German Household Dyes**; Rear of cabinet D.

A. **Peerless Dyes**; Dye cabinet; soft maple with roll-up front, c.1900, 22"W x 11"D x 36"H. $550-675

B. **Perfection Dyes**; Dye cabinet, ash cabinet with cherry finish, lithographed tin panel insert in door, *W. Gushing & Co., Foxcraft, Maine, USA*, c.1900, 17"W x 6"D x 24"H. $600-775

C. **Putnam**; "Fadeless" dye cabinet; wood with multi-colored tin (or paper) panel in door, shows Colonel Putnam chased by the redcoats, c.1910, 21"W x 9"D x 10"H. $175-250

D. **Putnam**; "Fadeless" dye cabinet; tin with front and back litho of Colonel Putnam, larger size, c.1915, 18-1/2"W x 7-3/4"D x 14-1/2"H. $175-250

A. **Putnam**; "Fadeless" dye cabinet; tin with front and back litho of Colonel Putnam, medium size, c.1915, 16"W x 8"D x 11"H. $165-235

B. **Putnam**; Interior view of A; shows 24 compartments, each with its own label for various dye colors and instructions on inside of front lid.

C. **Putnam**; "Fadeless" dye cabinet; wood countertop cabinet, tin litho (or paper) depicts trademark scene of British Red Coats chasing Col. Putnam, c.1900, 21"W x 9"D x 10"H. $175-250

D. **Rit**; Dye cabinet; tin, artificial wood grained multi-colored litho all sides, c.1920, 14"W x 11"D x 17"H. $225-300

A. **Camels Hair**; Lace cabinet; oak with glass lift top, 12 compartments varied sizes, transfer lettering, c.1920, 12"W x 6"D x 7"H. $275-325

B. **Lindsey**; Revolving ribbon cabinet; oak with revolving "remanufactured" center, adjustable interior shelves and bi-fold door, yardstick folds out to measure, c.1894, 28"W x 28"D x 42"H. $1000-1300

C. **Myra**; Velveteen display case; oak on original cast-iron base, made in Chicago, c.1895, 28"W x 20"D x 37"H. $1500-$2200

D. Ribbon cabinet; oak, four doors tip down, manufactured by *A.N. Russell & Sons Co., Ilion, NY,* c.1900, 27"W x 6"D x 26-1/2"H. $700-850

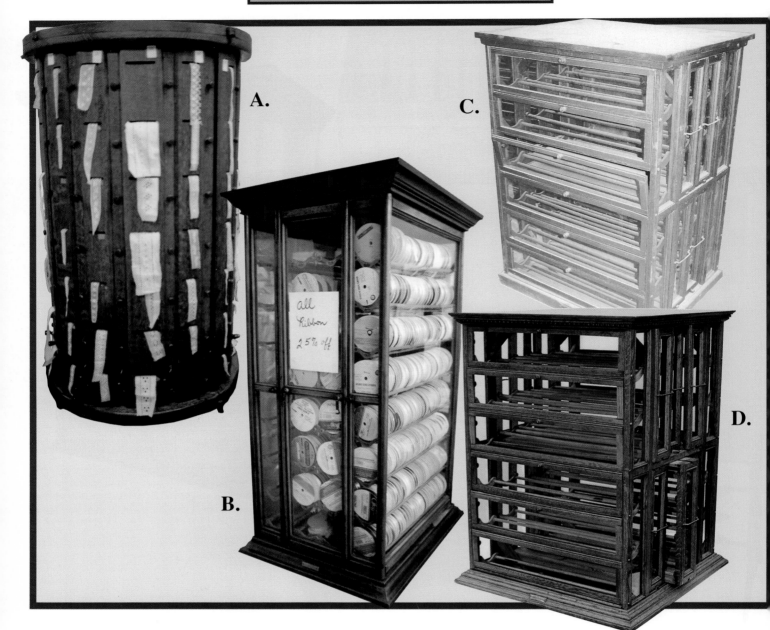

A. Ribbon cabinet; oak, cylindrical, ribbon rolls inside, with ribbon ends hanging through slots in the sides, holds 112 rolls, c.1890, 22"Dia. x 40"H. $900-1200

B. Ribbon display case; oak and glass, ribbon rolls on swing-out door racks, *Exhibition Show Case Co., Erie, PA. Henrich's pats. May 8, 1877*, c.1880, 25"W x 22"D x 47"H. $700-850

C. Ribbon cabinet; oak and glass, six doors tip out on each side, four end racks slide out each end, 28"W x 22"D x 38"H. $1100-1400

D. Ribbon cabinet; oak, 12 tip-out drawers with glass fronts, six slide-out end racks, three over three, mfgr. *A.N. Russell & Sons, Ilion, N.Y. USA*, c.1910, 28"W x 27"D x 38"H. $1300-1600

A.   Ribbon cabinet; oak, cylindrical, smaller version, 80 rolls, manufactured by *David Lochner, Woodburn, IN*, Pat. 1912, 24"Dia. x 30"H. $800-1000

B.   Ribbon cabinet; oak and glass countertop display has three slide-out sections, c.1910, 27-1/2"W x 17"D x 26"H. $1000-1200

C.   Ribbon cabinet; oak, cylindrical, large version, 112 rolls, manufactured by *David Lochner, Woodburn, IN*, Pat. 1912, 24"Dia. x 40"H. $1000-1200

D.   Ribbon cabinet; oak, 10-sided for ribbon and lace, holds 100 rolls, c.1910, 22"W x 40"H. $1000-1300

A.   Ribbon cabinet; oak, door opens from back, manufactured by *H. Pauk & Sons Mfg. Co., St. Louis*, c.1890, 26"W x 14"D x 37"H. $650-900

B.   Ribbon or fabric floor showcase; oak, in use as bulk jelly bean case, c.1910, 48"W x 24"D x 41"H. $600-850

C.   Ribbon cabinet; oak, 36 compartments for ribbon, manufactured by *Lehnbeuter-Deichman Mfg. Co., St. Louis*, c.1909, 31-1/2"W x 13-1/2"D x 32"H. $800-900

D.   Ribbon cabinet; oak, 12 tip-down glass doors with two slide-out drawers on ends, c.1915, 28"W x 17-1/2"D x 37-1/2"H. $1000-1300

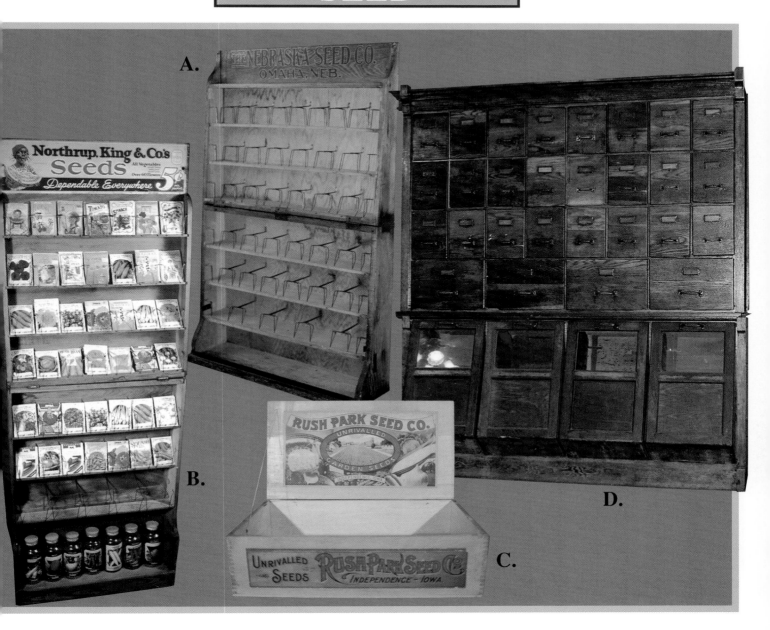

A. **Nebraska Seed Co.**; Seed display rack; ash and pine, folds in middle to close and ship, applied lettering, c.1915, 24"W x 9"D x 52"H. $450-500

B. **Northrup King & Co.**; Seed display rack; ash, with paper lithographed marquee, folds in middle to close and ship, c.1930, 25-1/4"W x 9"D x 68-1/2"H. $700-1000

C. **Rush Park Seed Co.**; "Unrivaled Garden Seed" counter display box; paper litho inside lid and front of box, c.1890, 24"W x 13"D x 6-1/2"H. $250-325

D. **Walker**; Seed cabinet; oak standing floor seed counter/cabinet, *Walker Bin Co, Pennyan, New York*, c.1890, 75"W x 24"D x 88"H. $2700-3200

A.   Mel. W. **"Webster's"**; Mammoth packet flower seed counter display box; paper litho label inside lid, c.1890, 9"W x 6-1/2"D x 3-1/2"H. $225-300

B.   Mel W. **"Webster's"**; Mammoth packet vegetable seed counter display box; paper litho label inside lid and on front, c.1890, 29"W x 15-1/2"D x 7"H. $285-375

C.   Bulk grain display counter; oak, "It Insures Pure & Clean Groceries", *Mfgr. Sheerer Gillette Co., Chicago*, Pat. Jan. 2, 1903, 124"W x 32"D x 34"H. $2100-2700

D.   Seed cabinet; painted pine and tin, handmade, 35 tin drawers with seed labels and metal pulls, c.1920, 54"W x 12"D x 38"H. $800-110

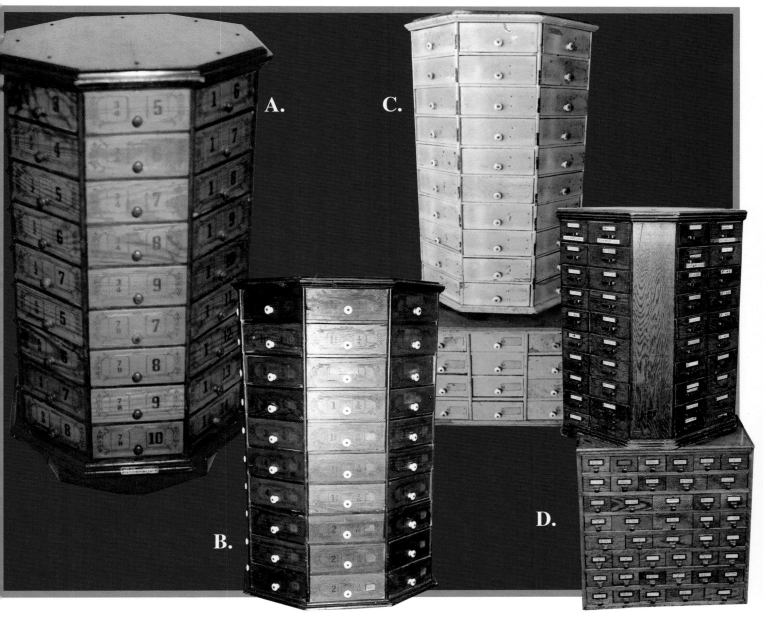

A. Hardware cabinet; octagon, revolves, 72 pie-shaped drawers, ash and soft maple, wood pulls, manufactured by *The American Bolt & Screw Case, Dayton, Ohio*, Pat. Apr. 27 `80 - May 12 `03, 21-1/2"W x 33"H. $2000-2400

B. Hardware cabinet; 80-drawers, same mfgr. as A, but porcelain pulls with brass washers, c.1910, 30-1/2"W x 30-1/2"D x 64-1/2"H. $1800-2000

C. Hardware cabinet; top section revolves, porcelain pulls, painted pine, basswood, 80 drawers above, 24 drawers below, c.1900, 30-1/2"W x 30-1/2"D x 64-1/2"H. $1200-1400

D. Two oak hardware cabinets; top has 80 drawers on four sides, 22"W x 22"D x 30"H. $650-800

Lower cabinet, oak, 48 drawers, 22"W x 20"D x 24"H. $275-350

A. **Keen Kutter**; Cutlery and tool cabinet; oak with die-cut metal logo, *E.C. Simmons-Keen Kutter-Cutlery and Tools* on top of each door, inside cabinet also has metal logo on drawer and Keen Kutter decals, 23-1/2"W x 8"D x 31"H. $500-700

B. Revolving hardware cabinet; cast iron, eight sizes per 10 levels, each level turns, holds 80 different size screws/bolts, c.1890, 21"Dia. base x 24"H. $1300-1600

C. Revolving hardware cabinet; cast iron, eight sizes per 13 levels, each level turns, holds 104 different size screws/bolts, c.1890, 21"Dia. base x 31"H. $1400-1800

NUT/BOLT/HARDWARE

A.

A.   Hardware wall display; oak, three running
sections, each running section has three
vertical sections–lower, middle and top,
center running section has bulk nail bins
in bottom of the section, other sections for
various nuts, bolts and hardware items,
bulk storage in top of each section,
Warren Manufacturing, c. 1900, each
section is 8'W x 30"D x 11"H.
$3200-3800 per three piece vertical
section.

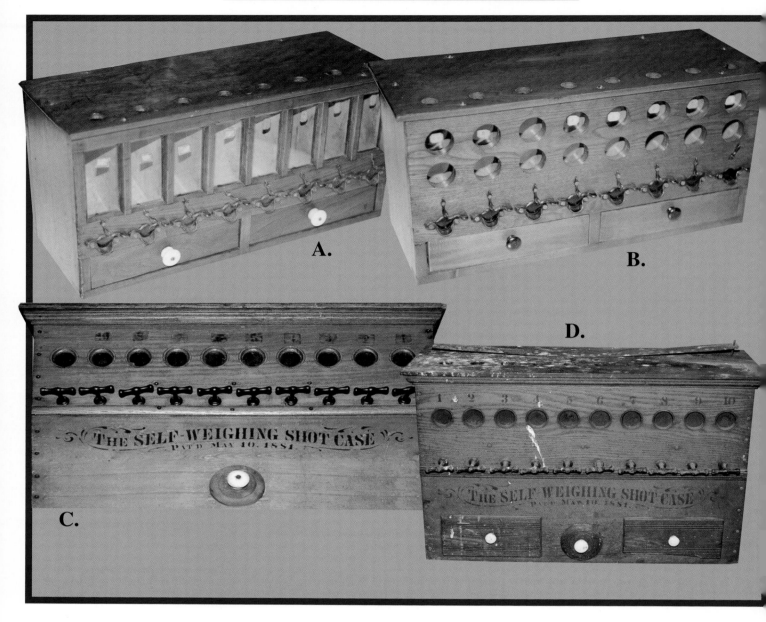

A.   Shot cabinet; ash, rectangular glass windows with iron lever releases for eight different sizes of shot, c.1890, 25"W x 10"D x 12-1/2"H. $700-800

B.   Shot cabinet; ash, round glass windows and iron lever releases for eight different sizes of shot, c.1890, 25"W x 10"D x 12-1/2"H. $800-900

C.   **The Self Weighing Shot Case**; ash, unusual – it doesn't have the two drawers at the bottom, Pat. May 10, 1881, 29"W x 10"D x 18"H. $1700-1800

D.   **The Self Weighing Shot Case**; ash, as found, has plate on top that covered holes to shot compartments, original porcelain pulls, Pat. 1881, 31"W x 11"D x 19"H. $1200-1300

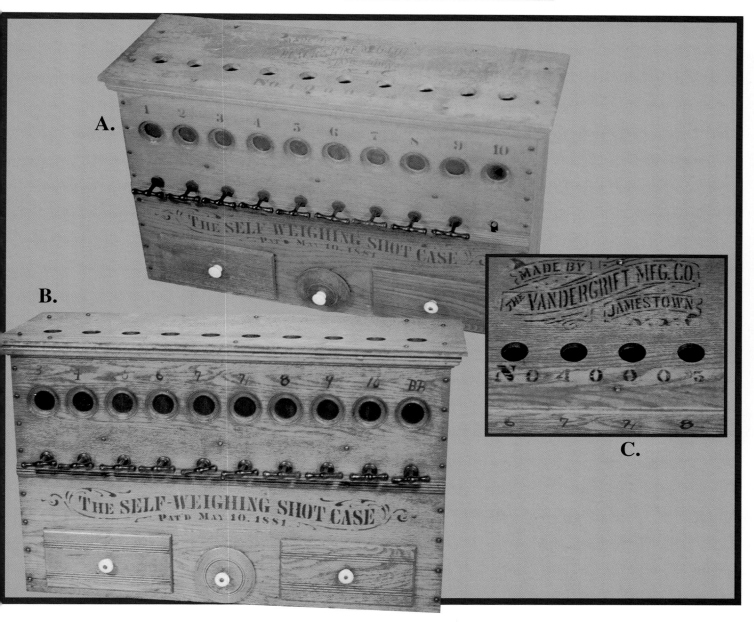

A. **The Self Weighing Shot Case**; manufactured by *Blackstone Mfg. Co., Jamestown*, Pat. May 10, 1881 No. 10023, 31"W x 11"D x 19"H. $1300-1500

B. **The Self Weighing Shot Case**; ash, manufactured by *Vandergrift Mfg. Co., Jamestown*, Pat. May 10, 1881, No. 40005, 30-1/2"W x 10-1/2"D x 18"H. Mint condition, $1600-1800

C. **The Self Weighing Shot Case**; top view of lettering on shot case B.

A. **DeLaval**; Cream separator parts cabinet; oak with tin litho panel in door "The World's Standard", interior has drawers for parts, early version, c.1900, 17-1/2"W x 10-1/2"D x 23-1/2"H. $950-1150

B. **DeLaval**; Cream separator parts cabinet; oak with tin litho panel in door "The World's Standard, One million in use", interior has drawers for parts, later version, c.1910, 17 1/2"W x 10-1/2"D x 23-1/2"H. $800-1000

C. **DeLaval**; Interior of separator parts cabinet; drawers hold parts.

A. **P. Lorillard & Co.**; Tobacco countertop display cabinet; wood, two drawers underneath the front doors, reversed etching on glass front doors, fancy marquee and hardware, c.1890, 34"W x 18-1/2"D x 42-1/2"H. $2500-3500

B. **P. Lorillard & Co.**; Tobacco countertop display cabinet; walnut, reversed etching glass and applied lettering on doors, c.1890, 31-1/2"W x 17"D x 44-/2"H. $4500-6000

C. Tobacco standing wall display case; cherry, *Brunswick Balke Collender Co., Billiard & Pool Tables, Bank, Office & Saloon Fixtures, Chicago, New York, Cincinnati, St. Louis*, c.1900, 72"W x 20"D x 112"H. $8000-9000

A.   **Milward's**; Needle counter display; ash, c.1910, 11"W x 11-1/2"D x 8"H. $75-100

B.   **Milward's**; Needle cabinet; walnut one drawer with applied lettering, 15-1/2"W x 11"D x 3"H. $225-300

A. **Dr. C.N. Barber's;** Vet remedies cabinet; tin with litho on front panel, door tips down, c.1910, 18"W x 9-1/2"D x 15"H. $1300-1600

B. **Brown's**; Horse healer vet medicine case; stenciled lettering on pine case, c.1890, 14"W x 6"D x 30"H. $1400-1800

C. **Dr. Claris**; Vet medicines cabinet; oak with glass door, marquee with applied letters, c.1900, 18"W x 9"D x 24"H. $450-750

D. **Columbia**; Vet remedies cabinet; birch, walnut finish, tin litho in door, *The F.C. Sturtevant Co., Hartford, Conn.*, c.1915, 18"W x 9"D x 24"H. $950-1200

E. **Dr. Daniels'**; Vet medicine cabinet; ash with colorful tin litho panel, c.1900, 21-1/2"W x 8"D x 28-1/2"H. $2300-2800

A. **Hanford's**, Balsam of Myrrh cabinet; oak with glass door on front, c.1890, 14-1/2"W x 9-3/4"D x 24"H. $450-525

B. **Humphreys'**; Vet specifics cabinet; oak and ash, multi-colored tin litho of various farm animals, c.1900, 21"W x 9"D x 34"H. $6500-7500

C. **Humphreys'**; Vet remedies cabinet; ash, multi-colored tin litho of horse head and other farm animals on front, c.1920, 17"W x 7"D x 24"H. $4000-5000

D. **Humphreys'**; Homeopathic specifics case; (medicines for people), walnut, blue flashed glass etched to clear, c.1900, 23"W x 17"D x 7"H. $4000-5000

E. **Humphreys'**; Vet specifics case; walnut, blue flashed glass etched to clear, with horse head, c.1900, 21"W x 16"D x 8-1/2"H. $5000-6000

A. **Humphreys'**; Vet specifics cabinet; walnut with embossed composition door panel, unusual version says Homeopathic Specifics, dated 12/14/87, 21"W x 10"D x 34"H. $5000-6000

B. **Humphreys'**; Inside of cabinet C; paper medicine list.

C. **Humphreys'**; Vet specifics cabinet; as found condition, ash, heavily embossed horse head on front, c.1900, 21"W x 10"D x 34"H. $5000-6000

D. **Humphreys'**; Vet specifics cabinet; excellent to mint original condition, ash, heavily embossed horse head on front, c.1900, 21"W x 10"D x 34"H. $7000+

E. **Humphreys'**; Inside of cabinet D; paper medicine list.

A. **Humphreys'**; Specifics medicine cabinet; (medicines for people), oak with blue tin litho panel in door, interior holds variety of 34 medicines, c.1900, 21-1/2"H x 7-1/2"D x 27-3/4"H. $750-1000

B. **Humphreys'**; Interior of specifics cabinet A; shows 34 drawers for various remedies.

C. **Humphreys'**; Specifics medicine cabinet; (medicines for people), ash, blue litho tin front, marquee top, c.1910, $1700-2000

D. **Humphreys'**; Vet box; lid open, large size c.1900, 15-1/2"W x 7"D x 9"H. $400-500

E. **Humphreys'**; Vet boxes; lids open, small size, c.1900, 9-1/2"W x 6"D x 6"H. $200-300 ea.

A. **Humphreys'**; Remedies cabinet; (medicines for people), tin, smaller size, two color litho on front, c.1930, 18"W x 6"D x 19"H. $400-500

B. **Humphreys';** Remedies cabinet; tin, larger size, two color litho on front, c.1930, 22"W x 6"D x 28"H. $400-500

C. **Humphreys'**; Homeopathic specifics cabinet; ash, litho with woman and lion on front, *Wells M. Hope Co., Phila. Pa.,* c.1890, 21"W x 10"D x 34"H. $7500+

D. **Dr. LeSure's** Famous Remedies; Vet cabinet; ash, tin litho of horse head in front, c.1910, 20-1/2"W x 6-3/4"D x 27"H. $3800-4500

E. **Dr. J.H. McLean's**; Display case; for "Strengthening Blood Cordial", walnut with curved glass door, letters painted on sides and marquee, c.1870, 18"W x 6-1/2"D x 28"H. $2500-3800

A. **Molax**; Laxative display case; glass, with wood back door, c.1920, 15"W x 9-1/2"D x 11-3/4"H. $225-375

B. **Munyon's**; Medicines cabinet; ash or oak, tin litho panel in door, 41 drawers pull out from back, c.1905, 18"W x 7"D x 24"H. $1100-1300

C. **Munyon's**; Homeopathic home remedies cabinet; lithograph on tin, "I would rather preserve the health of the nation, than be its ruler, Munyon", c.1920, 12"W x 13"D x 13"H. $625-750

D. **Pratts**; Vet remedies cabinet; ash, tin litho panel, c.1900, 17"W x 6"D x 34"H. $2000-2500

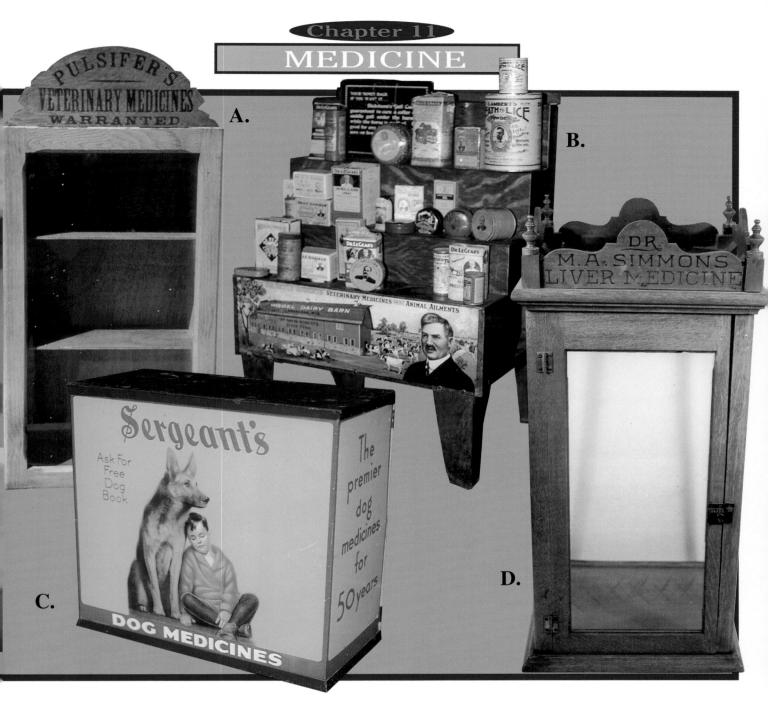

A. **Pulsifer's**; Warranted vet medicine cabinet; oak with glass door and marquee, applied letters, c.1890, 13"W x 6"D x 28"H. $3200-4000

B. **Dr. David Roberts**; Vet display; held medicine bottles, tin "stair step", *Beach Co., Coshocton, Ohio*, c.1900, 25"W x 18-1/2"D x 34-1/2"H. $2100-2500

C. **Sergeant's**; Vet cabinet; tin, multi-color litho, *Am Can Co., NY & Chicago*, c.1920, 15-1/2"W x 7"D x 14"H. $1200-1600

D. **Dr. M.A. Simmons**; Liver medicine cabinet; ash and pine, glass front, ornate gallery with turnings on top, c.1915, 15"W x 15"D x 31"H. $700-900

A.   Vet medicine cabinet; for wall or counter display, oak with beveled glass in doors, interior view with door and storage panel open, *W.D. Allison Co, Indianapolis, IN*, c.1915, 31"W x 11"D x 36"H. $725-975

B.   Vet medicine cabinet; front view.

C.   Drug store label dispenser; oak countertop dispenser, holds 96 rolls, *McCourt Label Cabinet Company of Bradford, PA*, Patented Aug. 9, 1904, 23"W x 7-1/2"D x 19"H. $300-450

D.   Druggist label cabinet; oak, holds 96 label rolls, c.1910, 45"W x 7-1/2"D x 15-1/2"H. $550-700

This store interior was likely taken in the autumn or winter, c.1920. It shows an orderly display area. Note the well-stocked shelves and a large upright baked goods display case, like the one on page 207.

This looks like a typical hardware store. It offers a nice assortment of tools, stoves and washers. The man standing on the right is leaning on a counter next to a Keen Kutter knife case like the one on page 131.

This Soda Fountain is decked out for the Fourth of July! You can see fresh chocolates in the slant front display case, Wrigley's gum, die-cut signs for soda products and even a portion of a match machine!

This Soda Fountain, probably in the Athens, Ohio area, c.1940, shows display cases full of potato chips and candy bars. Look for the pair of Coca-Cola display bottles standing on top of the back bar.

These two photographs are of the same Illinois Drug Store. This photo, taken around 1900-1910, shows the store with considerable unused floor space, probably early in its life. Note the three gentlemen pictured.

This photo, probably c.1920, shows the same three men. All appear older. The store is now well stocked. Notice the wonderful cigar cutter, the lighter and the Parker Pen "Lucky Curve" display case.

This store, c.1910, probably was in the Western U.S. It shows a variety of tobacco and cigar products. On the counter, at left, notice candy products and the Sun "Bicycle" cigar trade stimulator.

This is definitely a General Merchandise Store. Look at the range of goods. In the display case, front left, notice what looks like bulk wrapped taffy. Also note the Wrigley's Vassar gum box like the one on page 113.

Interior of the Bozeman Pharmacy, Bozeman, Mont.
THE MAIL ORDER DRUG STORE

Section 2

Gum & Candy
•
Pens
•
Razors / Knives
& Hardware

CASES, CONTAINERS &
DISPLAYS

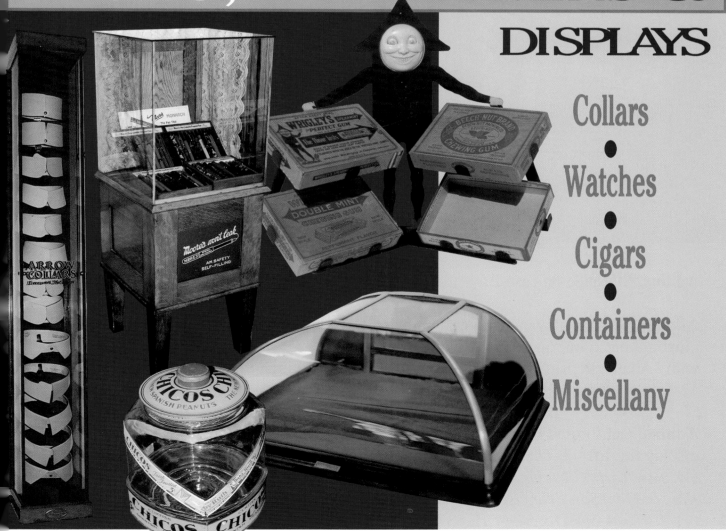

Collars
•
Watches
•
Cigars
•
Containers
•
Miscellany

A.   **Adams**; Marquee on case B.

B.   **Adams**; Gum display cabinet; oak with mirrored back, marquee on top embossed with "Adams Pepsin Tutti-Frutti", 12-1/4"W x 6"D x 17-1/2"H. $750-1000

C.   **Adams**; California Fruit Chewing Gum display tin; lift lid, *The American Chicle Co. New York, Cleveland, Chicago, Kansas City, San Francisco*, c.1920, 6-1/2"W x 4-3/4"D x 5-3/4"H. $375-550

D.   **Adams**; Pepsin Gum display tin; litho on four sides and top, lift lid, c.1920, 6-3/4"W x 4-3/4"D x 6"H. $500-600

E.   **Adams**; Spearmint display tin; litho on four sides and top, lift lid, c.1920, 6-3/4"W x 4-3/4"D x 6"H. $500-600

F.   **Adams**; Gum display cabinet; contemporary marquee for "Tutti Frutti", 12-1/4"W x 6"D x 17-1/2"H. $500-800

A.   **Beech-Nut**; Display; tin, litho of girl on back, metal pedestal, c.1920, 15"H. $1200-1600

B.   **Beech-Nut**; Display; Clown Beech-Nut Gum and Beechies, composition automaton, *Mfgr. by Wooten Studios, Long Island*, c.1930-40s, 22"H. $4000-5000

C.   **Beech-Nut**; Display; for mints, fruit drops and chewing gum, 11-1/2"W x 12-1/2"D x 11"H. $150-225

D.   **Beech-Nut**; Display; tin litho, for mints, fruit drops and chewing gum, c.1920, 9-1/2"W x 17"D x 13-1/2"H, $750-900

E.   **Blood Berry Gum**; Display jar; glass, paper label, c.1900, 12"H. $2000-2500

F.   **Buffalo Pepsin Gum**; Display case; metal frame with, clock, beveled glass panels, painted lettering, c.1900, 13"H. $2800-3500

A. **Chiclets**; Gum display box; cardboard with lid closure and glass lift lid beneath, for bulk gum, Chiclets brass spoon used to select gum tabs, c.1910, 10"W x 2"D x 7-3/4"H. $150-185

B. **Chiclets**; Gum display box; cardboard with glass lift lid, multi-color litho, c.1910, 7-1/2"W x 1-3/4"D x 5"H. $75-115

C. **Chicle**; Yucatan gum counter display tin; litho on four sides and top, lift lid, c.1920, 6-3/4"W x 4-3/4"D x 6"H. $500-600

D. **Clark's**; Teaberry gum change receiver; green depression glass with reverse applied decals and over painting, c.1920, 9"W x 6-1/4"D x 2"H. $250-325

E. **Clark's**; Teaberry tin; litho inside lid, 6-3/4"W x 5"D x 2-1/2"H. $450-525

A. **Cola-Cola**; Gum jar; embossed lid and
    lettering on jar, *Franklin Mfgr. Co.
    Richmond, Va.*, c.1910, 4-1/2"W x 4-1/4"D
    x 10-3/4"H. $1000-2000

B. **Coca-Cola**; Gum jar; Franklin Karo lid,
    no markings on jar, contemporary paper
    label, c.1910, 5"W x 5"D x 11"H.
    $800-1500

C. **Colgan's**; Taffy-Tolu gum counter display
    case; oak and glass, original paper applied

    to glass (front and side views shown), ad
    copy claims to be the "original" chewing
    gum, c.1900, 10"W x 9"D x 12" H.
    $1400-1800

D. **Colgan's**; Gum display case; oak with
    glass sides, reverse paint on glass, c.1910,
    9"W x 8"D x 17-1/2"H. $1000-1250

E. **Colgan's**; Taffy Tolu gum jar; figural jar
    top with lettering on jar, c.1910, 5-1/4"W
    x 5-1/4"D x 11"H. $325-425

A. **Colorado Fruit**; Gum display case; oak slant front, similar to the Zeno case, *H.E. Winterton Gum Co., Memphis-Chicago*, c.1900, 10-1/2"W x 8"D x 15-1/2"H. $700-1000

B. **Curtiss**; Change receiver for Baby Ruth Gum; glass, paper litho reverse applied and over painted, with litho tin gum holder on side, c.1930, 4-1/2"W x 6-1/4"D x 2"H. $300-400

C. **Curtiss**; Change receiver for Baby Ruth Gum; same as B, without tin gum tray, $225-275

D. **Fleers** Dubble Bubble; Ash tray; plaster, c.1920, 7-1/2"W x 6"D x 7-1/2"H. $425-550

E. **Gold Tip**; Chewing gum display; metal, four fold-down shelves, holds five flavors of gum, c.1920, 3-1/2"W x 3"D x 14"H. $325-500

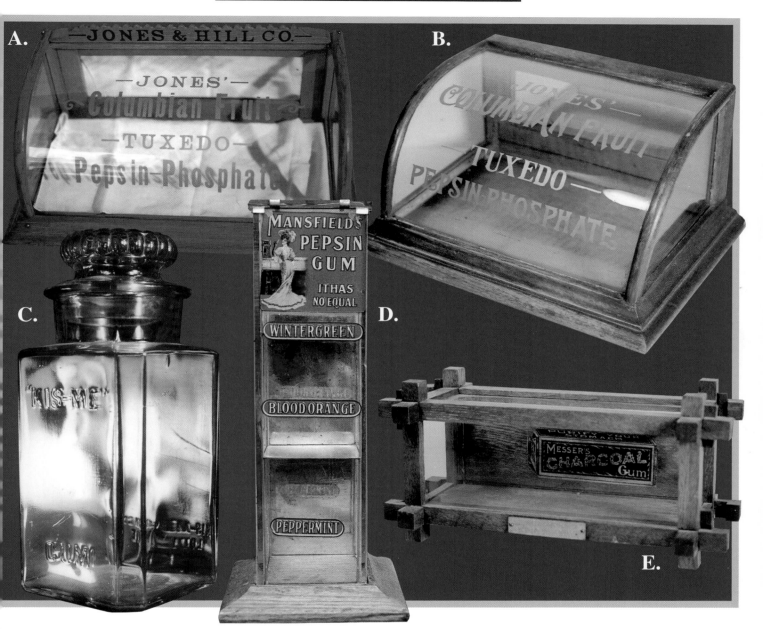

A. **Jones & Hill Co.**; Gum display case; oak and curved glass, reverse painted "Columbian Fruit - Tuxedo - Pepsin - Phosphate", c.1900, 17-1/2"W x 9-1/2"D x 7-3/4"H. $1000-1500

B. **Jones**; Gum display case; oak and curved glass, reverse paint "Columbian Fruit....", c.1900, 14"W x 10"D x 7"H. $1000-1500

C. **Kiss Me**; Gum jar; raised letters and molded lid, square with flat corners, c. 1900, 4-3/4"W x 11"H. $165-185

D. **Mansfield's**; Glass counter display; for Pepsin Gum, reverse applied decal, c.1900, 5"W x 5"D x 11-1/2"H. $1300-1600

E. **Messer's**; Gum display case; oak, for Charcoal Gum, applied decal on back door, brass tag on lower front, 13-1/2"W x 6-1/2"D x 6-1/2"H. $900-1100

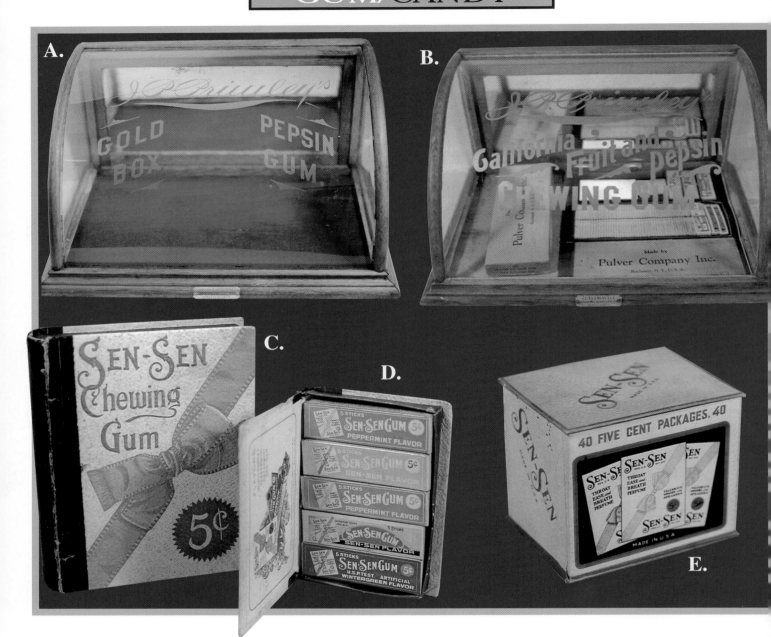

A.   **Primley's**; Gum case; "Gold Box Pepsin Gum", oak, curved glass with reverse etching, *J. Riswig, Chicago*, c.1910, 18-1/2"W x 12-1/4"D x 9-1/2"H. $900-1200

B.   **Primley's**; Gum case; "JP Primley's California Fruit and Pepsin Chewing Gum", oak, curved glass with reverse etching and paint, *J. Riswig, Chicago*, c.1910, 18-1/2"W x 12-1/4"D x 9-1/2"H. $825-1100

C.   **Sen-Sen**, Large gum display book; cardboard, for display of gum packs, c.1910, 6"W x 1-1/2"D x 7"H. $55-85

D.   **Sen-Sen**; Small gum display book; cardboard, includes individual packs of Sen-Sen flavored gum, c.1910, 4"W x 3/4"D x 5-1/2"H. $175-285

E.   **Sen-Sen**; Breath pellets display box; cardboard, fold-up lid, for packets, c.1920, 4"W x 3"D x 3-1/2"H. $135-185

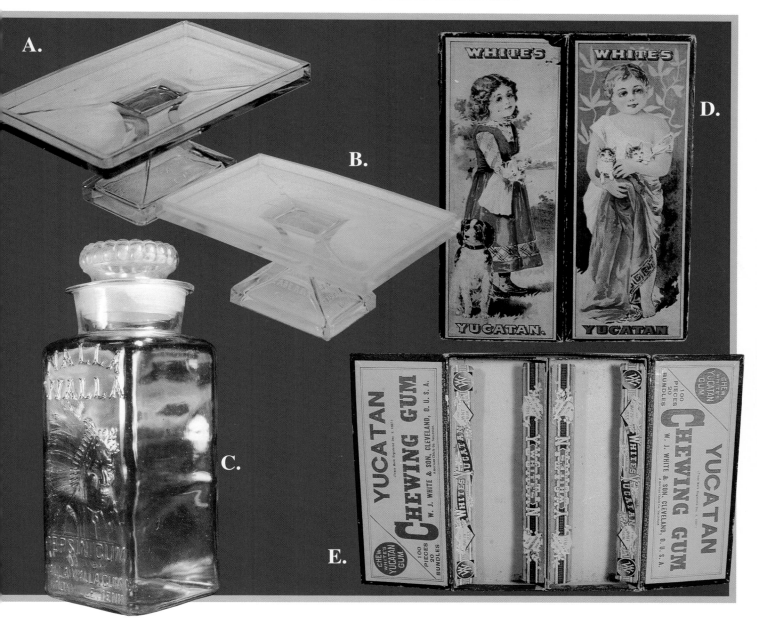

A.   **Teaberry**; Gum display stand/change tray; clear glass, c.1930, 7"W x 3"D x 4-3/4"H. $65-95

B.   **Teaberry**; Gum display stand/change tray; vaseline glass, c.1930, 7"W x 3"D x 4-3/4"H. $125-185

C.   **Walla Walla**; Gum jar; embossed Indian on front, c. 1915, 4-3/4"W x 4-3/4"D x 12-1/2"H. $225-300

D.   **White's**; "Yucatan" gum display box; cardboard, applied multi-color litho paper panels, hard to find, c.1900, 7"W x 3/4"D x 11"H. $300-375

E.   **White's**; display box open

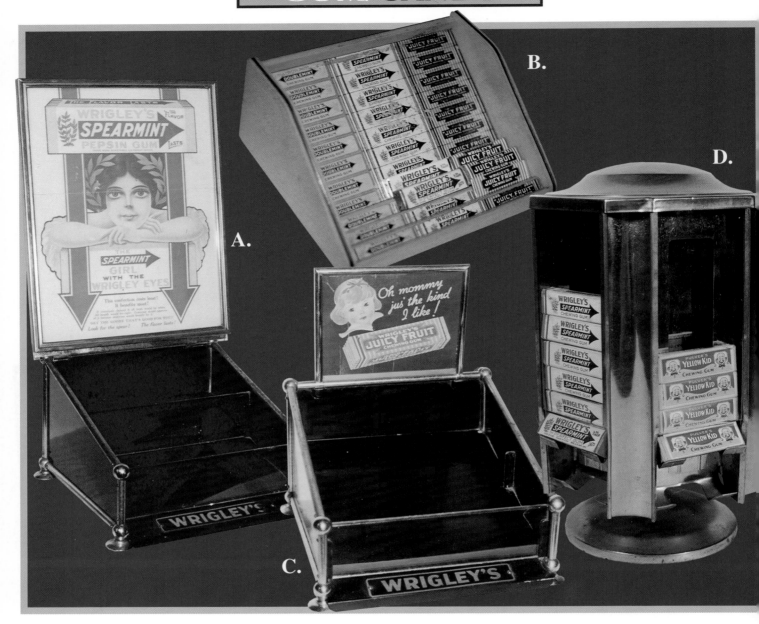

A. **Wrigley's**; Chewing gum display rack; slanted, metal and glass, three levels with header for sign, c.1920, 10"W x 10"D x 21"H. $325-450

B. **Wrigley's**; Gum counter display; maple with lithographed gum packs, holds three flavors, c.1930, 10"W x 8-1/2"D x 4-1/2"H. $155-225

C. **Wrigley's**; Chewing gum display rack; slanted, metal and glass, two levels with header for cardboard litho insert piece, c.1920, 10"W x 10"D x 12"H. $375-475

D. **Wrigley's**; Revolving gum display; nickel-plated metal, holds four flavors, c.1920, 8"Dia. x 14"H. $285-350

A. **Wrigley's**; Gum counter display; painted or dark finished wood with lithographed gum packs, holds three flavors, c.1930, 11"W x 8-1/2"D x 4-1/2"H. $145-200

B. **Wrigley's**; "Vassar" gum display box; cardboard, with lift lid, c.1915, 8-1/2"W x 1-1/2"D x 3-1/2"H. $135-185

C. **Wrigley's**; Santa Claus store premium; used as a giveaway with dealer gum purchases in the 30's, 27"H. $350-400

D. **Wrigley's**; Gum display; die-cut tin, "Moon-faced" figure holds gum display boxes, c.1920, 14"W x 6"D x 13"H. This piece is very price sensitive to condition. $800-1200 (add for paper on back, clear lettering on front, pink cheeks on face and display boxes)

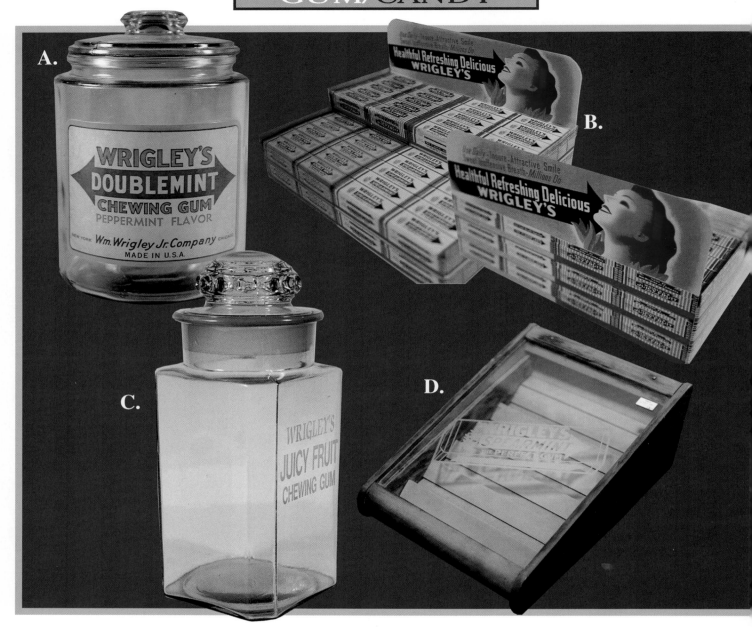

A. **Wrigley's**; Doublemint gum jar; paper labels, jar marked Wrigley's gum on bottom, c.1920, 6"Dia. x 8-1/2"H. $125-175

B. **Wrigley's**; Die-cut cardboard display; advertising Wrigley's Doublemint, Spearmint, and Juicy Fruit Gum, depicts lady on header card "Healthful Refreshing Delicious Wrigley's", c.1937, 12"W x 9"D x 6-3/4"H. $250-325

C. **Wrigley's**; Juicy Fruit jar; purple glass with etched lettering, ground top, c.1910, 5" square with flat corners x 11"H. $400-500

D. **Wrigley's**; Gum display case; ash/maple with reverse etched logo on glass and "Wrigley's Display" decal on back, c.1930 10-1/2"W x 14"D x 5-1/2"H. $375-450

A.   **Zeno**; Close up of marquee on case B.

B.   **Zeno**; Gum display case; oak with cut-out applied letters on marquee, mirror in back door, three glass shelves, c.1910, 10"W x 7-3/4"D x 18-1/2"H. $725-850

C.   **Zeno**; Close up of marquee on case D.

D.   **Zeno**; Gum display case; oak with pressed design in marquee, mirror in back door, three glass shelves, c.1910, 10"W x 7-3/4"D x 18-1/2"H. $775-1000

E.   **Zeno**; Gum counter display tin, litho on inside of lid, 9-1/2"W x 4-1/2"D x 2-1/4"H. $350-450

A. **Zeno**; Countertop case; lift-up lid, oak with reverse etched glass; 13"W x 9-1/2"D x 2-1/2"H. $250-350

B. **Zeno**; Gum lock box; tin, used to ship gum and as a document lock box, paper label on inside of lid, c.1910, 10-1/2"W x 6-1/2"D x 5-1/2"H. $35-85

C. **Belle Camp**; Candy case; ice cooled, ash or gum wood, c.1915, 24-1/2"W x 24-1/2"D x 62-1/2"H. $900-1300

D. **Belle Camp**; Close up of glue chip silver leaf panel in case C.

E. **Chase**; Candy counter display; tin, multi-color litho, *Chase Candy Co., St. Joseph, Mo.*, c.1927, 26"W x 14"D x 23"H. $1800-2500

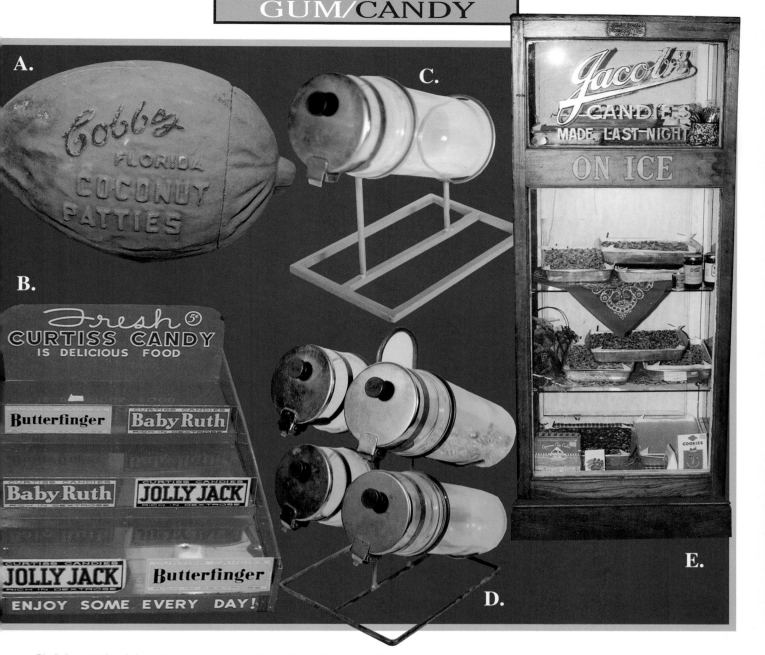

A. **Cobbs** (Florida) Coconut Patties; Candy display container; composition, end comes off, c.1930, 9"L. $75-125

B. **Curtiss**; Candy display; plastic and glass, c.1930, 15-1/2"W x 23"D x 12"H. $450-650

C. **Fazer**; Single countertop bulk display candy jar; 7-1/2"W x 12"D x 13"H. $125-175

D. **Fazer**; Counter top candy display; holds four jars, 10-1/2"W x 12"D x 17-1/2"H. $375-500

E. **Jacobs**; Candy case; ice cooled, ash with reverse gold lettering on glass, *Jacobs Candy Co., New Orleans*, c.1915, 28"W x 23"D x 72"H. $900-1300

A. **Life Savers**; Display; metal with bakelite sides, glass partitions, c.1940, 27"W x 16"D x 10"H. $285-375

B. **Life Savers**; Counter display; multi-color lithographed tin, c.1920, 12-1/2"W x 9"D x 9-1/2"H. $700-900

C. **Life Savers**; Counter display; multi-color lithograph tin, c.1920, 10"W x 15"D x 15"H. $900-1100

D. **Smith & Son's**; Counter display; oak and reverse etched glass "Smith & Son's Salted Nuts and Candies", 11"W x 9"D x 20"H. $325-400

E. **Sommer Richardson**; Cracker/candy glass display case; reverse etched glass, slant front, German silver, c.1890, 24"W x 24"D x 14"H.$550-800

F. **Whitman's** Chocolates; Display case; iron base and brass frame, reverse etched glass, c.1920, 12"W x 5"D x 6-1/2"H. $300-375

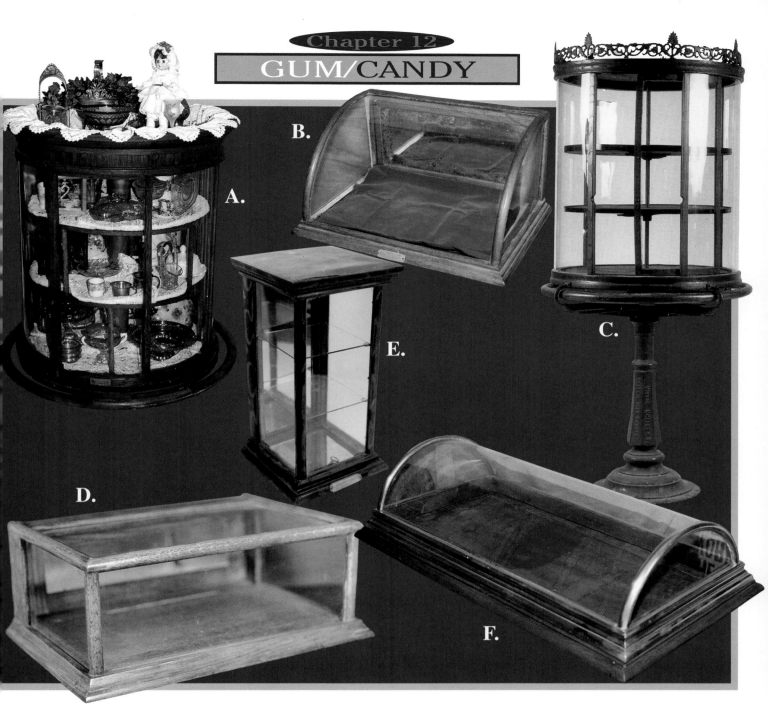

A. Revolving candy case; oak, mfgr. *Curtis, Goddard, Alliance, Ohio*, Pat., May 14, 1889, 32"Dia. x 38"H. $3500-4500

B. Gum or candy display case; curved glass and oak, *J.R. Reswig, Chicago,* 18"W x 12"D x 9"H. $350-450.

C. Display case; curved glass sides, Excelsior, oak on iron base, fancy cast-iron gallery top, *Crystal Case Co., Alliance, OH,* 24"Dia. x 34"H. $3000-4000

D. Countertop candy display case; oak and glass, mirror in back door, c.1910, 15"W x 10-3/4"D x 6"H. $275-350

E. Display case; metal frame with copper flashed finish, *Illinois Showcase Works, Chicago*, 8"W x 9"D x 17"H. $900-1100

F. Countertop gum display case; walnut, German silver trim, curved glass hinged top, c.1900, 27"W x 15"D x 7"H. $900-1100

A. Display case; Excelsior, oak on iron base (variation), curved glass sides, iron gallery top, *Crystal Case Co., Alliance, OH*, 24"Dia. x 34"H. $3000-4000

B. Display case; oak with acorn gallery, curved glass, *Crystal Case Co., Alliance, OH*, 26"Dia. x 34"H. $3000-4000

C. Display case; oak (standard base) with curved glass, iron gallery top, *Crystal Case Co., Alliance, OH, USA*, Pat. May 14, '89 - Jan. 5, '97, Jan. 29, '00, 24"Dia. x 34"H. $3000-4000

D. Display case; oak octagon candy display with revolving center pedestal, holds four shelves, "The Christmas Case" mfgr. by *J. G. Schumm*; pat'd. Dec. 25, 1894, 22-1/2"W x 44"H. $1800-2600

E. Display case; Excelsior, oak, countertop, *Crystal Case Co., Alliance, OH*, 24"Dia. x 34"H. $3000-4000

A. **Conklin's**; Self-filling fountain pen floor display case; quartersawn oak and glass with mirrored sliding doors in back, applied reverse transfer on glass, c.1920, 30"W x 24"D x 41-3/4"H. $400-525

B. **Conklin's**; Close up of reverse transfer.

C. **Crocker**; Counter display; "Ink Tite" self-filling fountain pens, c.1920, 15-1/2"W x 9"D x 3-1/2"H. $275-325

D. **Eberhard Faber** Microtomic Van Dyke; Large display pencil; soft wood, painted, 60"L. $400-450

E. **Eisenstadt's**; "Incomparable" floor pen case; cherry stained maple with reverse etched front glass, rare, c.1915, 16"W x 17"D x 42"H. $375-450

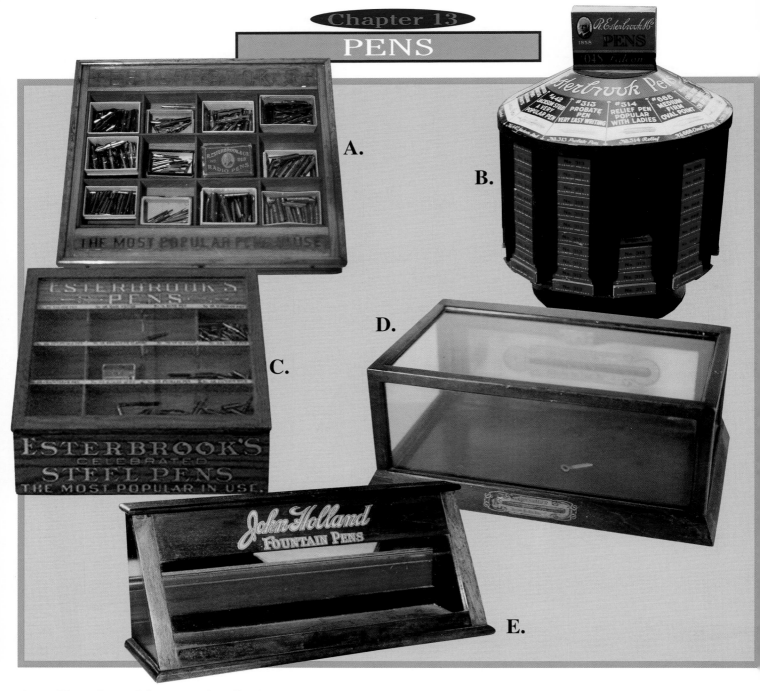

A. **Esterbrook's**; Pen tip display case; oak, 12 compartments for pen tips, c.1920, 13-1/4"W x 11-1/4"D x 2-1/4"H. $200-285

B. **R. Esterbrook & Co.**; Pen point counter display rack; revolves, lithographed tin, c.1920, 14"Dia. x 16"H. $225-300

C. **Esterbrook's**; Counter display case; wood, compartments for various metal tips for steel pens, stenciling in front and top of case, c.1920, 13-1/2"W x 5"H. $125-200

D. The **Grieshaber**; Counter showcase; "Keeps to the Write", birch with mahogany stain, applied decal on front and mirror back, c.1915, 17-1/2"W x 11-1/2"D x 7"H. $375-450

E. **John Holland**; Counter display case; birch with walnut stain, c.1920, 20"W x 6"D x 10"H. $225-275

A.   **Hunt's**; Pen cabinet; oak, applied gold lettering, c.1920, 22"W x 15"D x 6"H. $325-400

B.   **Hunt**; Pen point display case; wood and glass, large decal on glass, "Round Pointed C. Howard Hunt Pen Co. Tip", pull-out drawer, 16 compartments, c.1920, 12"W x 10"D. $150-250

C.   **Matchless**; Fountain pen countertop display case; oak and glass, holds one tray of pens, c.1910, 9-1/4"W x 8-1/4"D x 3-1/2"H. $185-275

D.   **Moore's**; "Won't Leak" fountain pen floor case; oak with etched glass, c.1910, 16"W x 16"D x 42-1/2"H. $350-450

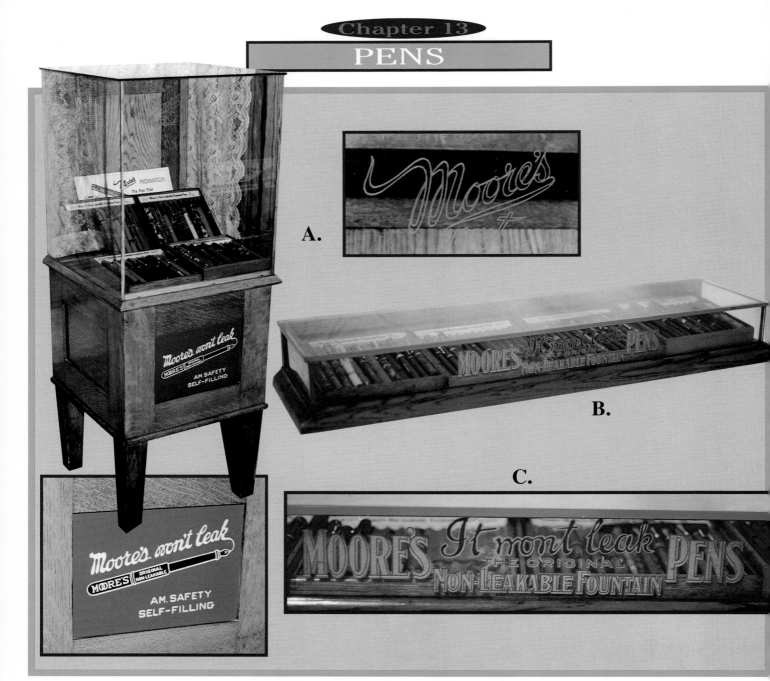

A.

B.

C.

A. **Moore's**; "Won't Leak" fountain pen single floor case; oak, etched glass front, porcelain insert panel below, c.1910, 16-1/4"W x 16-1/4"D x 42"H. $550-650

B. **Moore's**; "It Won't Leak" fountain pens countertop display case; oak and glass, holds four trays of pens, reverse applied transfer, c.1910, 31-3/4"W x 8-1/2"D x 4-1/2"H. $225-300

C. **Moore's**; Reverse applied decal on front glass of B.

A.   **Parker**; "Lucky Curve" fountain pens and pencils floor display case; single wide, oak and glass with reversed etching, holds six trays of pens or pencils, c.1915, 16-1/2"W x 23-1/4"D x 42"H. $350-450

B.   **Parker**; "Lucky Curve" fountain pen floor case; oak and etched glass with door below, c.1915, 17-1/2"W x 23-1/4"D x 42"H. $425-550

C.   **Parker**; "Lucky Curve" fountain pen countertop display case; oak and glass, holds two trays of pens, 12 each, gold transfer lettering on back door, c.1910, 15-3/4"W x 8-1/2"D x 7"H. $375-500

A.   **Sanford's**; Inks display box; wood box that advertises "Sanford's Inks" on four sides, 13-1/2"W x 7"D x 6"H. $35-60

B.   **Sanford's**; Inks display case; wood and glass countertop display with "Sanford's Inks" decals on three sides, 12"W x 10"D x 17-1/2"H. $350-500

C.   **Sanford's**; Inks display case; birch with walnut stain; applied letters and reverse decal, doors open from angled sides, 23"W x 13"D x 33"H. $325-400

D.   **Sanford's**; Inks display case; oak, applied reverse decal, 12-1/2"W x 11"D x 16-1/2"H. $500-600

E.   **Sanford's**; Inks display case; wood and glass countertop display with "Sanford's Inks" decal on front, 8"W x 6"D x 11"H. $300-400

F.   **Sanford's**; Inks display case; oak, applied reverse decal, 11"W x 8"D x 16"H. $500-600

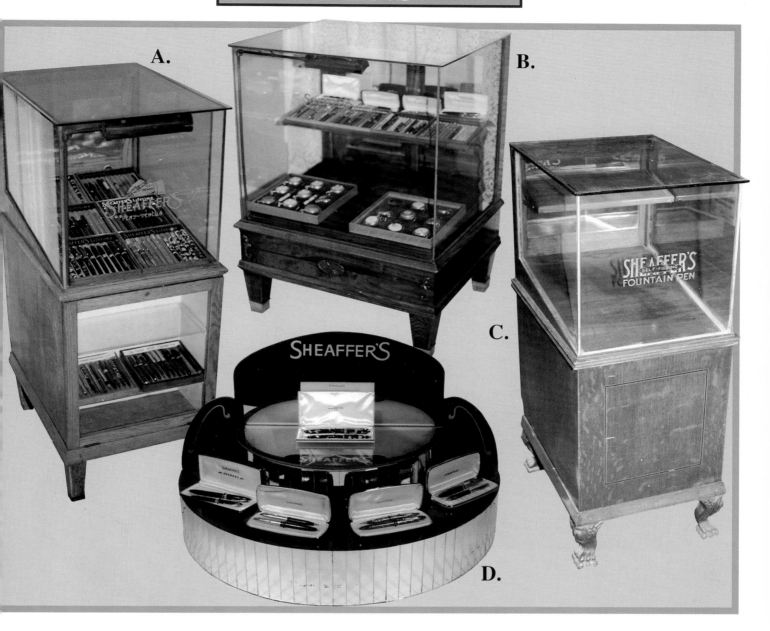

A.   **Sheaffer's**; Floor display case; single wide, oak and glass, interior lighted, glass door in front lower, reverse etched front glass, c.1920, 16-1/2"W x 23-1/2"D x 42"H. $450-550

B.   **Sheaffer's**, Floor display case; double wide, lighted, birch with cherry stain, reverse applied lettering inside glass, c.1920, 30-1/2"W x 26"D x 42"H. $475-600

C.   **Sheaffer's**; "Self-filling" floor display case; oak with etched glass, cast-iron claw feet, c.1920, 17"W x 23"D x 42-1/2"H. $400-475

D.   **Sheaffer's**; Counter display stand; glass, top level lit from below. mirrored panels on front of two levels, c.1950, 29"W x 18"D x 18"H. $325-375

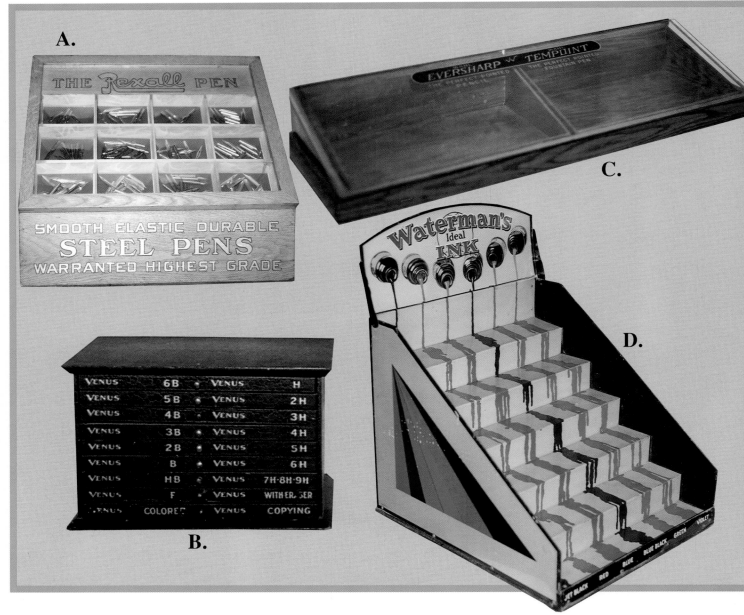

A. **Rexall**; Steel pen point counter display case; oak with transfer letters, 12 compartments for pen points and drawer in back, c.1915, 14"W x 14"D x 8"H. $250-275

B. **Venus;** Pencil cabinet; birch, nine drawers, c.1920, 14"W x 8"D x 8"H. $185-215

C. **Wahl Eversharp/Tempoint**; Pen and pencil display case; oak and glass, slant top, etched and reverse painted glass, two removable wood trays for pens or pencils, c.1920, 26"W x 8"D x 4"H. $185-225

D. **Waterman's**; Ink counter display; tin multi-color litho, *H.D. Beach Co., Coshocton, OH*, c.1905-1910, 15"W x 17"D x 20"H. $725-800

PENS

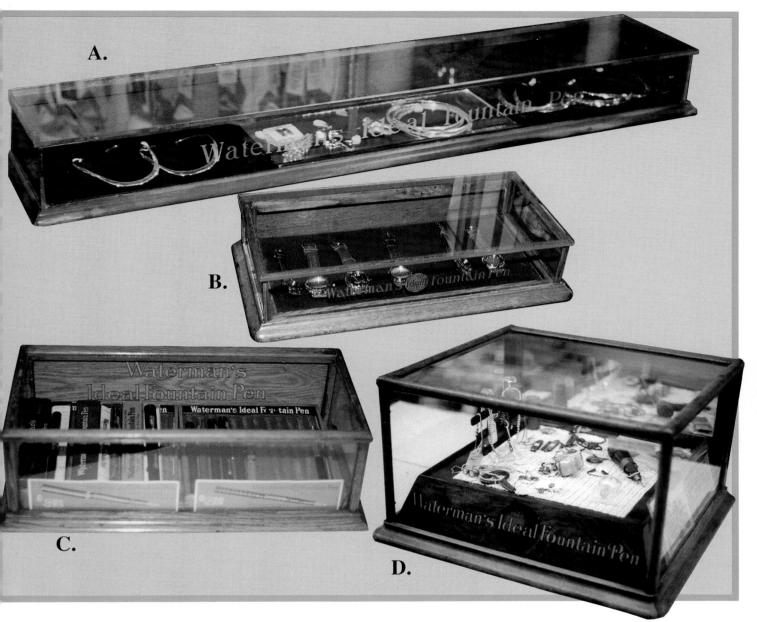

A. **Waterman's**; "Ideal" counter display case; walnut with etched glass front, reverse transfer letters, unusually large, c.1910, 47"W x 9"D x 5"H. $500-600

B. **Waterman's**; "Ideal" counter display case; oak and glass, letters and logo applied reverse inside, c.1910, 17"W x 8"D x 4"H. $325-375

C. **Waterman's**; "Ideal" fountain pen case; oak and glass, holds two trays of pens, applied transfer lettering inside door, c.1910, 17-3/4"W x 8-1/2"D x 7-1/2"H. $375-425

D. **Waterman's**; "Ideal" fountain pen display case; oak and glass, platform riser on interior, transfer with logo on front of riser, mirrored back door, c.1910, 22"W x 20"D x 10"H. $425-550,

A. **Carborundum**; Display case for pocket hones; triangular, oak and glass, two windows have trademark Indian head in center, 23" x 23" x 27" x 41"H. $1200-1600

B. **Carborundum**; Sharpening stones display case; medallion is embossed with Indian head, inside of front door, shelves in cabinet, 24"W x 19-1/2"H. $1500-1800

C. **Cattaraugus**; Knife display case; soft wood, pins to hold knives, applied lettering, 32"W x 12"D x 14"H. $600-800

D. **Cattaraugus**; Cutlery display case; wood, unusual "fan" countertop case with ornate hardware, paper advertising on two sides, 11"H. $600-900

E. **Clauss Shear Co.**; Counter display case; ash, reverse etched glass, 15-1/4"W x 15-1/4"D x 31-1/2"H. $600-700

A.   **Ever-Ready** Safety Razor; Display; simulated wood grained tin, trademark die-cut marquee of man shaving face, 12-1/2"W x 9"D x 11"H. $700-1100

B.   **Howard's Cutlery**; Counter display case; walnut with German silver trim, reverse etched glass, 24-1/2"W x 12-1/2"D x 12-3/4"H. $750-900

C.   **Howard's Cutlery**; Display case; oak, curved glass, c.1910, 16"Dia. x 26"H. $575-800

D.   **Keen Kutter Kutlery**; Knife display case; oak with etched glass front, interior shaped to hold knife boxes, c.1910, 53-1/2"W x 28"D x 17-1/2"H. $700-900

E.   Steel saws display case; oak and glass rotating floor model, doors open on two sides, 22-1/2"W x 23"D x 38"H. $700-1100

A. **Keen Kutter**; Scissor display case; oak and glass, reverse etched front, glass panel in door, 14-3/4"W x 13-3/4"D x 30-3/4"H. $475-550

B. **Keen Kutter**; Countertop display case; oak, mirrors in sliding back doors, reverse etched glass in front, *Simmons Hardware Co., Mfgr. & Distributors, St. Louis, Mo.,* 33-1/2"W x 24"D x 12-1/2"H. $500-725

C. **Keen Kutter**; Display case; oak with reverse etched glass, 14"W x 12"D x 26"H. $400-600

D. **Norvell-Shapleigh Hardware Co.**; Display case; wood and etched glass countertop display, Diamond-Edge trademark, 14-1/2"W x 24"H. $400-600

E. **Norvell Shapleigh**; Hardware display case; oak with plated iron trim, *Norvell Shapleigh Hardware, St. Louis,* c.1900, 48"W x 22"D x 42"H. $475-650

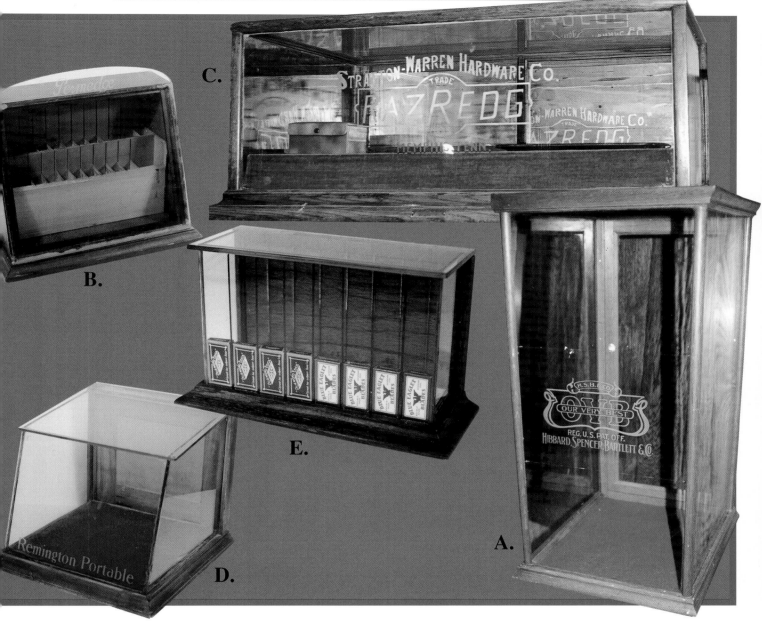

A. **OVB**, Our Very Best; Cutlery display case; oak, reverse etched glass front, *Hibbard, Spencer, Bartlett & Co.*, c.1910, 14"W X 14"D x 28"H. $350-475

B. **Permedge**; Counter razor display case; reversed etched glass at top, 14-1/2"W x 8"D x 13-1/2"H. $85-135

C. **RAZREDG**; Display case; Stratton-Warren Hardware Co., Memphis, TN, oak display for razors, reverse etched front glass, *H. Pauk & Sons, St. Louis, MO,* c.1900, 41-1/2"W x 28"D x 17-1/2"H. $450-600

D. **Remington**; Counter case for "Portable Razors"; birch, reverse etched glass front, 15-1/2"W x 14-1/2"D x 12"H. $185-225

E. **OVB,** Our Very Best; Razor display, oak, "Order blades.....from" *Hibbard, Spencer, Bartlett & Co. Chicago,* 12"W x 4-1/2"D x 7"H. $185-250

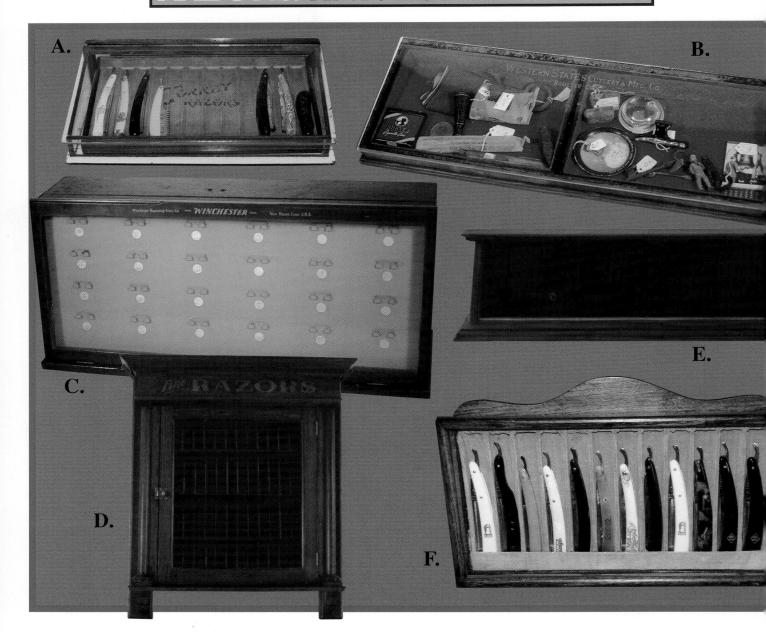

A.   **Torrey**; Razor counter display; oak and glass with reverse etched glass, holds 13 razors,15"W x 8"D x 14"H. $175-225

B.   **Western State Cutlery & Mfg. Co.**; Cutlery case; walnut, *Boulder, Co.*, 29"W x 10"D x 3-1/2"H. $275-350

C.   **Winchester**; Knife case; birch, 31-1/2"W x 9-1/2"D x 15"H. $550-675

D.   Razor display case; "Fine Razors", oak, columns beside beveled glass door, displays individual straight razors, 36"W x 8"D x 41"H. $1400-1700

E.   Razor display case; wood, holds straight edge razors, restored, 24-1/2"W x 7"D x 6-1/2"H. $175-250

F.   Razor counter display case; oak with walnut finish, holds 12 razors in velvet lined compartments, c.1910, 15"W x 8"D x 2"H. $150-225

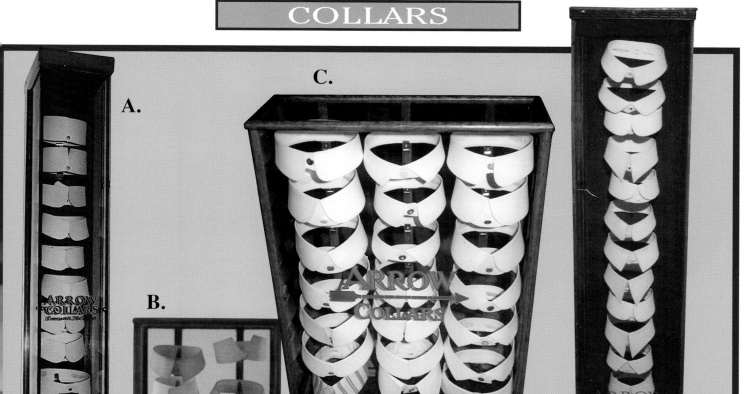

A. **Arrow**; Collar display case; exterior, copper and glass, reverse transfer on glass. *Reinle, Salmon Co., Baltimore, Md.,* c.1910, 7"W x 8"D x 50"H. $1000-1200

B. **Arrow**; Collar countertop display case; wood and glass, two columns of collars, reverse transfer letters, c.1910, 12"W x 8-1/2"D x 25-1/2"H. $500-700

C. **Arrow**; Collar counter display case; oak frame with glass on four sides, reverse transfer lettering on front, three columns of collars, c.1910, 19"W x 7"D x 26"H. $775-900

D. **Arrow**; Collar display case; used on exterior of store, single column of collars, metal and glass, c.1910, 2-1/4"W x 7-1/2"D x 49-1/2"H. $875-950

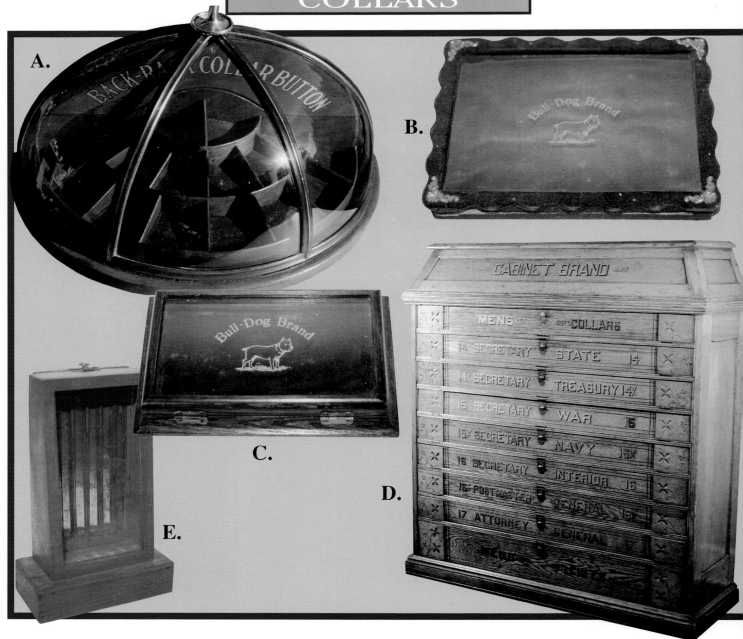

A. **Back-Rack**; Collar button counter display case; unusual curved glass, metal and wood frame, Pat'd July 12, 1910, 14"W x 9"H. $1600-2000

B. **Bulldog Brand**; Collar button display; velvet covered wood with fancy brass trim and reverse painted glass, c.1900, 9-1/2"W x 7-1/2"D x 1-1/4"H. $115-165

C. **Bulldog Brand**; Collar button display; oak with reverse painted glass in lid, c.1900, 8"W x 5"D x 2"H. $125-175

D. **Cabinet Brand**; Collars/cuffs cabinet; oak, 9-drawer, very unusual, c.1900, 41"W x 14"D x 45"H. $5500-6500

E. **King's**; Collar button display; small, oak with glass front, opens from back, drawer below, reverse painted letters on glass, 6"W x 3"D x 9-1/2"H. $185-250

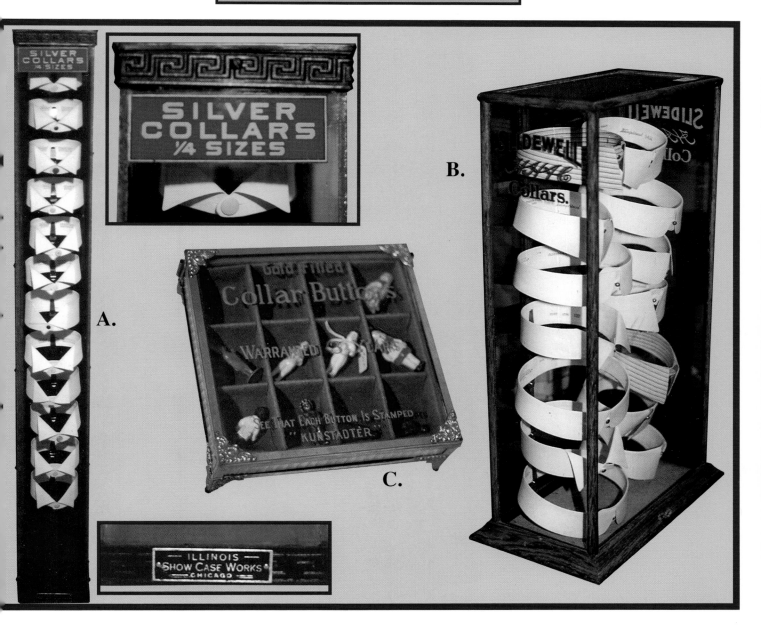

A.   **Silver**; Collar display case; used on exterior of store, single column of collars, metal and glass, made by *Illinois Showcase Works*, c.1910, 6-1/2"W x 7-1/2"D x 49-1/2"H. $600-750

B.   **Slidewell H.H.A. & E.**; Collar display case; reverse etched side panels, *Illinois Showcase Works, Mfgr., Chicago*, c.1910, 14-1/2"W x 8-1/2"D x 25-1/2"H. $1100-1300

C.   Collar button display case; metal with brass legs, reverse etched glass with gold leaf lettering, 12 compartment drawer pulls out, c.1890, 7-3/4"W x 7-3/4"D x 2"H. $275-325

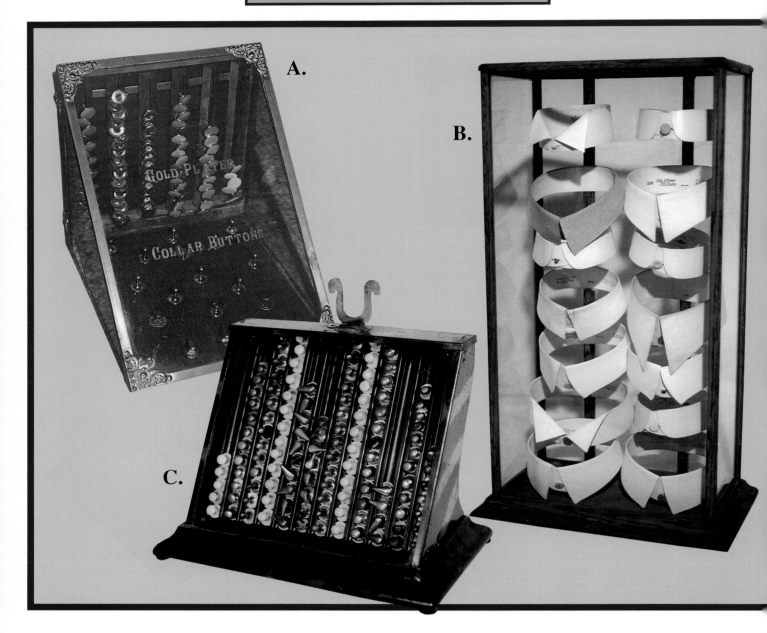

A. Collar button counter display case; metal frame with slant front and glass sides, etched gold reverse painted letters, c.1890, 6-1/2"W x 6-1/2"D x 6-1/2"H. $125-175

B. Collar display case; oak and glass, collars put in through removable bottom panel, holds two rows with seven each, c.1910, 14-1/2"W x 8-1/2"D x 25-1/2"H. $475-600

C. Collar button counter slant front display case; metal with flash copper plating and glass, made to hold cardboard point of purchase sign, c.1910, 9-1/2"W x 5-1/2"D x 7"H. $150-225

A. Watch display case; oak and glass, base velvet covered ash with relief for watches, this case was used with a variety of different watch manufacturers glass in it, as well as no advertising, c.1910, 9"W x 9-1/2"D x 9"H. $85-125

B. **Uncle Sam**; Watch display case; slant fronted, birch with walnut stain, reverse paint on glass, interior formed to hold watches, c.1920, 9"W x 9-1/2"D x 9-1/2"H. $600-800

C. Watch spring cabinet; oak, three drawers, "Swiss & American Mainsprings" applied decal lettering, spiral front trim, 15"W x 10"D x 12"H. $285-375

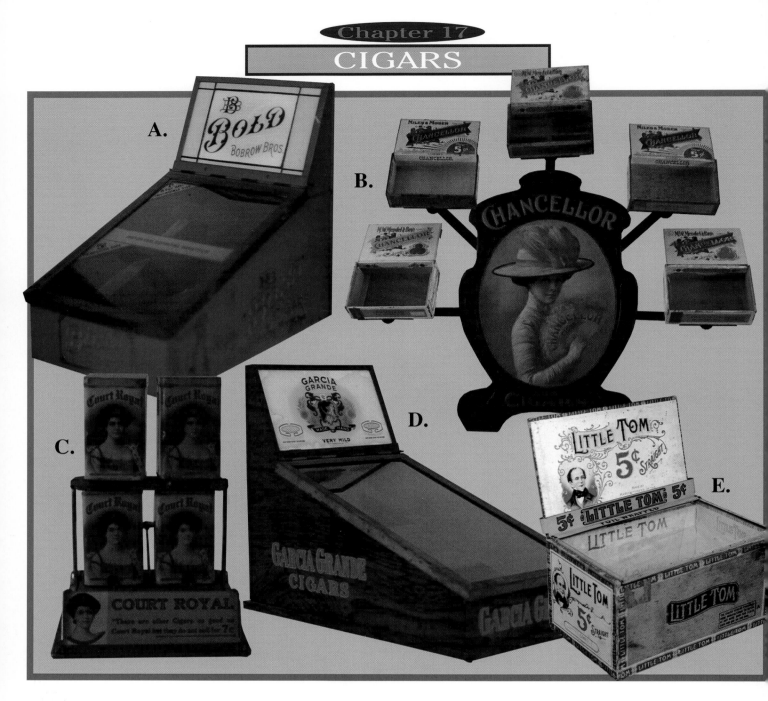

A. **Borrow Bros.**; Cigar display humidor for "Bold" cigars; glass and metal, 10"W x 16"D x 15"H. $250-375

B. **Chancellor**; Cigar tin display; die cut shows lady in hat with fan, five display arms, very rare, *Mayer & Lavenson Co.* 40"W x 35"H. $18000+

C. **Court Royal**; Cigar display; holds four tins, when handle in back is pushed down, two lower cans tilt forward so customer can take out cigars, and bell rings, base is embossed cast iron, paper under glass on lower front, 9-1/2"W x 7"D x 8-1/2"H. $1000-1500

D. **Garcia Grande**; Cigar display humidor for "Garcia Grande" cigars; glass and metal, 10"W x 16"D x 15"H. $250-375

E. **Little Tom**; Cigar box; tin framed glass lid that holds up cigar box lid, 8-1/2"W x 5-1/2"D x 5"H. $35-55

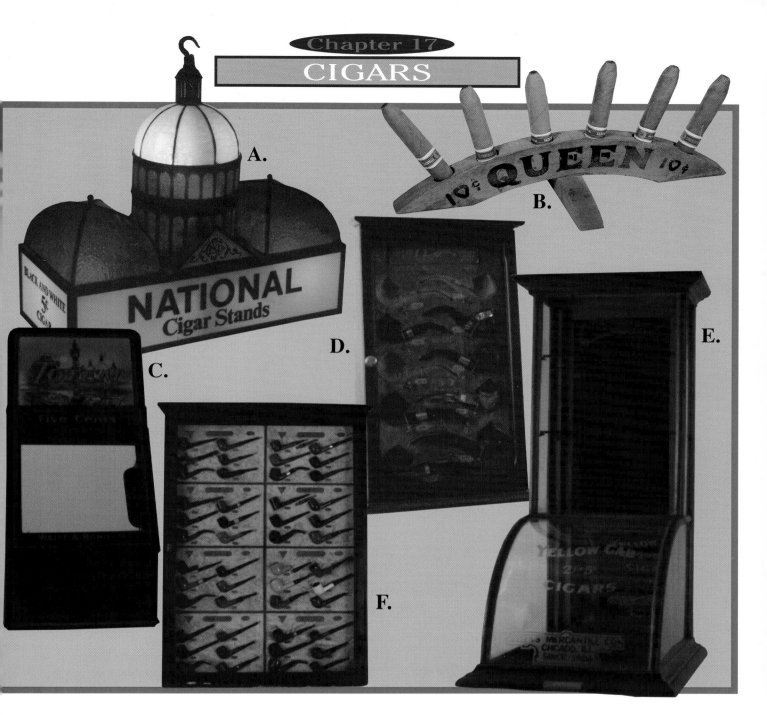

A. **National**; Cigar store lamp; stained glass shade, original ad panels are debossed and painted, c.1910, 23"W x 11"D x 23"H. $3500-4000

B. **Queen**; Cigar display stand; wood with twist-out wooden foot, holds six cigars, c.1900, 12"W x 1"D x 2"H. $115-165

C. **Totem**; Cigar display; die-cut tin marquee, holds boxes of Waitt & Bon Totem cigars, 8-1/2"W x 7"D x 13-1/2"H. $250-375

D. **Wellbore**; Pipe display; glass and wood, for Genuine French Briar Wellbore Pipes, 11"W x 6-1/2"D x 18"H. $350-500

E. **Yellow Cab**; Cigar display case; etched curved glass and wood, (some of these cases have contemporary glass), *H. Pauk & Sons Mfg. Co. St. Louis, MO.*, 21"W x 16"D x 34"H. $1000-1300

F. Pipe display case; wood and glass wall mounted holds 48 pipes, 30"W x 4-1/2"D x 40"H. $500-650

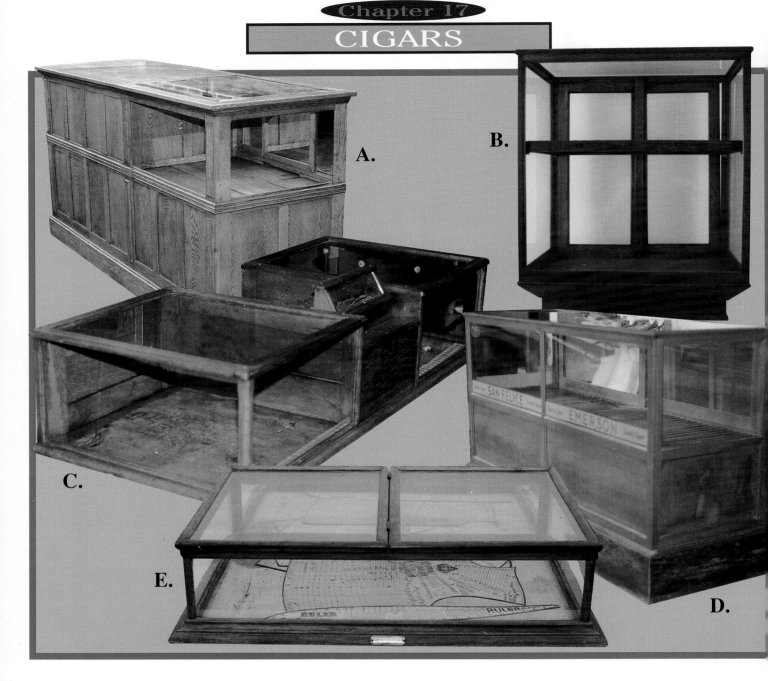

A. Counter and cigar humidor display; oak, hotel registration counter, *Keystone, Dubuque, Iowa*, c.1910, 85"W x 30"D x 44-1/2"H. $1600-1800

B. Cigar display case; oak and glass, floor model, sliding glass doors in back, one shelf, 34-1/2"W x 21-1/2"D x 42"H. $300-500

C. Registering showcase; oak countertop case, commonly used to hold cigars, cash register in center section, 52-1/2"W x 22"D x 11-1/2"H. $600-750

D. Floor cigar humidor showcase; "San Felice Cigars", birch with cherry stain, c.1920, 71"W x 24"D x 42"H. $750-900

E. Countertop cigar case; oak, with lifting top panels, *H. Pauk & Sons Mfg., Co., 1327 N. Fifteenth St., St. Louis, MO*, c.1900, 34"W x 23-1/2"D x 8-3/4"H. $450-650

A. **Aridor**; Display jar; on aluminum stand, used for bulk crackers, Pat. 1917, 10"H. $125-150

B. **Chico's**; Display jar; original paper, c.1930, 8"W x 8"D x 11"H. $450-600

C. **Diamond;** Spice bin; metal, four compartment, stenciled with applied lettering, c.1890, 54"W x 21"D x 40"H. $750-900

D. **Gun Powder**; Tea display canister; tin with litho'd and applied lettering, *Merchant Mills, Milwaukee, WI.*, c.1870, 18"W x 18"D x 20"H. $750-925

A. **J.H. Allen & Co's**; Coffee display bin; tin lithographed bulk store display, St. Paul, Minn, c. 1890, 13-1/2"W x 14"D x 22-1/2"H. $350-450

B. **Monarch**; Tea bin; tin, multi-colored litho front and top, c.1900, 13"W x 12"D x 15"H. $575-700

C. **Portable Pantry**; tin with cylindrical vertical canisters; painted design and lettering, c.1890, 32"W x 39"H. $500-650

D. **Ramon's**; Medicine jar; glass with tin lid, applied lettering, c.1930's, 8"Dia. x 10"H. $135-175

E. **Squirrel Salted Nuts**; Display jar with paper label; 5-1/2"W x 5-1/2"D x 9-1/4"H. $175-225

A. Cane case; oak, wrought iron interior cane holder with tiered pedestal bottom, 24"W x 24"D x 46"H. $1100-1300

B. Cane case; oak, stick and ball insert, 25-1/2"W x 18-1/2"D x 46"H. $750-800

C. Cane and umbrella case; oak with glass on four sides and top, *Russell and Sons Co., Ilion, NY,* c.1910, 30"W x 14"D x 45"H. $625-700

D. Cane and umbrella store counter display case; walnut with etched glass panels, *Exhibition Showcase Co.- Erie, PA*, Pat. Nov. 17, '89, 32"W x 27-1/2"D x 49-1/2"H. $1800-2200

E. Close up of glass panel "Ladies Choice Umbrellas and Parasols".

F. Close up of glass panel "Mens Choice Canes and Umbrellas".

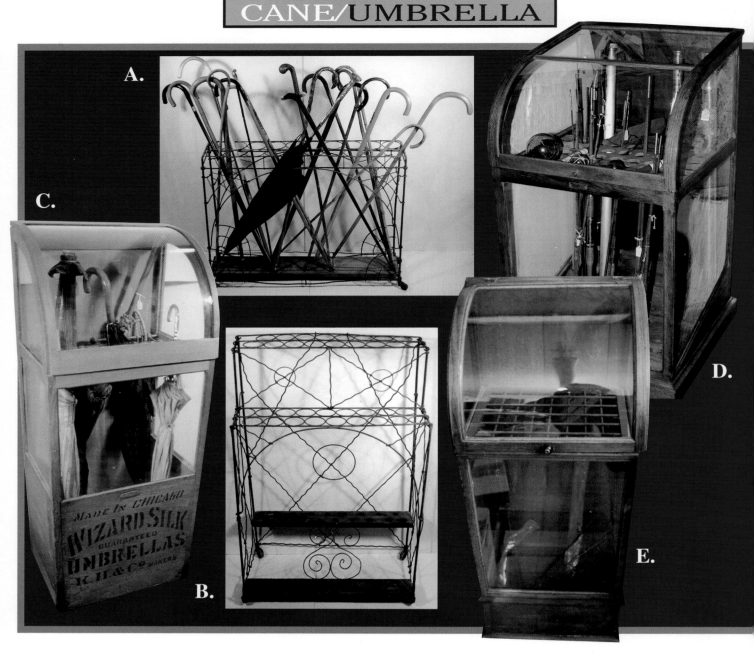

A. Cane and umbrella rack; wire and wood, unusual, c.1880, 32"W x 7-1/2"D x 23-1/2"H. $450-500

B. Cane and umbrella rack; wire and wood, two levels, unusual, c.1880, 23-1/2"W x 36-1/2"D x 12-1/2"H. $525-650

C. **Wizard Silk Umbrellas**; Display case; oak, stenciled lettering, *Mfgr. Alex H. Revell & Co., 431-437 5th Ave, Chicago,* c.1890, 19"W x 14"D x 47"H. $600-750

D. Umbrella case; oak, slanted top with curved glass, *Mfgr. Joe Knittel Showcase Co, Quincy, Il.,* c.1900, 28-1/2"W x 28-1/2"D x 49"H. $900-1100

E. Umbrella display case; oak and glass with curved glass lifting door, c.1900, 20"W x 16"D x 30"H. $650-800

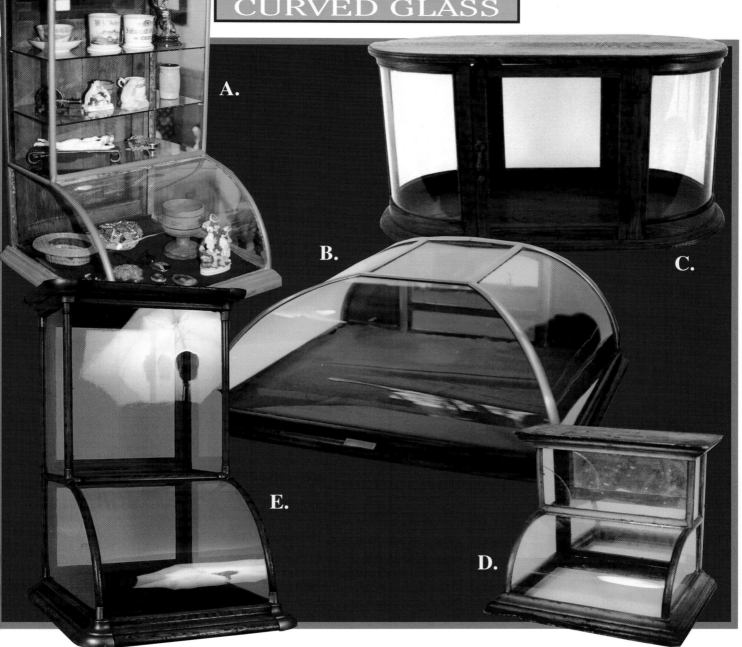

A.

B.

C.

E.

D.

A.   Display case; single tower oak, German silver, *C. McJohn & Co., N.W. Showcase Mfg. 47 to 49 St., Chicago, Il.*, c.1890, 24"W x 24"D x 34"H. $900-1100

B.   Display case; walnut and German silver, curved glass on three sides, *Excelsior Showcase Works, Jos. Knittel Proprietor, 54 to 60 N. Third St., Quincy, Il.*, c.1890, 24"W x 24"D x 14"H. $1000-1400

C.   Display case; oak and glass oval counter case, single opening back door, unusual shape, c.1910, 30"W x 16"D x 16"H. $500-750

D.   Jewelry case; German silver, curved glass, small, *N.Y. Showcase Co, 58 W. Broadway, NY*, c.1900, 17-1/2"W x 12"D x 15"H. $600-950

E.   Display case; single tower, walnut with German silver trim, c.1900, 24"H x 24"D x 40"H. $1300-1600

A.   Curved glass tower showcase; walnut with German silver trim, c.1900, 24"W x 21"D x 31"H. $1200-1400

B.   Display case; curved glass, German silver frame, c.1900, 21"W x 21"D x 12"H. $300-375

C.   Display Case; floor, *L. Paulle Maker, Minn., MN,* c.1900, 20"W x 20"D x 72"H. $1100-1500

D.   Display case; walnut, curved glass, mirror in back door, *Mfgr. Excelsior Showcase Works, Quincy, Il., St. Louis, Mo.,* 24"W x 21"D x 12"H. $350-450

E.   Display case; German silver, double curved glass, c.1890, 8'-3"W x 27"D x 23"H. $2800-3500

F.   Display case; double tier German silver counter case, unusual curved front center section widens at bottom, c.1900, 60"W x 24"D x 48"H. $2200-3000

A. Display case; oak with glass slant top, opens from hinges at front, probably for hardware, *Henry L. Hanson Co.*, c.1930, 18"W x 12-1/2"D x 9"H. $135-200

B. Display case; birch with walnut stain jewelry store case, slant front, *Columbus Showcases, Columbus, Ohio*, c.1920, 24"W x 24"D x 58"H. $450-600

C. Display case; slant front oak and glass countertop case, sliding glass doors in back, two interior shelves, c.1920, 36"W x 22"D x 32"H. $300-450

D. Display case; metal and glass counter case with embossed plated corner trim, door tips down in back, c.1900, 13"W x 8-1/2"D x 7-1/2"H. $125-175

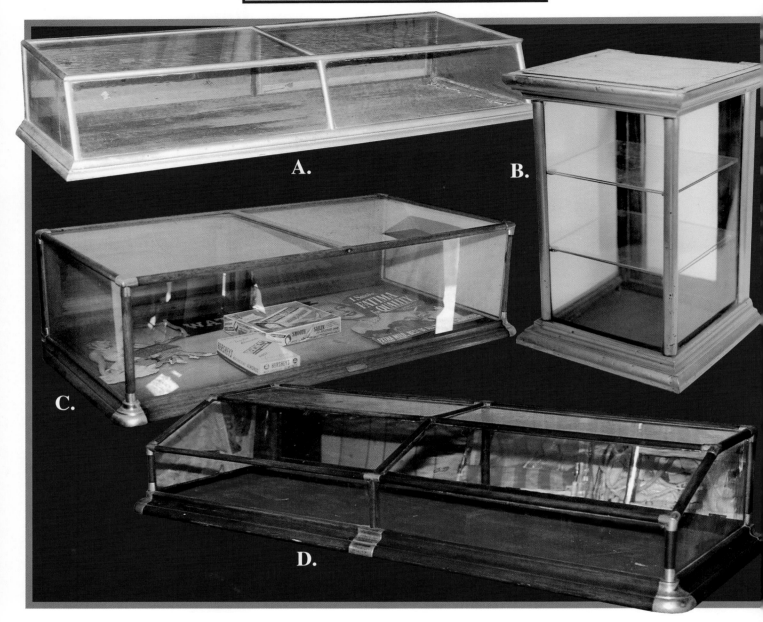

A. Display case; double wide German silver counter display for silver or jewelry, slant front, c.1900, 72"W x 26"D x 13"H. $550-800

B. Display case; German silver counter case with unusual slide up back door, c.1900, 12-1/2"W x 11-3/4"D x 19"H. $400-600

C. Display case; double wide oak and glass counter display with German silver corner trim. *Quincy Showcase Works, 127-135 Main St Quincy, Ill*, 48"W x 24"D x 13"H. $550-650

D. Display case; walnut with German silver trim, *Excelsior Showcase Works Mfgr. Jos Knitte Prop. No. 100-106 N. 3rd St., Quincy, Il Branch House, 313 No. Main St., St. Louis, Mo.*, 73"W x 27"D x 14"H. $1100-1400

Chapter 19
GENERIC CASES

A. Display cases; matching, walnut, cherry and maple inlay, glass sides, mirror back door, c.1880, 11"W x 8"D x 21-1/2"H. (pair), $1100-1300

B. Display case; metal and glass, counter case, c.1910, 16-1/2"W x 8"D x 6"H. $115-175

C. Display case; countertop German silver case, *Borneman & Co, Phila.*, c.1900, 14"W x 7"D x 5-1/2"H. $200-275

D. Display case; countertop German silver case, c.1900, 4-1/2"W x 7-1/2"D x 12-1/2"H. $325-400

E. Display case; triangular walnut and glass case with lift top, c.1900, 10"W x 10"D x 4-1/2"H. $325-450

A. Display case; German silver counter case, *A.H. Revell Mfg. Co. 431-437 5th Ave. Chicago*, c.1890, 20"W x 21"D x 31"H. $350-450

B. Display case; oak with bevel glass, countertop jewelry case, three drawers slide from both sides, c.1910, 15-1/2"W x 9"D x 4-1/2"H. $275-375

C. Display case; small wood and glass countertop case, c.1900, 21"W x 14-1/2"D x 10"H. $250-350

D. Display case; German silver, unusual tip-up top doors, *Schmitt & Co. 55 & 57 Main St., Cinn., Ohio*, 36"W x 22"D x 9"H. $550-650

E. Display case; small glass and wood countertop case, *Alfred Noack High Grade Showcases, Oakland, Cal.*, 27-1/2"W x 8"D x 8-1/2"H. $175-300

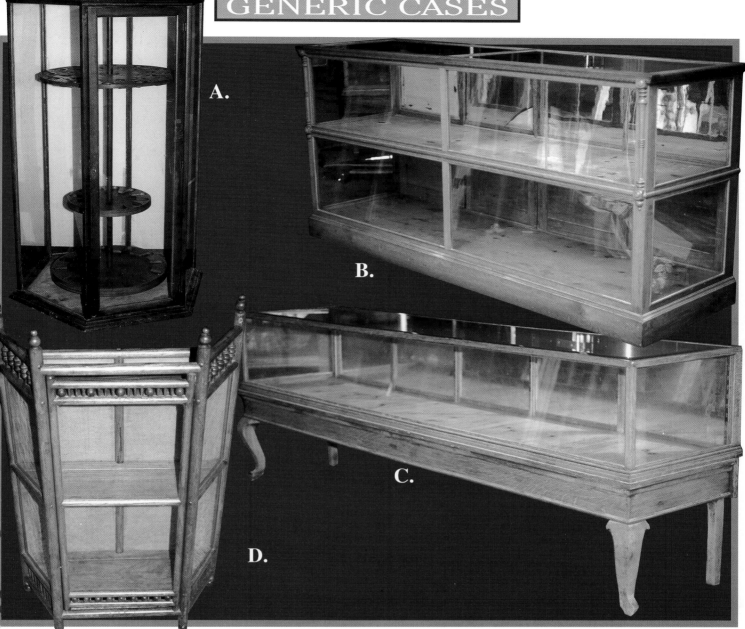

A. Gun display case; fumed oak hexagonal, *Mfgr. H. Pauk & Sons, Mfgr. Co., 327 N. 15th St., St. Louis*, c.1890, 32-1/2"Dia. x 55"H. $1350-1700

B. Display case; floor, oak and glass, with mirrored sliding rear doors, *The Nauman Co., Makers, Waterloo, Iowa*, c.1910, 96"W x 28"D x 45"H. $475-650

C. Floor jewelers showcase; oak, Queen Anne legs, single piece bevel glass top and front, slide down doors in rear, *The Nauman Co. Makers, Waterloo, IA*, c.1910, 122"W x 28-1/2"D x 42"H. $800-1000

D. Wall or counter display case; oak, stick and ball with glass panels, c.1915, 18"W x 7"D x 29"H. $500-600

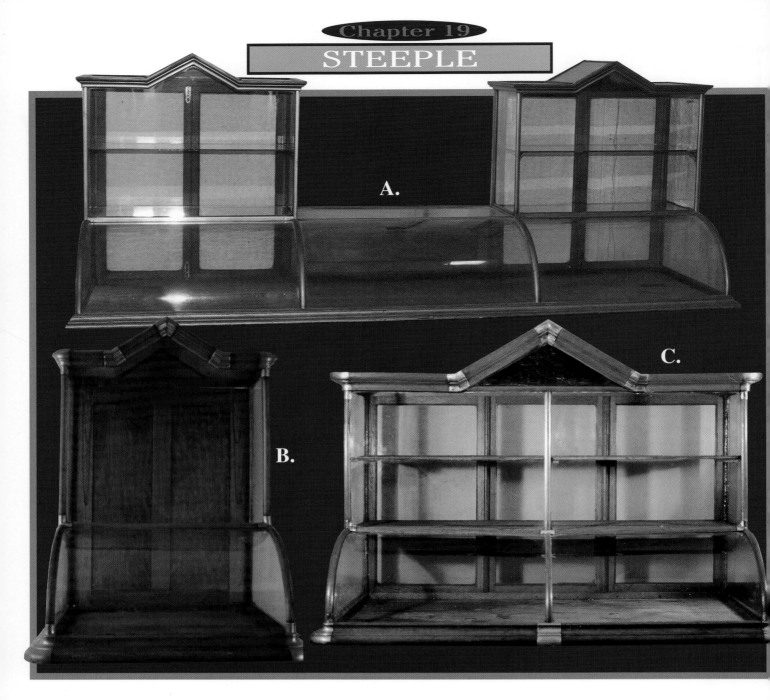

A.   Display case; double steeple curved glass case with German silver frame, c.1880, 96"W x 28"D x 39"H. $3200-3500

B.   Display case; single tower with curved glass front, walnut with German silver trim, c.1890, 28"W x 30"D x 39"H. $1100-1400

C.   Display case; double wide, single steeple, oak with German silver trim, mirror in steeple, *Nashville Showcase Co.*, c.1890, 59"W x 29"D x 44"H. $3200-3700

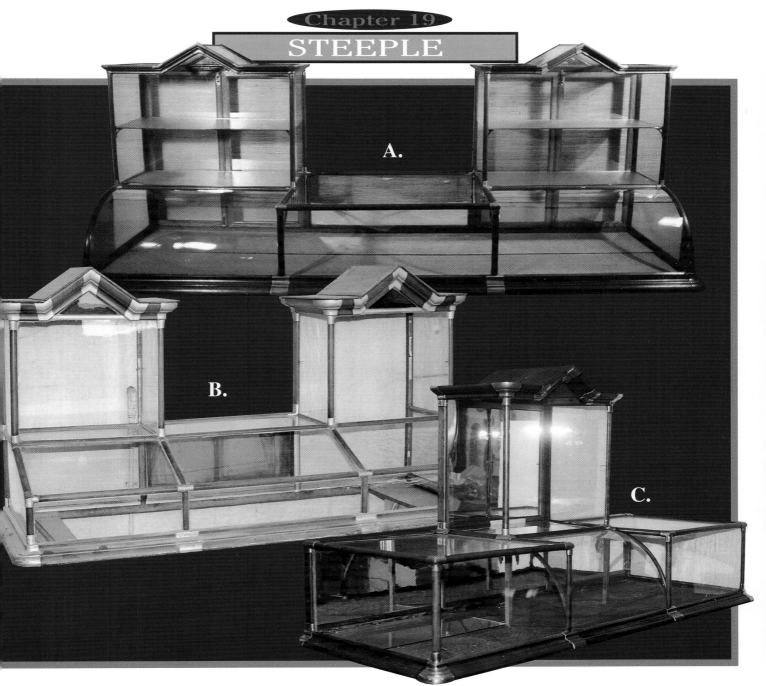

A. Display case; double steeple, unusual walnut with German silver trim, two ends have curved glass, center section has flat top and front, applied lettering in steeple, #60 Excelsior case, *Claes & Tehnbeuten, St. Louis*, c.1880, 8'W x 28"D x 39"H. $3300-3600

B. Display case; double steeple, walnut with German silver trim, *Eureka Showcase, Manuf's, Monk & Co. Prop's 48 Lake Street, Chicago*, c.1890, 72"W x 27"D x 37"H. $2800-3300

C. Display case; single steeple with curved glass, cherry wood with German silver trim, very unusual with curved glass center section, mfgr. *Dixon Borgeson & Co. Makers, Portland OR & San Francisco, CA*, c.1910, 72"W x 25"D x 39"H. $3500-5000

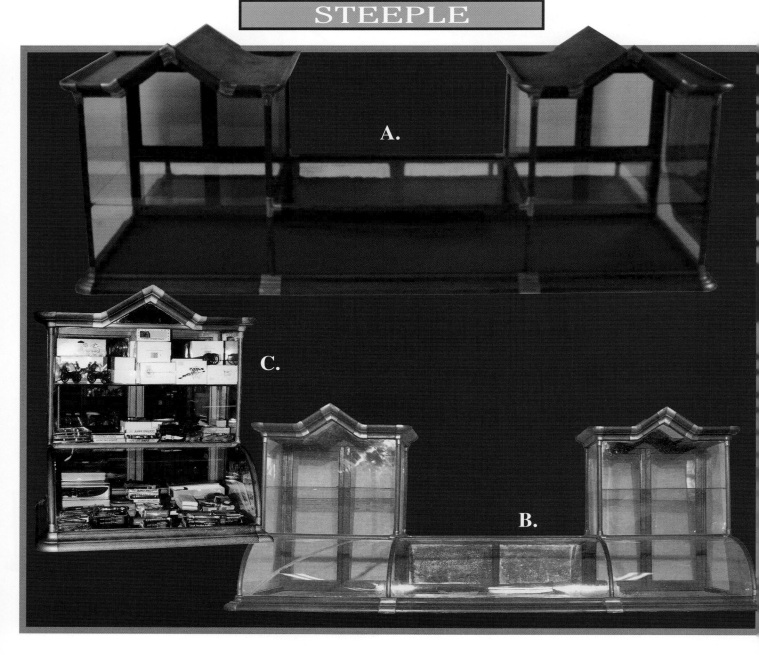

A. Display case; double steeple, wood with German silver trim, *Quincy Showcase Works, Quincy, Ill.*, 96"W x 26-1/2"D x 38-1/2"H. $3500-4500

B. Display case; double steeple mahogany showcase with German silver trim, curved glass, c.1900, 7'W x 28"D x 39"H. $3200-3500

C. Display case; single steeple, oak with German silver trim, c.1890, 33"W x 24"D x 40"H. $1100-1400

This store, believed to be on Armitage Ave. in Chicago, c.1920, shows an indiscernible die-cut string holder, turned just a bit too much to identify. Next to it hangs a cast-iron string holder.

This Grocery Store and Meat Market, c.1920, shows a customer just exiting. It also shows three different barrel meat scales at the meat counter. These cases were refrigerated with block ice.

This photo is full of things! Look for the Zeno gum case, as seen on page 115, and the Humphreys' Specifics cabinet as seen on page 94. On the counter, front right, sits a Mills "Jockey" trade stimulator.

This General Merchandise Store is staffed with what looks like a young group of clerks. There is a broad assortment of soft goods, but the cigar lighter on the left indicates tobacco was sold as well.

This saloon, c.1880, is probably from Virginia City, NV. The man in the top hat is dressed for formal entertainment. The bar and back bar are painted and ornately trimmed. Note the elaborate chandeliers.

This saloon interior, probably Nevada in the 1890's shows what a gentleman's saloon would have looked like. The hanging towel was to wipe the draft "froth" from mustaches!

This Butcher Shop, c.1920, shows butcher, cleaver in hand, standing by his Dayton or Toledo scale. In front of the scale is a one cent Bluebird Gumball vendor. The mirror, at right, reflects the front of a Model T.

This saloon interior, c.1940, shows several die-cut cardboard signs. It also shows a Coca-Cola cardboard sign illustrated by Haddon Sundblom. Look close on the back bar, you also see an Alka-Seltzer dispenser.

Buster Brown
•
Red Goose
•
Uncle Josh
•
Etc.

CHARACTERS

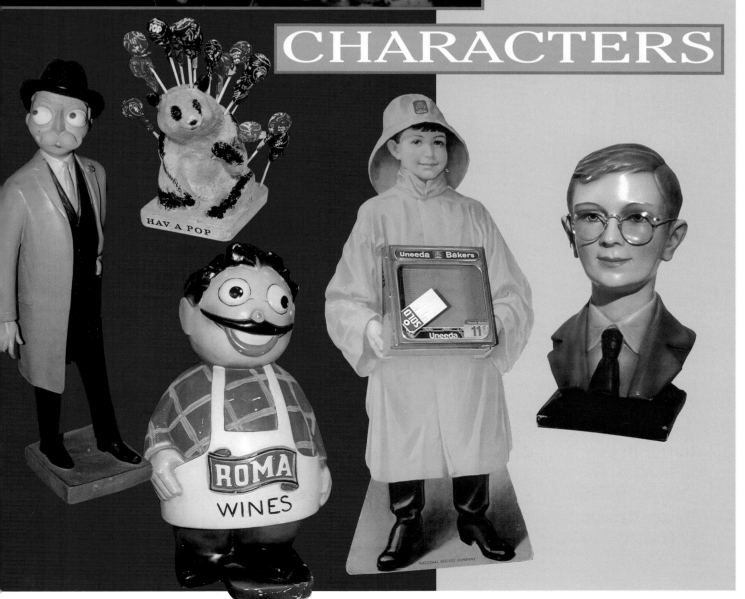

Chapter 20

CHARACTERS

A.   **Buster Brown**; Store balloon inflator; life size, fiberglass head, plastic clothes cover helium tank, c.1960's, 64-1/2"H. $850-1100

B.   **Buster Brown**; Rug; c.1955, 54"Dia. $425-475

C.   **Buster Brown**; Neon two-sided exterior store sign; c.1950, 55"W x 40"H. $3500-4500

D.   **Clayton's** Dog Remedies; Display; countertop composition bull dog with embossed lettering on both sides, comes with a booklet "Dr. Clayton's Treatise on all Breeds of Dogs", c.1920, 27"W x 19-1/2"H. $1500-2000

E.   **Clayton's** Dog Remedies; Display; mache figure (in the manner of King Kong products), c.1920, 29"L x 14-1/2"H. $1000-1300

A. **GE**; Store figure; hard rubber, c.1950, 40"H. $1700-1900

B. **Hills Bros. Coffee**; Store figure; painted plaster, c.1930, 19"H. $1000-1300

C. **Johnson Halters**; Horse head display figure; composition with glass eyes, c.1900, 22"H. $600-800

D. **Kool** Cigarettes; Store figure; composition "Willy", with monocle on eye, c.1930, 14-1/2"H. $600-750

A. **Majestic Radios**; Composition store eagle figure; c.1930, 41"W x 12"D x 28"H. $1800-2200

B. **Model** Cigar; "Esquire" man; painted plaster, missing cigar, c.1930, 25"H. $1000-1300

C. **National's** Eagle Blended Whiskey; Composition store figure; *NAPCO, Nat'l Advertising Products Co, N.Y.*, c.1940, 10"H. $45-100

A.   **OshKosh**; "Uncle Josh", life size die-cut cardboard display, half body with overalls, c.1935, 27"W x 81"H over all. $900-1100

D.   **Peruvian** Horse Salve; Plaster figure; highly detailed, c.1890, 7"W x 5"D x 10"H. $1400-1600

B.   **OshKosh**; Counter display sign; die cut, pressed composition, c.1930, 7"W x 14"H. $375-450

E.   **Poll Parrot Shoes**; Plaster counter figure; used to display kid's shoes, c.1940, 6"W x 7"D x 12"H. $185-225

C.   **Mr. Peanut**; Figural penny scale; cast aluminum Mr. Peanut over Hamilton scale, 20"W x 24"D x 48"H. $12000+ (*Note; these have been remanufactured.*)

F.   **Poll Parrot Shoes**; Store figure; plaster painted, c.1920, 11-1/2"H. $425-500

A. Proud owner sitting astride his Red Goose riding toy, c.1928.

B. **Red Goose Shoes**; Display figure; electric, head nods up and down, composition with fabric grass and glass eyes, c.1940, 11"W x 24"D x 20"H. $650-900

C. **Red Goose Shoes**; Globe; white milk glass with debossed red goose on one side and "Friedman-Shelby All Leather Shoes" on other side, 12"W x 10"H. $300-500

D. **Red Goose Shoes**; Child's riding goose; painted wood, glass eyes, metal wheels with rubber tires, c.1925, 20"L x 16"H. $1400-2200

A. **Robin Hood** Shoes; Display figure; plaster, painted, c.1920, 15"H. $375-450

B. **Roma** Wines; Store display figure; plaster, painted, c.1950, 20"H. $175-250

C. **Seaforth**; Display figure; plaster, painted, Scotsman holds sample bottle of after shave, c.1930, 13-1/2"H. $275-350

D. **Stevens**; Store figure; composition dog, "Everything for the Dog", c.1920, 17-1/2"W x 8"D x 19-1/2"H. $900-1100

A.   Sucker holder; plaster, painted, "Hav a Pop" polar bear, this one is very difficult to find, c.1940, 5"W x 6-1/2"D x 8"H. $475-600

B.   Sucker holder; plaster, painted, "Chief Watta Pop", c.1940, 8-1/2"W x 5"D x 9-1/2"H. $375-525

C.   Sucker holder; plaster, painted, puppy "Watta Pop", c.1940, 5-1/2" W x 7"D x 7-1/2"H. $350-400

A. **Thomas** Inks; Store figure; composition or plaster cat with glass eyes, 10"W x 12"D x 20"H. $1200-1600

B. **Uneeda** Biscuits; Die-cut figure; "Slicker Boy", litho cardboard, easel back, c.1920, 20"W x 49"H. $1000-1300

C. **Weatherbird**; Store display figure; plaster, multi-colored, c.1940, 8-1/2"W x 12"D x 24"H. $750-900

D. **White Owl**; Cigar figure; plaster with glass eyes, c.1930, 14"H. $325-450

A.   Display figure; plaster, "Wear Apple Caps", *Apple Hat Mfg. Co., St. Louis*, c.1914, 24"H. $1100-1400

B.   Composition standup store display figure; for Gossard Foundations, c.1950, 16"W x 6"D x 24"H. $325-450

C.   Lingerie store figure; for Lily of France, white metal with brass wash, c.1940, 12"H. $275-350

D.   Composition standup store display figure; for Madame Grace Foundations, c.1950, 9"W x 9"D x 34"H. $300-400

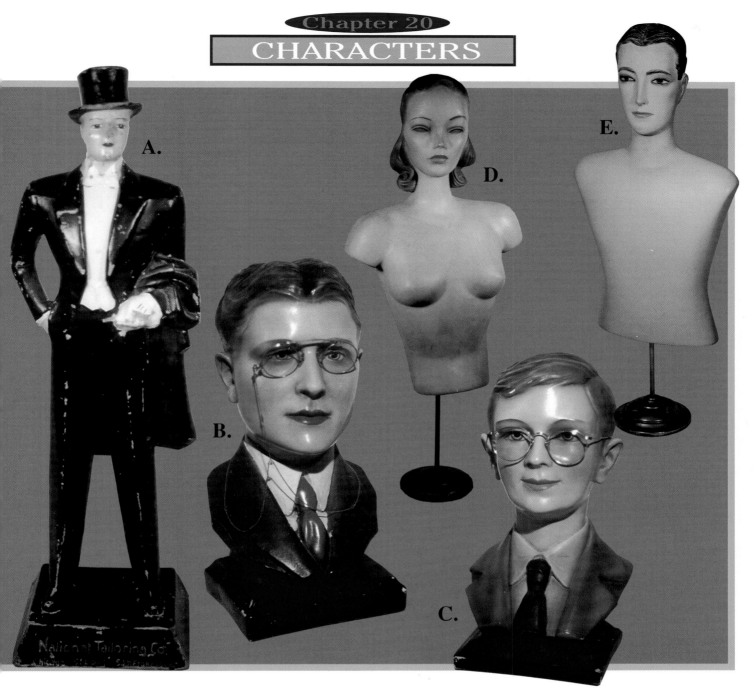

A. Composition store figure; mache-like material, *National Tailoring Co., Chicago, St. Louis, San Francisco*, c.1910, 9"W x 7"D x 31"H. $850-1200

B. Eyeglass display figure; plaster, man's bust from jewelry store, c.1920, 8"W x 7"D x 20"H. $450-525

C. Eyeglass display figure; plaster, boy's bust from jewelry store, c.1920, 7"W x 6"D x 17"H. $450-525

D. Female half mannequin; composition on iron base, c.1950, 40"H. $200-275

E. Male half mannequin; composition on iron base, head is life size but depth has been flattened, c.1950, 40"H. $200-275

This Cigar Store interior, probably c.1920 shows "High End" display cases. This is most likely a "City" cigar store. Note the clock in the upper left. It's actually a "Wizard" clock cigar trade stimulator.

Another "City" Cigar Store. This shows a wide variety of smoking goods. This looks very much like the smoke shops found in city hotels. Note the Mansfield gum vendor on the counter at right.

This Cigar Store and Pool Hall photo, c.1909, shows a group of men engaged in one of the favorite pastimes of the day. Notice the "Hance" peanut vendor on the cigar case at left.

This Pool Hall could be in a rural community. The gent at center looks to be a farmer in town for a game of billiards. Look closely, front right. You see part of an early coin operated arcade boxing machine.

This Cafe interior, taken at 1:45 P.M., shows a variety of cigar, gum and soda related material. A Beechnut Gum bulk pack hides in the display case. On top of the counter sits a rare Mills "Umpire" trade stimulator.

This Cigar Store Soda Fountain, c.1920, shows a nice onyx fountain head and a large selection of candy jars. Also, the "dice" cup sits on the cigar counter, waiting for a customer that feels lucky!

COUNTERS/BACK BARS

A.   Back bar; flame birch, reverse lit stained
     glass on front and under canopy, metal
     trim on top of support columns, 144"W x
     20-1/2"D x 115"H. $40000+

B.   Back bar; mahogany with onyx columns,
     marble top, leaded glass with concave
     initialed center piece, reverse lit, 158"W.
     $50000+

A.

B.

A.   Back bar; walnut barber shop back bar and
     mug rack, c.1880's. 50"W x 92"H.
     $1800-2400

B.   Back bar; quartersawn oak soda fountain
     back bar, corbel brackets hold up canopy
     with hanging lights, c.1920, 96"W x 96"H.
     $3200-3800

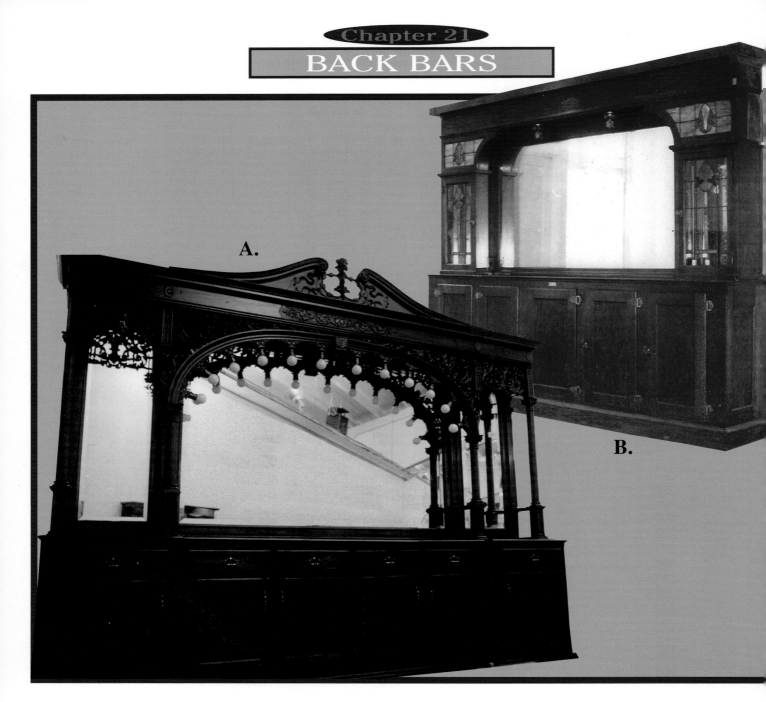

A.   Back bar; Saloon, oak, with dark
     mahogany stain, very ornate upper section,
     major contemporary reconstruction, basic
     unit, c.1910, 16'W x 10'H. $10000-12000

B.   Back bar; Soda Fountain, oak, some
     quartersawn, leaded glass and mirrored
     side cabinets, typical of c.1920 soda
     fountain, 10'W x 8'H. $5000-6000

A. Back bar; Soda fountain, mahogany with marble top, onyx columns, and marble center dispenser section, dispensers probably *Lippincott & Co.,* triple mirror center section, highly ornate, mirror crown, c.1890, 8'W x 8'H. $7500-9000

B. Back bar; Soda fountain, mahogany with marble top, and marble center dispenser section, dispensers probably *Lippincott & Co.,* nickel over brass hardware, triple center back bar mirror section, c.1890, 8'W x 8'H. $7500-9500

A.   Front and back bar; Soda Fountain,
     mahogany/cherry front and back bar,
     leaded, stained glass fountain head, three
     section back bar mirror, paneled front bar,
     c.1900, 12'W x 10'H. $11000-13000

B.   Back bar; Soda Fountain, oak, with black
     marble, probably *Lippincott & Co.* syrup
     dispenser, white milk glass in lower
     front, single mirror upper section, c.1890,
     6'W x 9'H. $7500-9500

C.   Front and back bar; Soda Fountain,
     oak, with marble, probably *Lippincott &
     Co.* syrup dispensers, three section back
     bar mirror, paneled front bar, c.1890, back
     bar 6'W x 9'H, front bar, 8'W.
     $12000-14000

A. Front and back bar; Soda Fountain, oak, with marble bar tops, marble *Lippincott & Co.* syrup dispensers, leaded beveled glass upper section supported by fancy turned oak columns, quartersawn oak paneled front bar with marble kick plate, c.1890, 12'W x 10'H. $40000+

B. Back bar; Soda Fountain, center section, oak, marble & onyx *Lippincott & Co.* syrup dispensers, nickel over brass hardware, c.1890, 40"W x 9'H. $6000-8000

C. Back bar; Soda Fountain, center section, painted wood, marble & onyx *Lippincott & Co.* syrup dispensers, very ornate upper section, c.1890, 48"W x 10'H. $9000-10000

A. **Monarch Foods**; Display stand; metal with painted sides, c.1920, 25"W x 19"D x 31"H. $650

B. **Monarch Foods**; Sweet pickles display; metal with four round stoneware inserts in top, each is marked Reid, Murdock & Co., all have glass covers, c.1915, 63"W x 16"D x 32-1/2"H. $2600-3500

C. Display counter; quartersawn oak, display for soft goods, c.1940, 72"W x 42"D x 30"H. $725-950

D. Bulk spice display counter; oak, glass front, 12 drawers that slide out, each drawer has applied lettering, c.1900, 60"W x 14"D x 42"H. $2200-3000

A. Floor display counter; oak with bulk grain bins, unusual, with glass upper display area, *Sherer Display Equip.*, patents 1903-1924, 120"W x 31"D x 42"H. $2500-3500

B. Grain display case; oak, sits on table or counter, lift-up doors and pull-out drawers, c.1910, 60"W x 20"D x 19"H. $525-650

C. Grain counter; oak, drawers in back, c.1910, 72"W x 31"D x 40"H. $1100-1400

D. Post Office Box mail counter; oak with brass combination door fronts and two clerk windows, *Saddler Co. Baltimore, Md., Indianapolis, Ind., Kansas City, Mo.,* c. 1915, 108"W x 12"D x 48"H. $2200-2800

This store is filled with wonderful merchandise and display material. Find the Calumet clock, the National Biscuit rack and the sack rack similar to the one on page 300.

This Grocery Store shows a variety of food items and related display material, including, die-cut Dutch Cleanser and Jello signs. Look for the unusual pickle containers on the counter, lower foreground.

This photograph shows the interior of a Hardware Store in Southwestern Iowa. The "Warren" cabinets, on the left, are the same cabinets as those pictured on page 85.

This Cigar Store interior, c.1910, shows a wonderful humidor back bar. You can also see a reverse paint on glass cigar sign and a Mills "Commercial" poker machine at the rear of the display counter.

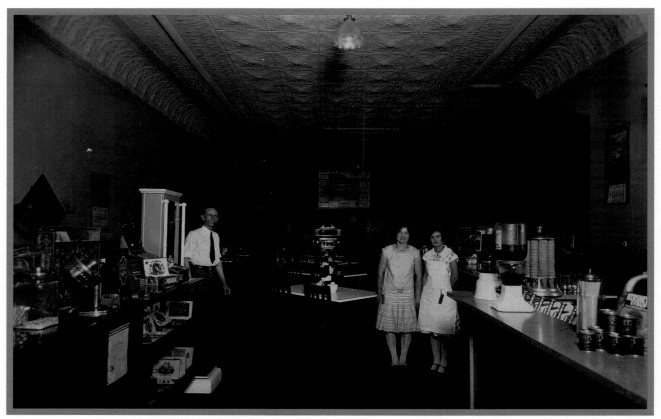

This photo shows a well-equipped 1930's Soda Fountain. Look for the syrup dispensers, the ice cream cone holder, the match machine, the rare Electromuse juke box, the cigar lighter and the coin operated scale.

This Soda Fountain, c.1920, shows a Hamilton King Coca-Cola tray on the ornate back bar. Also look for the wire soda fountain stools and chairs. Barely visible, in the lower left, is a Y-B cigar cutter.

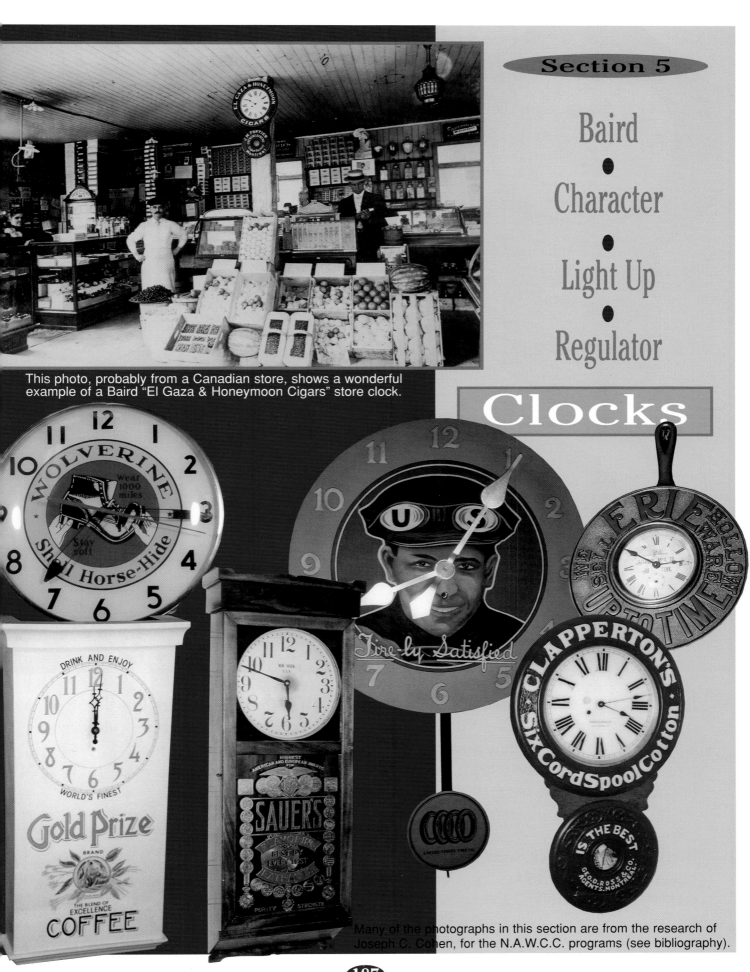

This photo, probably from a Canadian store, shows a wonderful example of a Baird "El Gaza & Honeymoon Cigars" store clock.

Baird
•
Character
•
Light Up
•
Regulator

Clocks

Many of the photographs in this section are from the research of Joseph C. Cohen, for the N.A.W.C.C. programs (see bibliography).

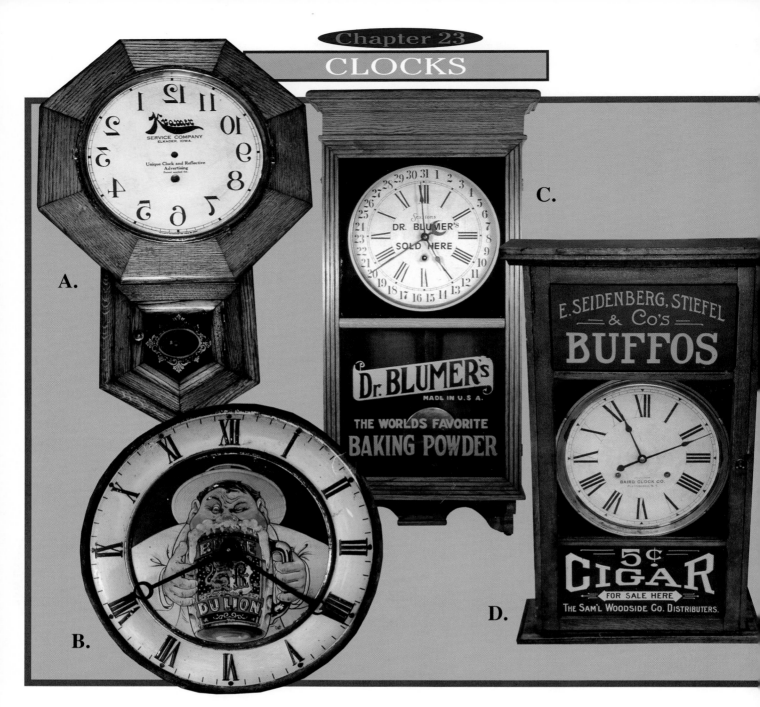

A. Regulator Barbershop Clock; reverse dial, (two versions of this clock, 9" dial and 12" dial, 12" rarest, 9" has been reproduced, repros have solid escape wheel) Kramer Service Co., Elkader, IA, c.1900, 14"W x 19"H. $1800-2000

B. **Biere Du Lion**; Clock; man with beer mug on front, paper litho face, German, c.1890, 24"Dia. $1800-2200

C. **Dr. Blumer's Baking Powder**; Regulator clock; oak, original face with reverse painted lower glass, manufactured by *Sessions Clock Co.*, c.1915, 16"W x 5"D x 36"H. $575-750

D. **Buffos** 5¢ Cigar; Clock, double-sided, *Baird Clock Co.*, (All Baird Clocks are correct with Seth Thomas works) c.1900, 16"W x 22"H. $2500-3000

A. **Buster Brown Shoes**; Clock; aluminum frame, reverse lit face, convex glass front, *Pam Clock Co.,* c.1950, 15"Dia. $425-675

B. **Calumet**; Full regulator clock; oak, reverse painted lower panel, *Gilbert Clock Co.,* c.1915, 16-1/2"W x 4-1/2"D x 37"H. $535-700

C. **Champion Spark Plugs**; Clock; back lit, plastic face, double neon, metal cabinet, c.1950, 30"W x 6"D x 35"H. $700-900

D. **Clapperton's** Six Cord Spool Cotton Is the Best; Clock; *Baird Clock Co., Montreal,* c.1888, 18"W x 30"H. $1600-2000

E. **Cream Mustard**; Clock; mahogany case, letters lithographed on clock face, earliest known example of mass produced American advertising clock, (ordered by George W. Mulford), *Ansonia Brass and Copper Clock Co.,* c.1871, 18"W x 28"H. $1600-1800

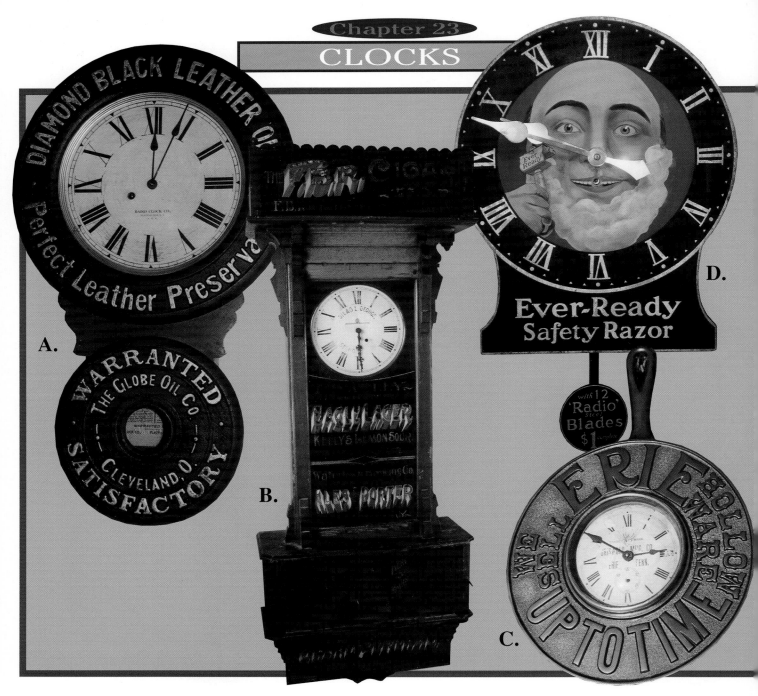

A. **Diamond Black Leather Oil**, Perfect Leather Preservative Warranted; Clock; *Baird Clock Co., Plattsburgh, NY,* c.1890, 18"W x 30"H. $1400-1800

B. **Eagle Lager**, Watertown Brewing Co.; Advertising clock; *Sidney Advertising Clock Co.,* c.1880, 20"W x 50"H. $5000-6000

C. **Erie Hollow Ware** - UPTOTIME; Iron frying pan clock; actual frying pan size, Griswold Mfg. Co., Erie, PA, *Waterbury Clock Co.,* c.1900, 16"H. $3000+

D. **Ever-Ready** Safety Razor; Clock; face of man shaving on front, painted on wood, (one version of Ever-Ready has been reproduced), *Mfgs. Gilbert, Sessions and Ingrahm Clock Co's.,* c.1918, 24"Dia. $2000-2400

A. **Folger's Coffee**; Clock; back lit, glass face, neon, metal cabinet, *Neon Products Inc., Lima, OH*, c.1950, 18"W x 7"D x 19"H. $600-800

B. **Gold Lion** Tonic; Calendar clock; walnut or cherry, long drop regulator, c.1900, 14"W x 24"H. $800-1200

C. **Gold Prize** Coffee, Drink & Enjoy World's Finest; Clock; painted wood, Lewis H. Frohman Co., Chicago, IL,

Gilbert Clock Co., c.1928, 14"W x 28"H. $2000-2400

D. **Jolly Tar** - Pastime, Old Honesty, Plank Road; Clock; *Baird Clock Co.*, c.1888, 18"W x 30"H. $1400-1800

E. **Mark Twain Flour**; Full regulator clock; oak, reverse transfer on lower glass, manufactured by *New Haven Clock Co.*, c.1910, 15-1/2"W x 5"D x 36"H. $450-585

A. **Merrick's** Spool Cotton; Clock; rosewood case, *New Haven Clock Co.,* c.1900, 16"W x 24"H. $800-1200

B. **Merwin** Electric Reminder Co.; Prototype electric reminder clock; used in hospitals and hotels, Sidney, NY, c. late 1890's, 18"W x 32"H. $800-1200

C. **Mother Seigel's** Curative Syrup Cures, Dyspepsia; Cast syrup bottle with clock in

front; raised letters on front, English, c.1900, 8-1/2"H. $400-600

D. **Moxie** Compound for the Nervous System; Clock; (this clock has been reproduced), *Baird Clock Co.,* c.1890, 18"W x 30"H. $1800-2000

A. **Nichols** Oriental Balm Rheumatis; Clock; *Baird Clock Co., Plattsburgh, NY*, c.1890, 18"W x 26"H. $ 1800-2200

B. **Old Mr. Boston** Liquors; Display bottle clock; white metal, painted, *Gilbert Clockworks*, c.1940, 10-1/2"W x 5"D x 22"H. $325-500

C. **Old Mr. Boston** Liquors; Display bottle clock; white metal, painted, *Gilbert Clockworks*, c.1940, 10-1/2"W x 5"D x 22"H. $325-500

D. **Oliver**; Clock; metal case, plastic dome, reverse lit neon, *Oliver Neon Products, Inc., Lima, OH*, c.1940, 16-1/2"Dia. $600-750

A. **OVB** - Our Very Best True Time Teller Alarms; Regulator clock; *New Haven Clock Co.,* c.1925, 18"W x 32"H. $500-700

B. **Poll Parrot Shoes**; Plastic, reverse lit face with glass dome, *Pam Clock Co.,* c.1950, 16"Dia. $485-575

C. **Reed's Tonic**; Clock; black, George M. Reed Bitter Co., *Yale Clock Co., New Haven, CT,* c.1880, 5"W x 17-1/2"H. $1200-1500

D. **Reed's Tonic**; Clock; ebony or natural finished wood, *Lupport Hubbel Clock Co. Bristol, CT,* c.1885, 14"W x 19"H. $1400-1800

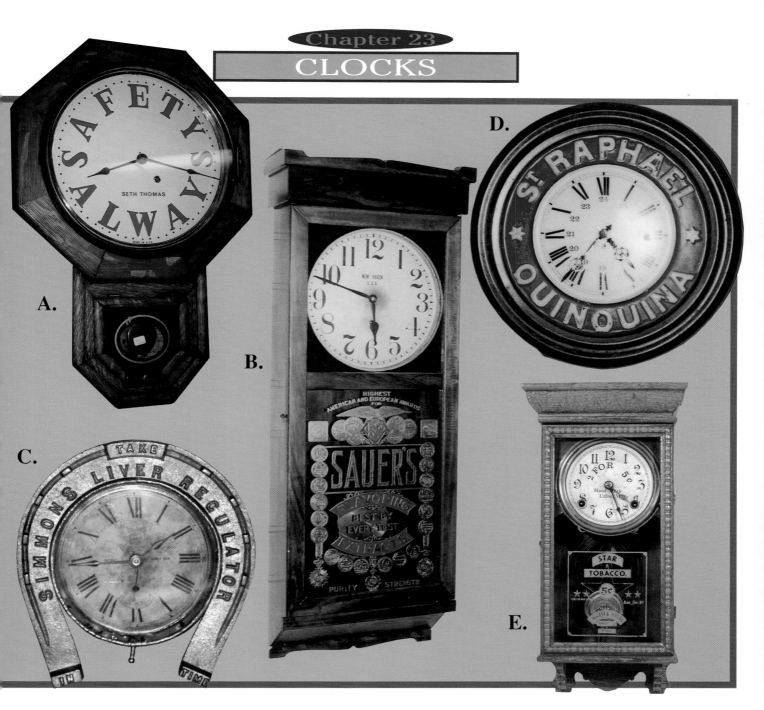

A. **Safety Always**; Short drop octagon regulator factory clock; *Seth Thomas Clock Co.*, c.1920, 18"W x 24"H. $500-600

B. **Sauer's**; Advertising regulator clock; walnut, reverse etched and gold leaf glass, *New Haven Clock Co.*, c.1915, 15"W x 3"D x 42"H. $1700-1900

C. **Simmons** Liver Regulator; Clock; bronze horseshoe, second earliest known mass produced American advertising clock, J.H. Zielen Co., *Ansonia Clock Co.*, c.1877, 6"W x 6"H. $450-700

D. **St. Raphael** Quinouina; Clock; lettering on red background, French, 24 hr. dial, c.1890, 16"Dia. $400-600

E. **Star Tobacco**; Quarter regulator clock; oak, unusual size, manufactured by *Seth Thomas Clock Co.*, 10"W x 4-1/2"D x 20"H. $725-900

A. **Star Tobacco**; Full regulator clock; oak, reverse painted lower glass, manufactured by *Sessions Clock Co.*, c.1910, 16"W x 5"D x 30"H. $375-550

B. **Telechron**; Advertising clock; metal sides, with walnut front, deeply etched glass face with neon ring, revolving drum with paper ad inserts and neon around perimeter, c.1930, 14"W x 9"D x 22"H. $725-850

C. **The Times** Philadelphia - Have You Read the Times; Clock; *Baird Clock Co., Plattsburgh and Montreal*, c.1890, 18"W x 30"H. $1400-1800

D. **Two Star**; Regulator clock; glass panel has L.I. Auto Lamp Supply Company trademark, dial has same trademark, 9516 Foster Avenue, Brooklyn, New York, 16-1/4"W x 34"H. $335-475

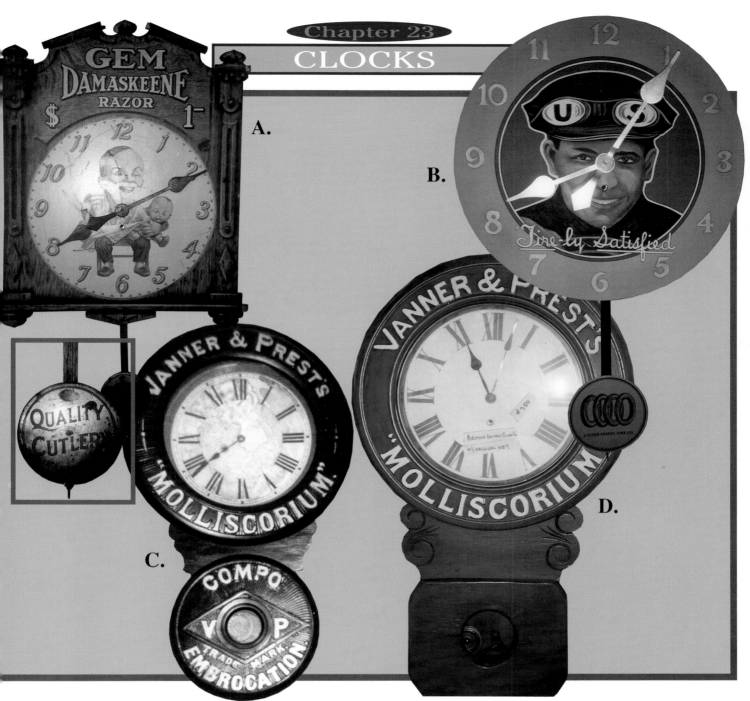

A. **"Ugly Baby"** Gem Damaskeene Razor; Clock; wood with painted face, *Sessions Clock Co.*, c.1910, 20"W x 24"H. $2500+

B. **U.S. Tire**-ly Satisfied; Clock; U.S. Tire Co., *Gilbert Clock Co.,* c.1918, 24"Dia. $3000-3500

C. **Vanner & Prest's** Molliscorium; Clock; *Baird Clock Co., Plattsburgh, NY*, c.1890, 18"W x 30"H. $1400-1800

D. **Vanner & Prest's** Molliscorium; Clock; *British United Clock Co.*, c.1900, 19"W x 30"H. $700-1000

A. Figural clock; German white metal with bronze flash finish, *M. Wallstein & Co., Inc.*, c.1900, 13"H. $350-475

B. **Winchester** Big Game Rifles and Ammunition; Clock; (this clock has been reproduced), *Baird Clock Co., Plattsburgh, NY*, c.1890, 18"W x 30"H. $2500-3000

C. **Wolverine Shoes**; Clock; composition case, reverse lit face with convex front glass, *Pam Clock Co.,* c.1940, 14-1/2"Dia. $375-500

D. **Woolf** Hats Clothing Shoes Madison and Halsted Sts., Chicago, IL; Clock; *Baird Clock Co., Plattsburgh, NY*, c.1890, 18"W x 30"H. $1800-2200

This saloon interior, from the Bushnell, IL area, c.1920, shows a very common, but very large, bar and back bar. The back bar has leaded and beveled glass side cabinets.

You could go to the pool hall for billiards, or a shave and a hair cut. This photo, c.1920, shows it all happening! On the wall is a movie poster for "The Gypsy Trail". On the right sits a Hance peanut vendor.

This store keeper, c.1910, stands next to a cigar and candy counter, well stocked with Wrigley's gum. His elbow rests on a Griswold trade stimulator. The curved glass case, front right, is patched with a Cinco tin.

This store interior, c.1890, looks to be very utilitarian. Although it looks to be a large store, there's little that suggests the "frills" of city life. That and the carbide light fixtures suggests a rural country store.

Section 6

Food
●
Ice Cream
Dippers
●
Syrup Bottles
●
Syrup Dispensers

CONSUMABLES

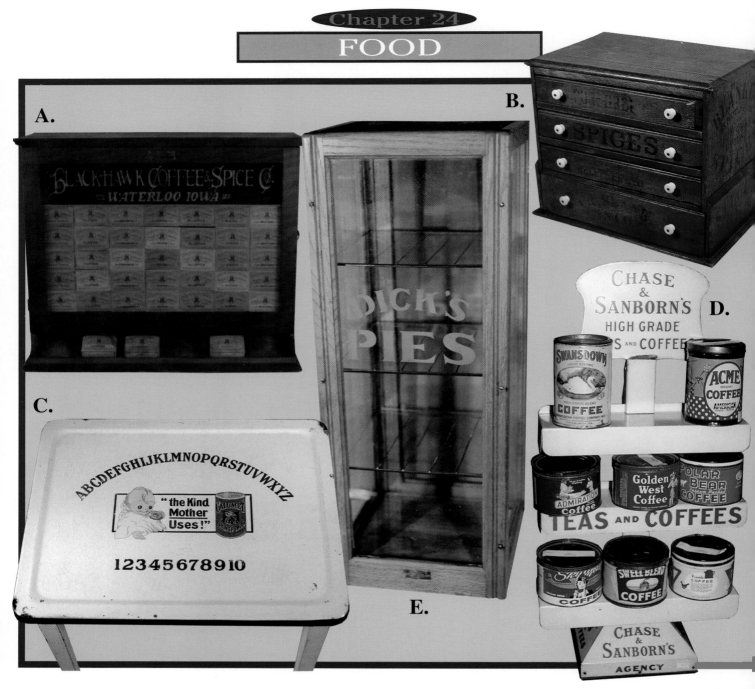

A. **Black-Hawk** Coffee & Spice; Display; wood with glass front door, *A.E. Cobb, Des Moines, Iowa*, Pat. March 26, 1901, 28-1/2"W x 12"D x 24"H. $900-1300

B. **Blanke's** Strickley Pure & Choice Grade Ground Spices; Spice cabinet; *C.F. Blanke & Co., St. Louis*, 22"W x 13-1/2"D x 19"H. $325-400

C. **Calumet** Baking Soda; Child's table; enamel top, painted wood frame and legs, c.1915, 20"W x 16"D x 18"H. $1100-1800

D. **Chase & Sanborn**; Coffee display; metal, *H.D. Beach Co., Coshocton, Oh.*, c.1910, 15-1/2"W x 4-3/4"D x 33"H. $600-725

E. **Dick's**; Pie cabinet; oak and glass, reverse etched glass front panel, wire shelves, *Miami Mfg, Peru, Indiana, Makers*, c.1930, 13"W x 12-1/2"D x 34"H. $275-350

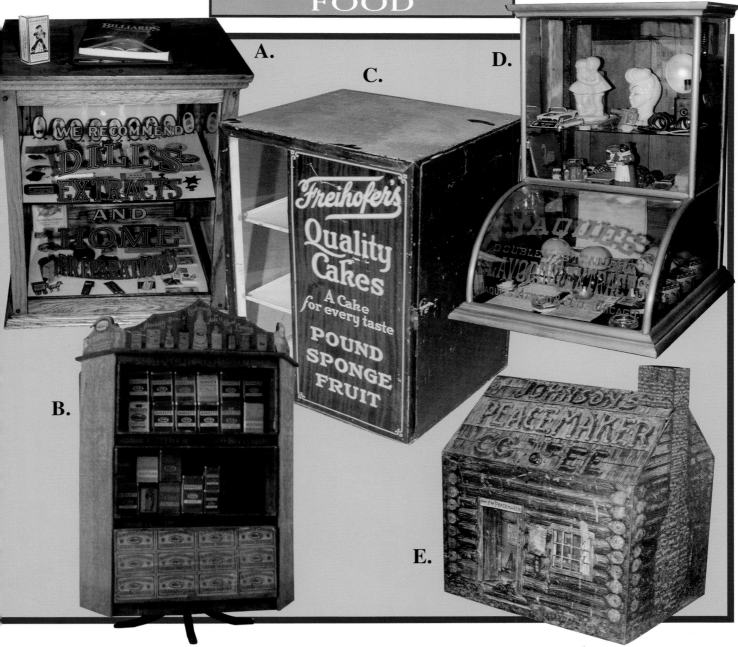

A. **Dill's** Extracts and Home Preparations;
Display case; oak and glass, reverse
transfer letters, c.1910, 14"W x 12"D x
18"H. $450-600

B. **E.R. Durkee**; Display cabinet; rotating
wood cabinet with marquee, sides are
embossed wood panels, 36"H. $800-1300

C. **Freihofer's** Quality Cakes; Display
cabinet; metal and glass, applied lettering,

17"W x 15"D x 22"H. $325-450

D. **Jaques** Double and Standard Flavoring
and Extracts; Counter display; German
silver with reverse etched glass, Jaques
Atwood & Co., Chicago, *J. Riswig Maker
44 & 46 State Street, Chi.*, $2400-2700

E. **Johnson's** PeaceMaker Coffee; Display;
lithographed tin, roof lifts, c.1900, 24"W x
18"D x 24"H. $900-1300

A.

B.

C.

D.

A. **Log Cabin** Maple Syrup; Display; wood log cabin with painted lettering on roof, c.1900, 18"W x 11"D x 12-1/2"H. $550-750

B. **Marquette Club**; Soda display; die-cut cardboard with relief for product, c.1920, 21-3/4"W x 5"D x 26"H. $150-200

C. **National Biscuit Company**; Floor display stand; oak, c.1910, 31"W x 25"D x 62"H. $700-1100

D. **National Biscuit Company**; Display rack; oak, five shelves (one is missing), c.1910, 46"W x 26"D x 60"H. $500-800

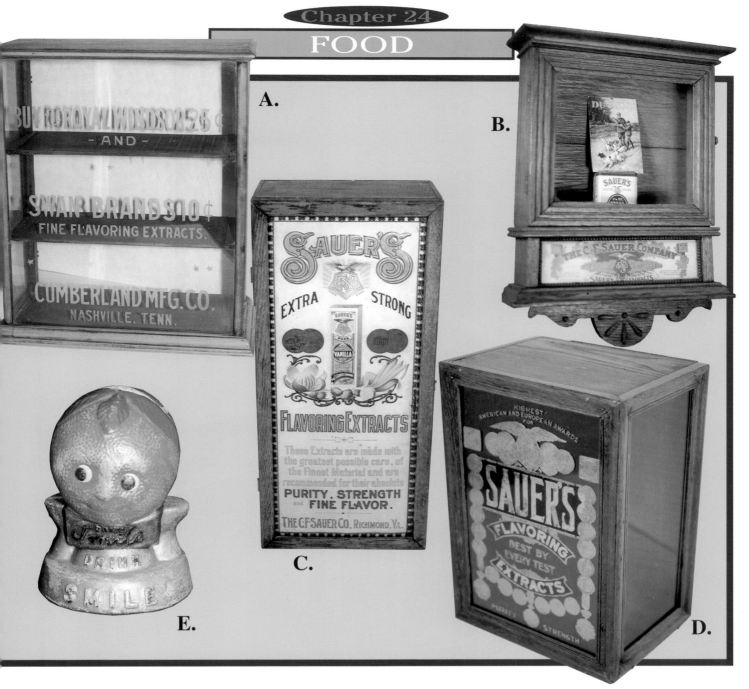

A.

B.

C.

D.

E.

Royal Windsor and **Swan Brand**; Extract counter display case; soft maple with reverse etched glass, *Cumberland Mfg. Co., Nashville, TN*, c.1920, 18-1/2"W x 8-1/2"D x 22"H. $425-600

C.F. Sauer Co.; Extract cabinet; oak and glass front, spoon carved, beaded trim, c.1910, 12"W x 4"D x 17"H. $550-700

Sauer's; Extract cabinet; oak with

embossed tin, c.1910, 12"W x 7-1/2"D x 26"H. $4000-5000

D. **Sauer's**; Extract cabinet; oak, glass sides and front, reverse painted gold lettering on front, 15"W x 10-1/2"D x 20-1/2"H. $750-900

E. **Smile** Soda; Menu holder; painted plaster figure of orange, c.1920, 6-1/2"H. $725-850

A. **Ward's** Cake; Counter display case; metal with multi-color lithograph, c.1910, 16-1/2"W x 13"D x 20-1/2"H. $3500-4000

B. **Washburn-Halligan** Coffee Co.; Counter display; basswood/soft maple with glass front, reverse paint on glass, c.1915, 28"W x 12"D x 24"H. $900-1300

C. **Dwinnell Wright Co.'s** Royal Spices; counter spice display; multi-color litho on tin, c.1890, 19"Dia. x 34"H. $2900-3400

D. Baked goods display; German silver, wire shelves, c.1900, 28"W x 21"D x 30"H. $350-425

FOOD

A. Countertop pie display case; metal ends with glass front and top, missing rear door, c.1930, 34"W x 9"D x 5"H. $115-175

B. Baked goods floor display case; oak and glass with four fold-down rear doors, *D.D. Royer Mfg. Co., Minneapolis, MN*, c.1910, 31"W x 22"D x 60"H. $850-1200

C. Bread case; oak with reverse etched glass, c.1910, 20"W x 14"D x 30"H. $325-450

D. Bread wrapper display; original wrappers from 1950's-60's, various sizes, brands, $7.50 each and up.

E. Bulk cheese display case with cutter; oak with curved glass, unusual front section hinged on top, lifts up, c.1910, 24"W x 26"D x 19"H. $900-1300

FOOD

A.

B.

A.   Baker's rack; ash with iron frame,
      manufactured by *The Combination Table
      Co., Bryon, OH*, Pat'd. June 6, 1893 and
      Feb. 4, 1896, 36"W x 25"D x 55"H, folds
      to table 32"W x 61"L. $750-1100

B.   Baker's rack; oak and pine, folds up for
      shelves, down to make table, c.1900,
      24"W. $575-$650

A. Counter coffee grinder; figural coffee pot, (front view) cast iron and aluminum, electrified, *American Duplex Co., Louisville, KY*, c.1930, 29"H. $725-900

B. Rear view of coffee grinder.

C. Pie showcase; oak and glass countertop showcase, screen back door and a pie rack insert, 26-1/2"W x 11"D x 28-1/2"H. $350-425

D. Popcorn and peanut wagon; *R.O. Stutsman Co., Des Moines, IA*, c.1910, $5500-6700

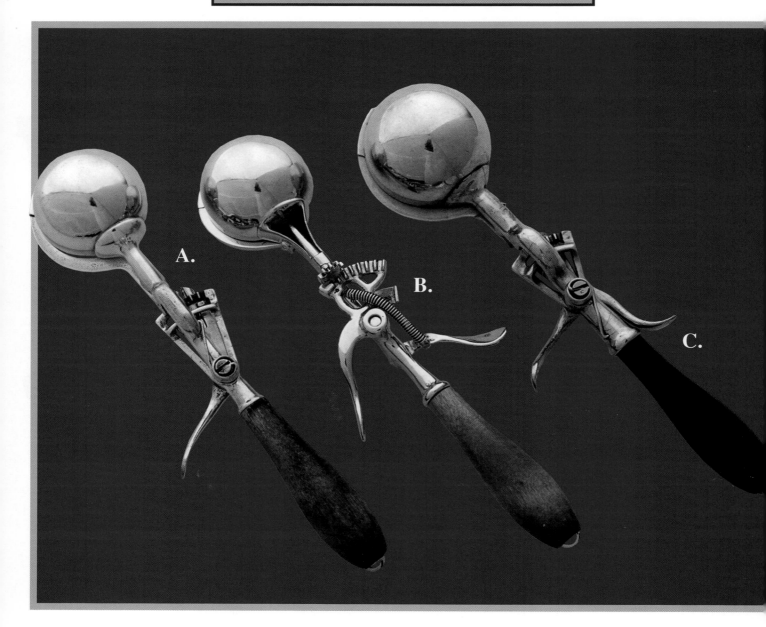

A.   Ice Cream Dipper; slicer, wood handle,
     nickel-plated brass, *Dover Mfg. Co.*, Pat.
     1924, 11"L. $500-600

B.   Ice Cream Dipper; slicer, wood handle,
     nickel-plated brass, *Grant & Holmes*,
     c.1916, 11"L. $1000-1500

C.   Ice Cream Dipper; slicer, wood handle,
     nickel-plated brass, *Dover Mfg. Co.*, Pat.
     1928, 11"L. $500-600

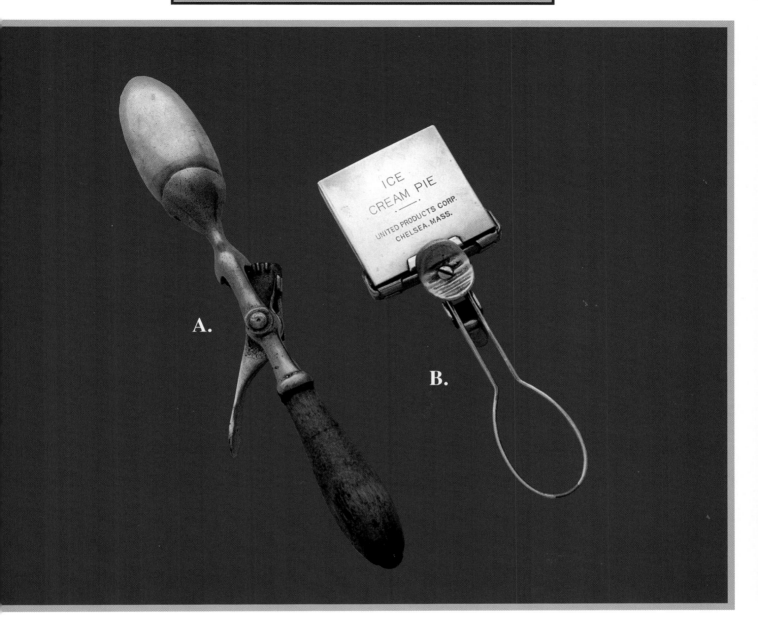

A. Ice Cream Dipper; for banana splits, wood
    handle, nickel-plated brass, *United
    Products Co.*, c.1930, 11-1/2"L. $600-700

B. Ice Cream Dipper; sandwich, nickel-plated
    brass, *United Products Co.*, c.1920's,
    7-1/2"L. $495-695

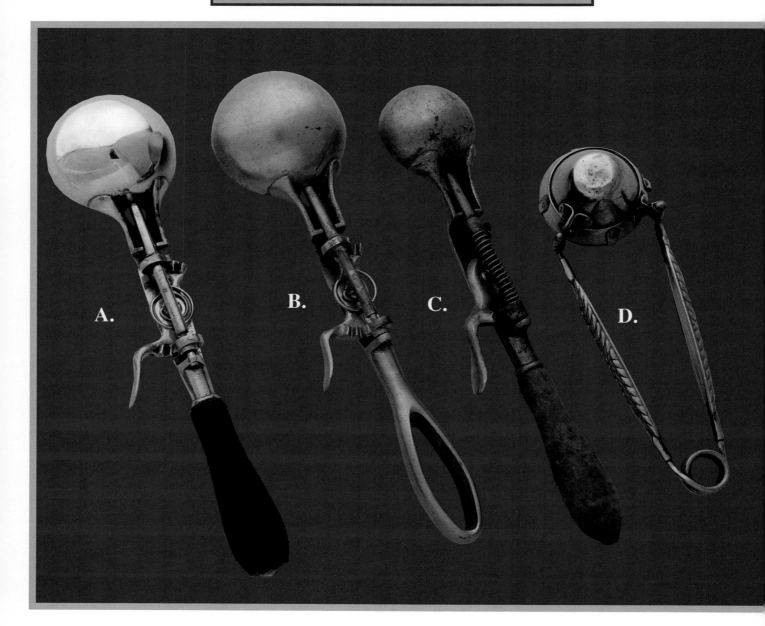

A. Ice Cream Dipper; wood handle, *Kingery Mfg. Co.*, 11"L. $200-300

B. Ice Cream Dipper; bronze loop, nickel-plated, *Kingery Mfg. Co.*, c.1908, 11"L. $225-350

C. Ice Cream Dipper; older spring, *Kingery Mfg. Co.*, 11"L. $200-300

D. Ice Cream Dipper; nickel-plated metal, *Kingery Mfg. Co.*, 8-1/2"L. $175-250

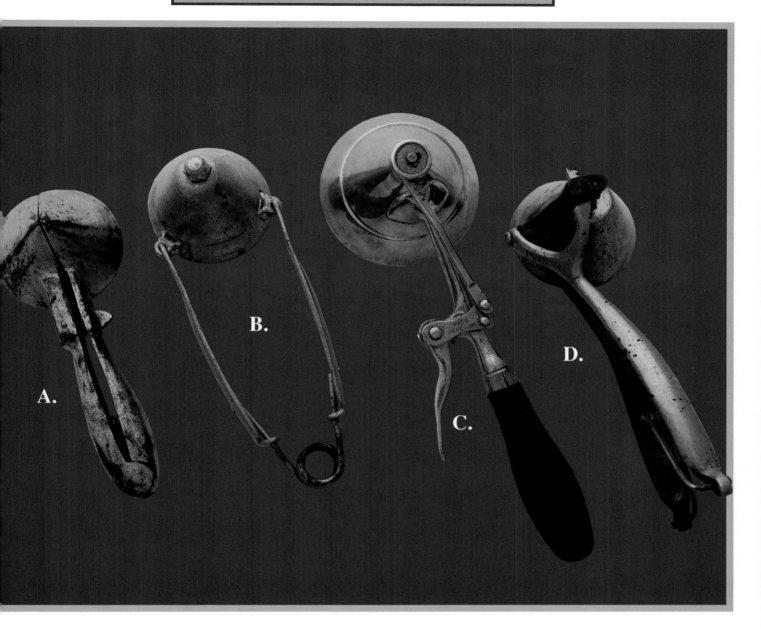

A.   Ice Cream Dipper; bowl splits in half,
     unknown maker, 6"L. $1000-1500

B.   Ice Cream Dipper; *Clemant-Baughman*,
     Pat. #525382, 7"L. $225-275

C.   Ice Cream Dipper; clipper #5, wood
     handle, nickel-plated brass, *F.S. Co.,
     Troy, NJ*, Pat. 1914, 10"L. $150-225

D.   Ice Cream Dipper; unknown maker, no
     marks, 7"L. $1200-1000

ICE CREAM DIPPERS

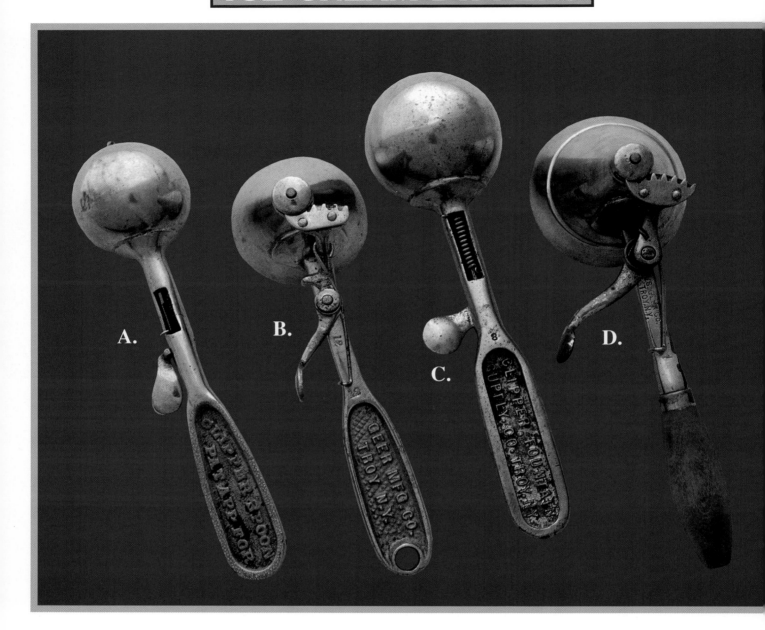

A. Ice Cream Dipper; nickel-plated brass, first Geer make, *Giles N Nielsen*, Pat. 1905, 9-1/4"L. $300-400

B. Ice Cream Dipper; nickel-plated brass, *Geer Mfg. Co.*, Pat. 1906, 9"L. $300-400

C. Ice Cream Dipper; nickel-plated brass, all metal, *Geer Mfg. Co.*, Pat. 1905, 9-1/4"L. $300-400

D. Ice Cream Dipper; large bowl with ring around it, wood handle with nickel-plated brass body, *Geer Mfg. Co.*, Pat. 1906, 9-1/2"L. $350-450

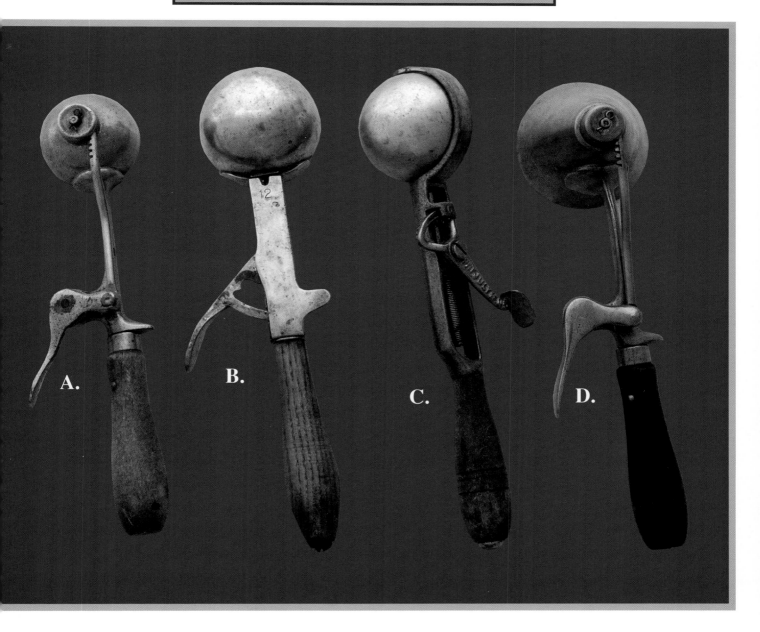

A.   Ice Cream Dipper; *Mosteller Mfg.*, mark
      #78, 10"L. $200-250

B.   Ice Cream Dipper; *Mosteller Mfg.*, mark
      #77, 11"L. $300-400

C.   Ice Cream Dipper; bowl flips, wooden
      handle with nickel-plated brass, *Mosteller
      Mfg.*, Pat. 1906, 11"L. $1200-1500

D.   Ice Cream Dipper; conical bowl, *Mosteller
      Mfg.*, mark #79, 10"L. $200-$250

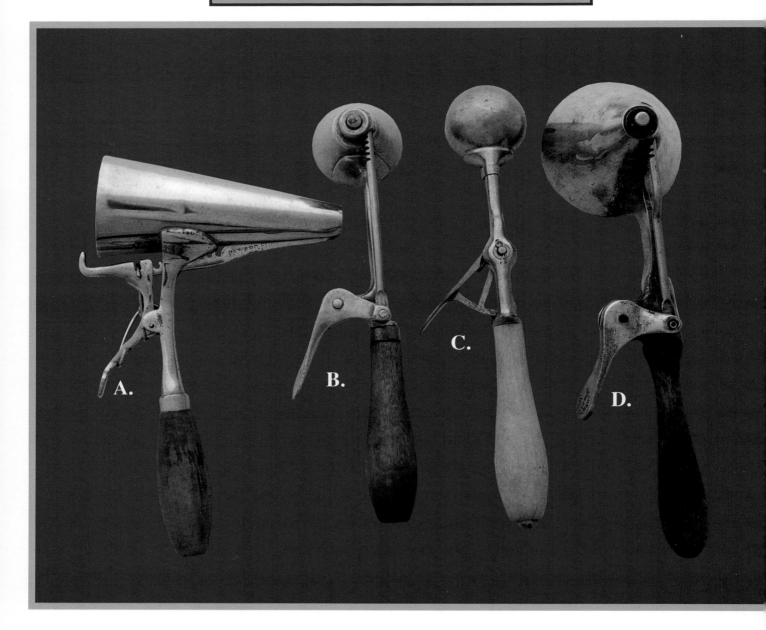

A. Ice Cream Dipper; cone holder, wood handle, nickel-plated brass, *Geer Mfg. Co.*, Pat. 1912, 8"L. $1500-1900

B. Ice Cream Dipper; wood handle, nickel-plated brass, *Gilchrist Co.*, Gilchrist #33, Pat. 1914, 10-1/2"L. $75-125

C. Ice Cream Dipper; wood handle, nickel-plated brass, *Gilchrist Co.*, Gilchrist #31, Pat. 1915, 11"L. $30-45

D. Ice Cream Dipper; aluminum, *Gilchrist Co.*, Gilchrist #32, c.1914, 12"L. $525-600

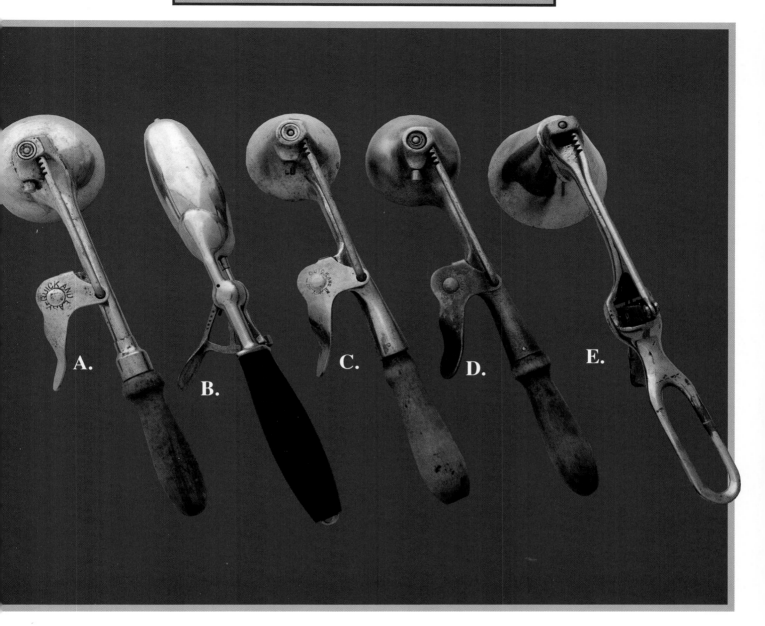

A. Ice Cream Dipper; wood handle, nickel-plated brass, *Erie Specialty Co.*, c.1915, 11"L. $125-150

B. Ice Cream Dipper; banana split, *Gilchrist Co.*, Gilchrist #34, c.1915, 11-1/2"L. $695-795

C. Ice Cream Dipper; round bowl, aluminum, *Erie Specialty Co.*, 11"L. $195-250

D. Ice Cream Dipper; round bowl, aluminum, *Erie Specialty Co.*, 11"L. $195-250

E. Ice Cream Dipper; brass loop handle, brass and copper, nickel-plated, *Erie Specialty Co.*, Pat. 1908, 11-1/4"L. $300-400

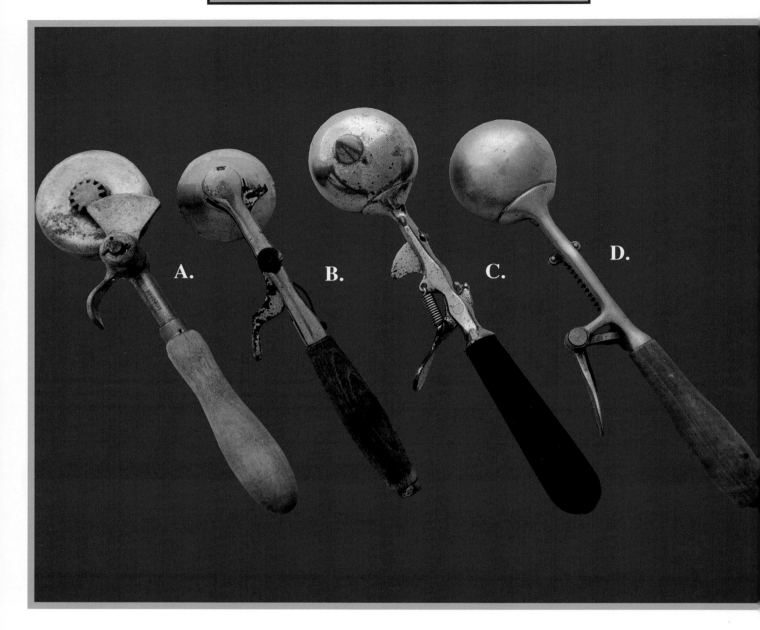

A. Ice Cream Dipper; wood handle, aluminum, marked "Economy", unknown maker, Pat. 1932, 10-1/4"L. $750-900

B. Ice Cream Dipper; *A.P. Olmstead*, 10"L. $450-500

C. Ice Cream Dipper; wood handle, nickel-plated brass, unknown maker, 11"L. $2000-2500

D. Ice Cream Dipper; wood handle, nickel-plated brass, *Guaranteed Disher Co.*, 11"L. $275-$395

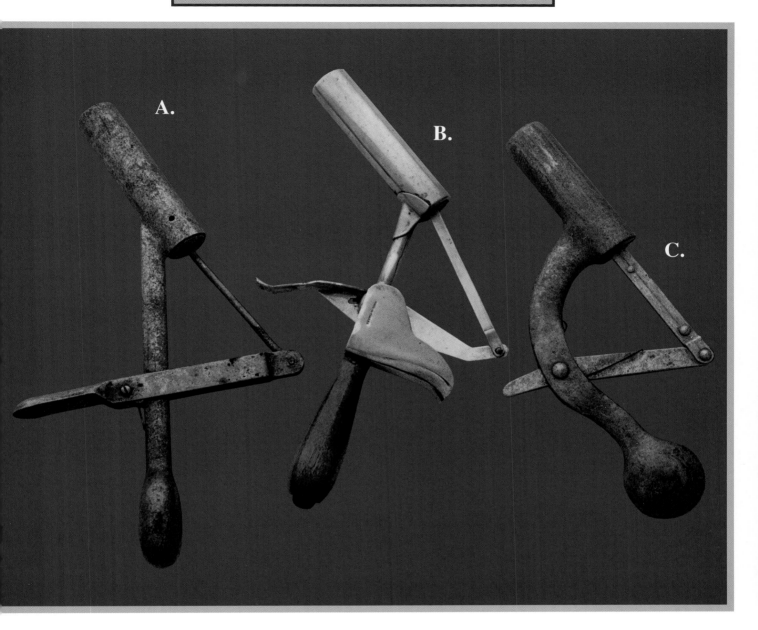

A. Ice Cream Dipper; unknown maker,
    9-1/2"L. $1000-1200

B. Ice Cream Dipper; cold dog scoop, wood
    handle, German silver over brass, *Fisher
    Motor Co.*, Pat. 1926, 9-1/2"L. $575-750

C. Ice Cream Dipper; aluminum, unknown
    maker, c.1920's, 9"L. $1000-$1200

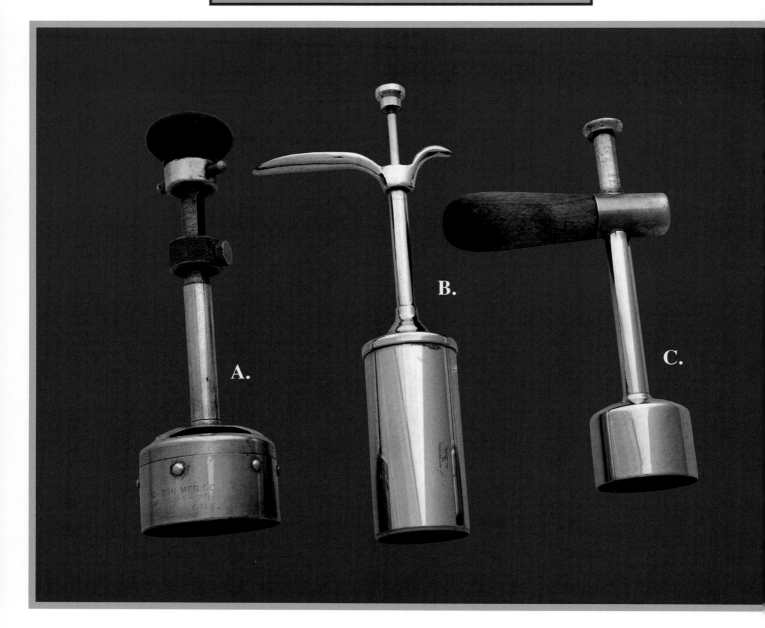

A.   Ice Cream Dipper; *Fro-zon Mfg. Co.*,
     Pat. 2/24/25, 7-1/2"L. $825-950

B.   Ice Cream Dipper; nickel-plated brass,
     Perfection Eq. Co., Pat. 1933, 8-1/2"L.
     $550-700

C.   Ice Cream Dipper; wood handle, nickel-
     plated, unknown maker, c.1931, 9"L.
     $1000-$1200

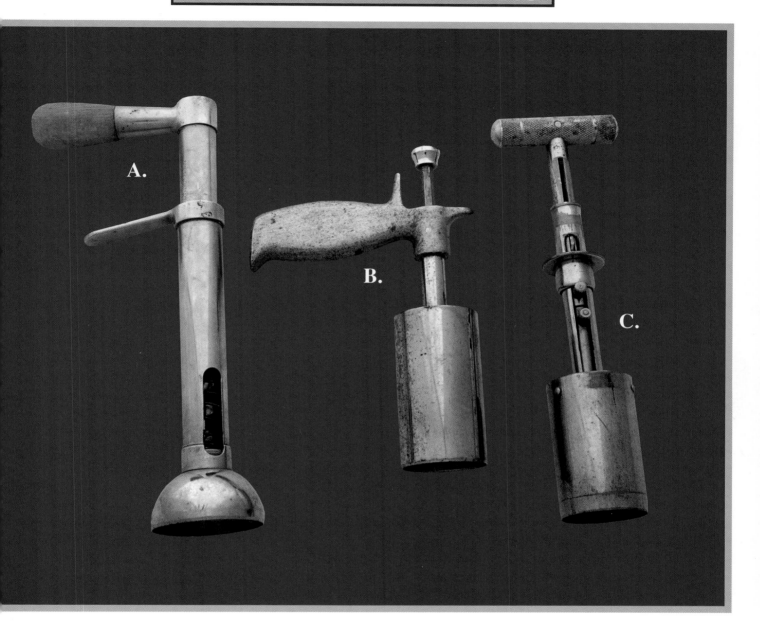

A. Ice Cream Dipper; "Fairy Vacuum Disher", wood handle, nickel-plated, *Fairbanks Sales Corp.*, 9"L. $1500-2000

B. Ice Cream Dipper; aluminum handle, unknown maker, similar to Perfection Eq., 5-1/2"L. $500-600

C. Ice Cream Dipper; aluminum handle, nickel-plated brass, *General Ice Cream Corp.*, Pat. 1925, 8"L closed, 11"L extended. $550-$675

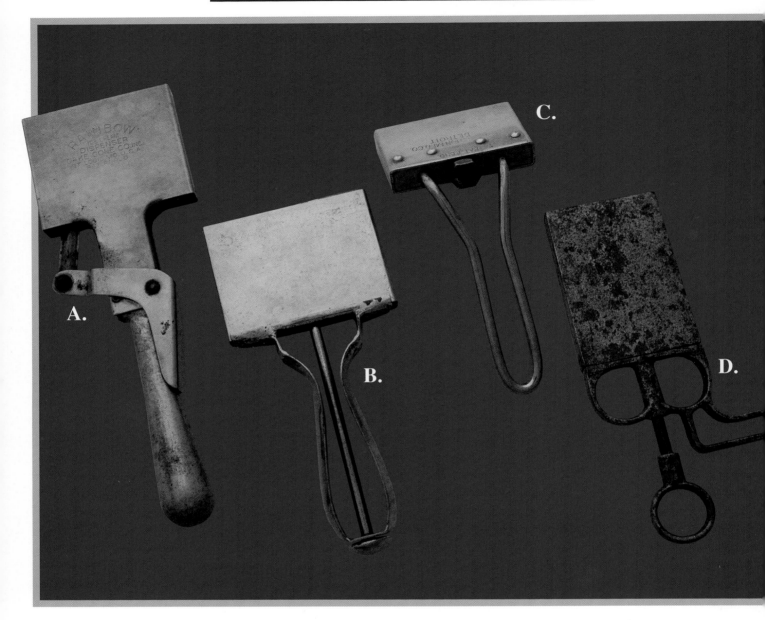

A. Ice Cream Dipper; marked "Rainbow Ice Cream Dispenser", rainbow has a thumb push which is difficult to find, aluminum handle, *Cake Cone Co.*, 9"L. $500-625

B. Ice Cream Dipper; open handle, for sandwich, metal strap, unknown maker, 8-1/2"L. $1000-1200

C. Ice Cream Dipper; metal, open rod handle for sandwich, *Bichon Mfg. Co.*, marked Pat. Pend., 7-1/2"L. $800-900

D. Ice Cream Dipper; aluminum, for sandwich, unknown maker, 8"L. $900-1000

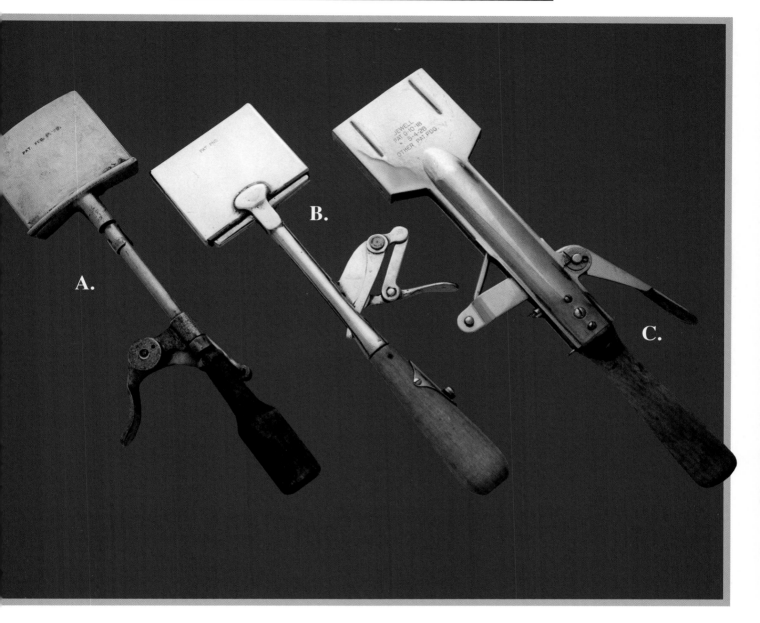

A. Ice Cream Dipper; wood handle, German silver, for sandwich, *Jiffy Dispenser Co.*, Pat. 1925, 12-1/2"L. $200-275

B. Ice Cream Dipper; "Ideal Ice Cream Sandwich Dipper", wood handle, nickel-plated brass, *Long Sales Co.*, 12"L. $1200-1600

C. Ice Cream Dipper; wood handle, white metal, for sandwich, *Bunker-Clancy Mfg. Co.*, Pat. 1927, and *Jewell,* Pat. 9-10-18, 5-4-26, 13-1/4"L. $1400-1600

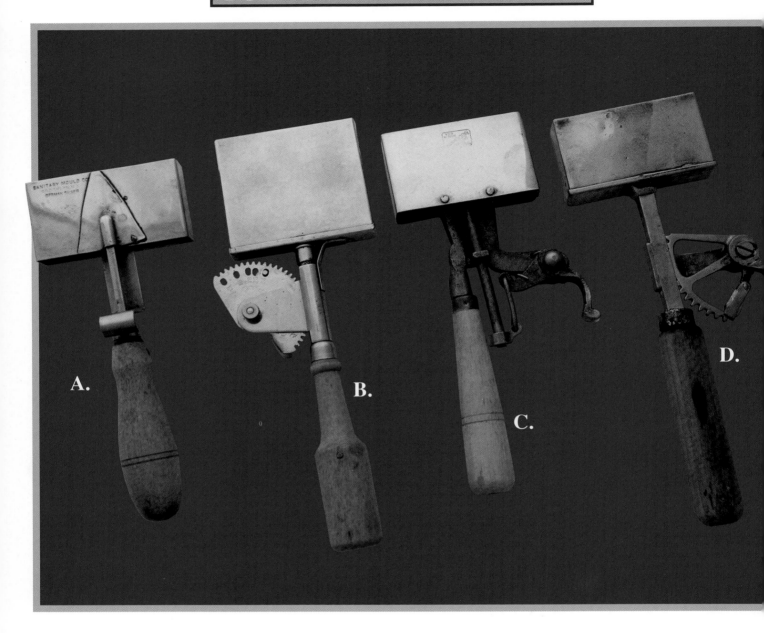

A. Ice Cream Dipper; wood handle, German silver, for sandwich, *Sanitary Mould Co.*, Pat. 1925, 8-1/4"L. $695-895

B. Ice Cream Dipper; wood handle, nickel-plated brass, *Mayer Mfg. Co., Chicago*, 9-1/4"L. $1000-1500

C. Ice Cream Dipper; scoop is marked,"The Original Rauch System, made in USA", wood handle, nickel-plated brass bowl, for sandwich, unknown maker, 8-1/4"L. $1000-1200

D. Ice Cream Dipper; smaller bowl, wood handle, nickel-plated brass, unknown maker, (could be Polar-Pak), 9-1/4"L. $500-695

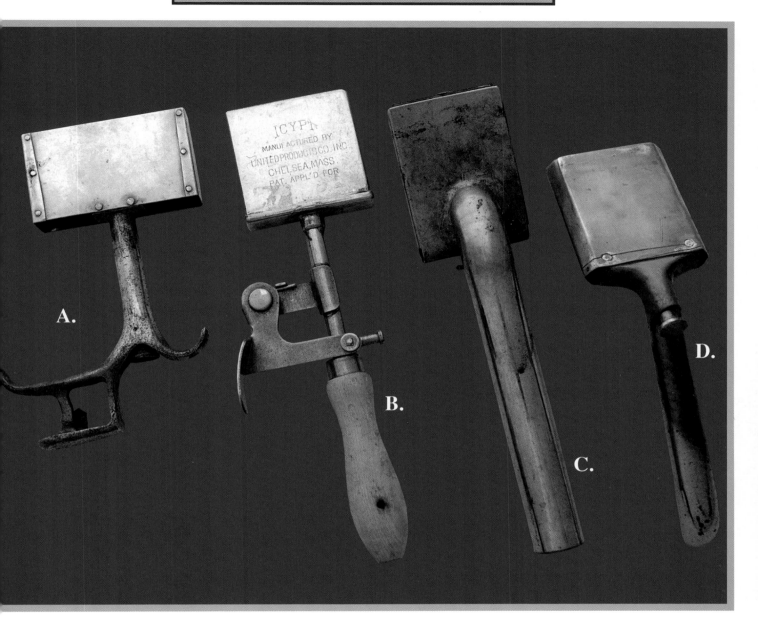

A. Ice Cream Dipper; aluminum and stainless steel, for sandwich, *Johannes Schloemer, NY*, Pat. 1926, 6-1/2"L. $900-1200

B. Ice Cream Dipper; Icypi sandwich, wood handle, nickel-plated brass, *United Products Inc.* (hard to find United), 10"L. $250-350

C. Ice Cream Dipper; mark on end of metal handle and bowl, for sandwich, *J.S. Anderson*, 10"L. $1000-1200

D. Ice Cream Dipper; nickel-plated metal handle and bowl, for sandwich, *Co-La-Pie*, 8-1/4"L. $750-895

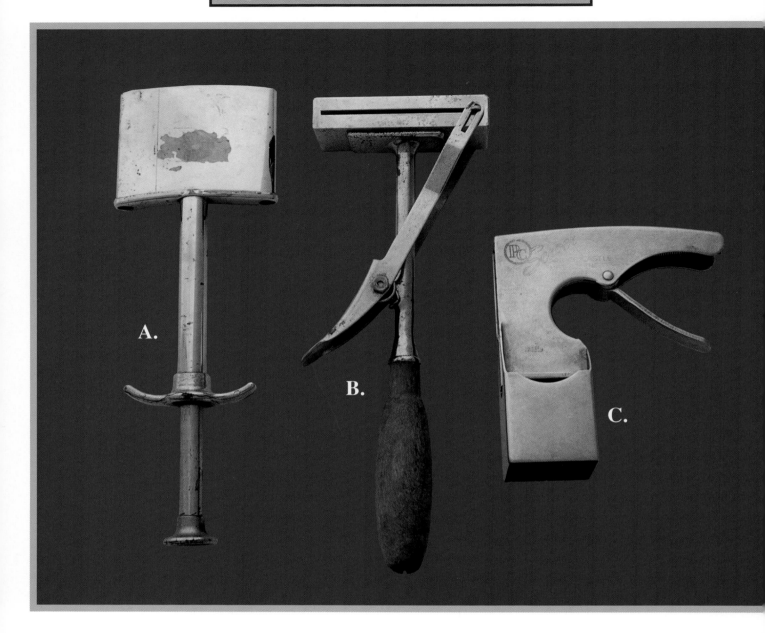

A.   Ice Cream Dipper; metal handle, nickel-plated brass, for sandwich, *W.F. Wendel*, Pat. 1927, 9"L. $1000-1200

B.   Ice Cream Dipper; wood handle, nickel-plated brass, for sandwich, dips at 90 degrees, unknown maker, 9-1/2"L. $1500-2000

C.   Ice Cream Dipper; stainless steel, for sandwich, *Prince Castle Mfg.*, 5"L. $175-250

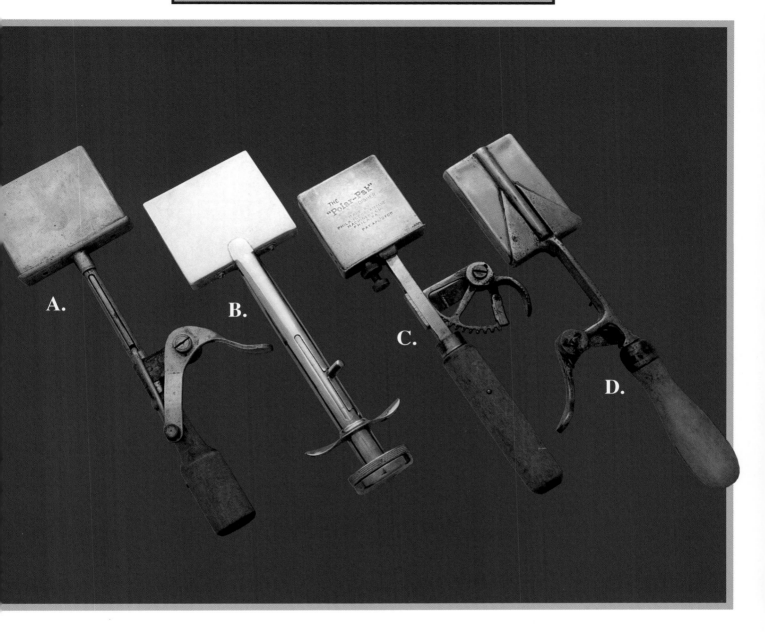

A. Ice Cream Dipper; wood handle, German silver, for sandwich, *Mayer Mfg. Co.*, 12"L. $200-275

B. Ice Cream Dipper; metal handle, nickel-plated brass, for sandwich, *Dan Dee Dipper Co.*, Pat. 1920, 11-1/2". $1300-1500

C. Ice Cream Dipper; wood handle, nickel-plated brass, for sandwich, marked Polar-Pak, *Philadelphia Ice Cream Cone*, 10-1/2"L. $500-695

D. Ice Cream Dipper; wood handle, nickel-plated brass, for sandwich, *Mark File Co.*, 11-1/2"L. $1000-1200

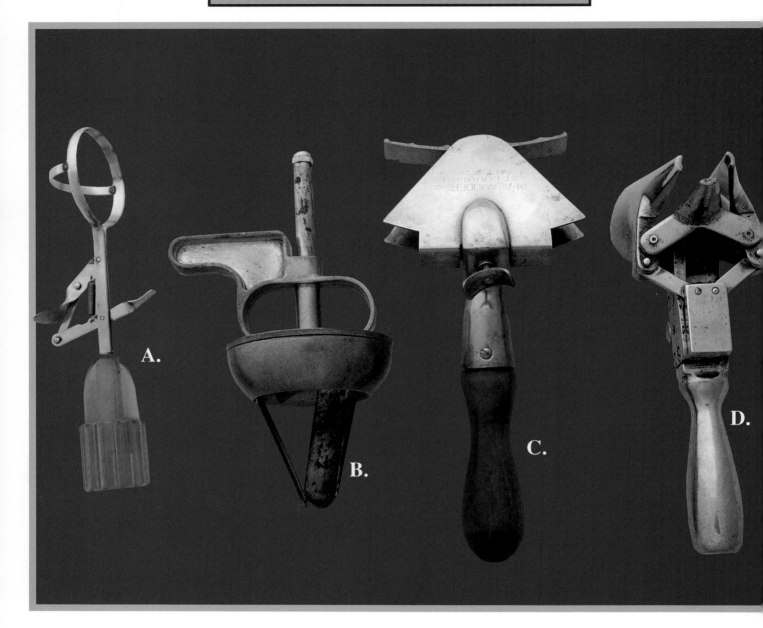

A. Ice Cream Dipper; plastic handle, stainless steel, *H.A. Alheit*, Pat. #2,444,486, c.1945, 7"L. $650-750

B. Ice Cream Dipper; white metal handle, *M.L. Burkhardt*, Pat #1,042,080, c.1919, 7"L. $2500-3000

C. Ice Cream Dipper; wood handle, 45 degre angled dipper, aluminum, *Pi-Alamoder, Inc.*, c.1926, 10"L. $2500-3000

D. Ice Cream Dipper; aluminum handle and body, *Feller Cone Co.*, c.1941, 7-1/2"L. $2500-3000

A. Syrup bottle; Coca-Cola, label under glass, c.1910, 12-1/4"H. $750-850

B. Syrup bottle; Coca-Cola, enamel on bottle, c.1910, 11-3/4"H. $550-650

C. Syrup bottle; Pepsi-Cola, foil label, c.1910, 12-1/4"H. $1450-1550

D. Syrup bottle; Pepsi-Cola, label under glass, c.1910, 12"H. $750-850

E. Syrup bottle; Hires Flavored with Malted Milk, label under glass, c.1910, 12-1/4"H. $750-850

F. Syrup bottle; Dr. Pepper, foil label, c.1910, 12-1/4"H. $750-850

G. Syrup bottle; Christo-Cola, enamel on bottle, c.1910, 11-1/4"H. $350-450

H. Syrup bottle; Peacock, enamel on bottle, c.1910, 11-1/4"H. $350-450

A. Syrup bottle; Grape Smash, label under glass, c.1910, 12-1/4"H. $500-600

B. Syrup bottle; Cherry Smash, label under glass, c.1910, 12-1/4"H. $500-600

C. Syrup bottle; Cherry Smash, painted label, c.1910, 12-1/4"H. $300-400

D. Syrup bottle; Nu Grape, label under glass, c.1910, 12-1/4"H. $300-400

E. Syrup bottle; Emerson's Ginger Mint Julep, label under glass, c.1910, 12-1/4"H. $300-400

F. Syrup bottle; Kola Mint, label under glass c.1910, 12"H. $300-400

G. Syrup bottle; Tango-La, label under glass, c.1910, 11"H. $300-400

H. Syrup bottle; Miner's Iced Mint, label under glass, c.1910, 11"H. $300-400

A. Syrup bottle; Birchola, label under glass, c.1910, 12-3/4"H. $300-400

B. Syrup bottle; Douglas Grapefruit, label under glass, c.1910, 12"H. $300-400

C. Syrup bottle; Gin Gera, label under glass, c.1910, 12-1/4"H. $300-400

D. Syrup bottle; Jersey Creme, foil label, c.1910, 12-1/4"H. $300-400

E. Syrup bottle; Howel Orange Julep, label under glass, c.1910, 11-3/4"H. $350-450

F. Syrup bottle; Howel Orange Julep, foil label, c.1910, 11-3/4"H. $300-400

G. Syrup bottle; Howel Orange Julep, foil label, c.1910, 11-3/4"H. $300-400

H. Syrup bottle; Johnstone's Orange Julep, label under glass, c.1910, 12"H. $350-450

A. Syrup bottle; Orange Whistle, label under glass, c.1910, 12-1/4"H. $200-300

B. Syrup bottle; Daggett's Orangeade, label under glass, c.1910, 11-1/2"H. $200-300

C. Syrup bottle; Sheehan's Orangeade, label under glass, c.1910, 12"H. $200-300

D. Syrup bottle; The Three Miller's Orangeade, label under glass, c.1910, 11-1/2"H. $200-300

E. Syrup bottle; Drink Cherry-Cheer, label under glass, c.1910, 12"H. $350-450

F. Syrup bottle; Howel's Cherry Julep, label under glass, c.1910, 12"H. $350-450

G. Syrup bottle; Cherry Red, label under glass, c.1910, 11"H. $150-250

H. Syrup bottle; Cherry Chaser, label under glass, c.1910, 12"H. $150-250

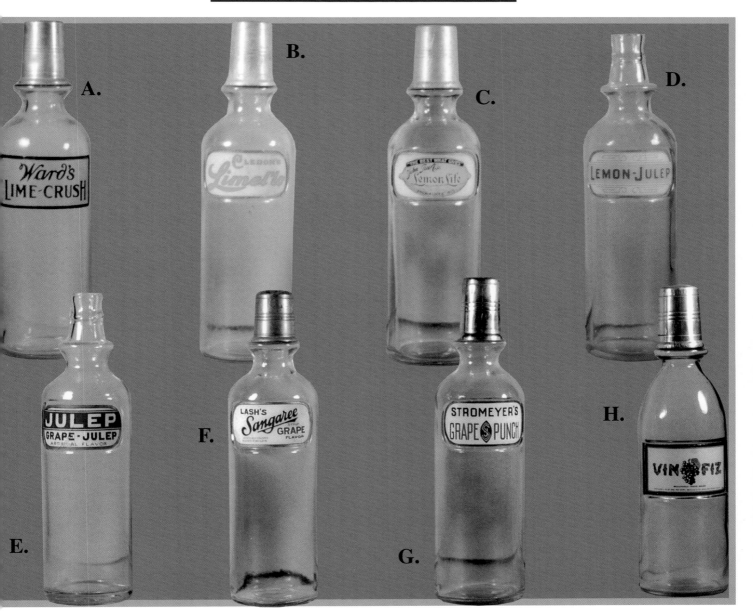

A. Syrup bottle; Ward's Lime Crush, silk screened painted label, c.1910, 12-1/4"H. $250-350

B. Syrup bottle; Cledon's Limel'lo, label under glass, c.1910, 12-1/4"H. $200-300

C. Syrup bottle; John Graf Co. Lemon Life, label under glass, c.1910, 12-1/4"H. $350-450

D. Syrup bottle; Lemon Julep, label under glass, c.1910, 12-1/4"H. $200-300

E. Syrup bottle; Julep Grape-Julep, label under glass, c.1910, 12"H. $200-300

F. Syrup bottle; Lash's Sangaree Grape, label under glass, c.1910, 12"H. $200-300

G. Syrup bottle; Stromeyer's Grape Punch, label under glass, c.1910, 12-1/2"H. $200-300

H. Syrup bottle; Vin Fiz, label under glass, c.1910, 12"H. $250-350

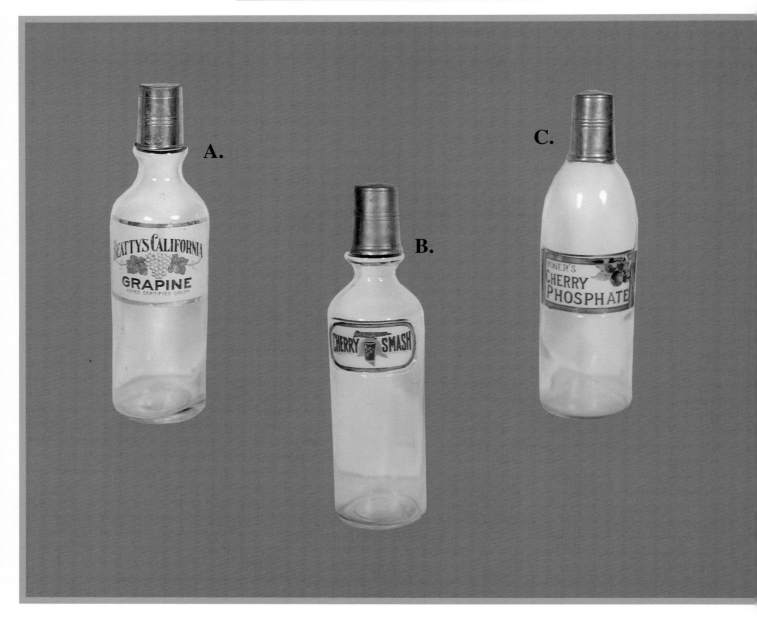

A.   Syrup bottle; Beatty's California Grapine,
     label under glass, c.1910, 12"H. $500-600

B.   Syrup bottle; Cherry Smash, label under
     glass, showing 5¢ glass, c.1910, 12-1/2"H.
     $650-750

C.   Syrup bottle; Miner's Cherry Phosphate,
     label under glass, c.1910, 11-1/2"H.
     $500-600

A. **Almond Smash**; Syrup dispenser; ceramic, c.1910, 14"H. $3500-5000

B. **Birchola**; Syrup dispenser; ceramic, c.1910, 14"H. $1800-2500

C. **Buckeye** Root Beer; Syrup dispenser; black, *The Cleveland Fruit Juice Co.*, c.1910, 15"H. $1600-1800

D. **Buckeye** Root Beer; Syrup dispenser; ceramic, shows buckeye, c.1910, 14"H. $1900-2400

E. **Buckeye** Root Beer; Syrup dispenser; *The Cleveland Fruit Juice Company, Cleveland, Ohio*, c.1910, 14"H. $1700-2200

A. **Buckeye** Root Beer; Syrup dispenser; ceramic, shows "Dancing Centaurs", c.1920, 15"H. $1900-2600

B. **Buckeye** Root Beer; Syrup dispenser; ceramic, tree trunk figural, c.1930, 14-1/2"H. $750-1200

C. **Buckeye** Root Beer; Syrup dispenser; ceramic, Buckeye is in raised lettering, c.1910, 15"H. $2500-3000

D. **Cannon's** Orange Punch; Syrup dispenser; ceramic, shows orange, front and back, c.1910, 14"H. $5500-7000

E. **Cardinal Cherry**; Syrup dispenser; ceramic, product of *J. Hungerford Smith Co., Rochester, NY*, c.1910, 14"H. $4500-5500

A.   **Chero Crush**; Syrup dispenser; ceramic,
       Cherry figural, c.1910, 14"H. $8500+

B.   **Cherri Bon**; Syrup dispenser; ceramic,
       c.1910, 12"H. $ 4500-6500

C.   **Cherry Chic**; Syrup dispenser; ceramic,
       c.1910, 12"H. $4500-6500

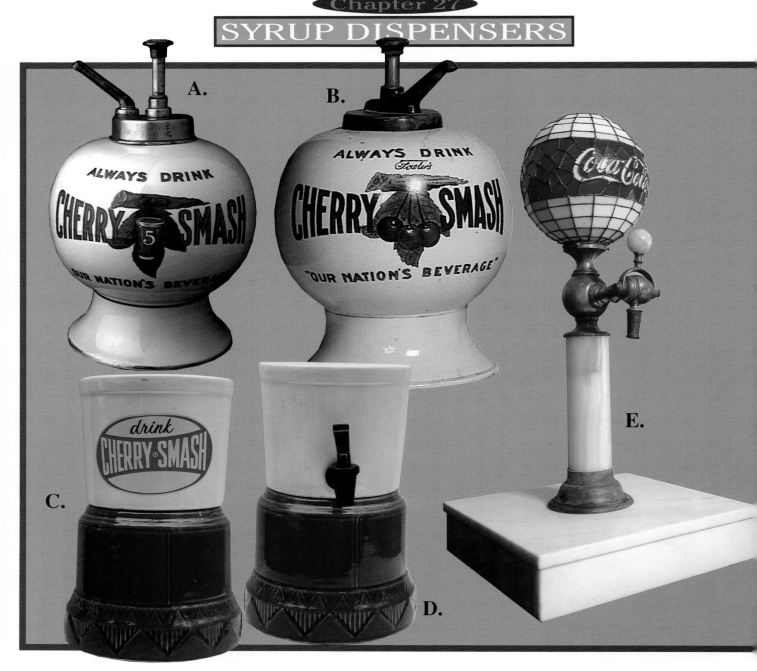

A. **Cherry Smash**; Syrup dispenser; ceramic, "version with the 5¢ glass", c.1900, 16"H. $2000-2500

B. **Cherry Smash Fowler's**; Syrup dispenser; ceramic, "version with three cherries", c.1900, 16"H. $1800-2300

C. **Cherry Smash**; Syrup dispenser; for bulk syrup bottle, applied transfer, c.1930, 11"H, 19"H with bottle. $150-225

D. **Cherry Smash**; front of syrup dispenser C.

E. **Coca-Cola**; Syrup dispenser; fountain head, marble, onyx with leaded glass globe, c.1910, 22"H. $4000-5000

SYRUP DISPENSERS

A. **Coca-Cola**; Syrup dispenser; ceramic, three-piece: lid, dispenser and base, *Wheeling Pottery*, c.1895, 12"Dia. x 23"H. $12000+

Coca-Cola; Syrup dispenser; ceramic, three-piece: lid, dispenser and base, contemporary, c.1970, (Coca-Cola authorized version is marked, value 15-20% more) 12"Dia. x 23"H. $1200-1600

C. **Dr. Pepper**; Syrup dispenser; ceramic, three-piece: lid, dispenser and base, c.1910, 12"Dia. x 23"H. $11000+

D. **Dr. Pepper**; Syrup dispenser; ceramic, three-piece: lid, dispenser and base, contemporary, c.1985, 12"Dia. x 23"H. $1400-1900

A. **Crawford's** Cherry-Fizz; Syrup dispenser; ceramic, "one cherry version", c.1910, 15-1/2"H. $5000-6000

B. **Crawford's** Cherry-Fizz; Syrup dispenser; ceramic, "three cherry version", c.1910, 15-1/2"H. $5000-6000

C. **Dr. Swett's** Root Beer; Syrup dispenser; pottery bottle with spigot, c.1900, 14"H. $1600-2200

D. **Dr. Swett's** Root Beer; Syrup dispenser; ceramic, tree stump figural, c.1900, 14"H. $5500-7000

A. **Fan-Taz**; Syrup dispenser; ceramic, baseball figural, c.1900, 16"H. $8000+

B. **Fowler's** Root Beer; Syrup dispenser; ceramic, c.1910, 15"H. $2000-3000

C. **Fru-Tola**; Syrup dispenser; "It's Fine", etched glass, with glass lid, porcelain vase (missing legs), c.1910, 7"Dia. x 16"H. $1000-1400

D. **Ginger-Mint** Julep; Syrup dispenser; brown ceramic, barrel-shaped, c.1920, 13-1/2"H. $750-1000

E. **Ginger-Mint** Julep; Syrup dispenser; white ceramic, barrel-shaped, c.1920, 14"H. $750-1000

A.   **Grape Crush**; Syrup dispenser; purple glass, c.1920, 14"H. $2800-3500

B.   **Grape Fruitola**; Syrup dispenser; ceramic, *F.M. Willams*, c.1913, 14"H. $2500-3000

C.   **Grape Kola**; Syrup dispenser; china, with lid, bulbous pedestal shape, c.1900, 20"H. $1800-2800

D.   **Grape Julep**; Syrup dispenser; ceramic with bulk glass bottle container, *Property of Southern Fruit Julep Co., Chicago, Phil., Ft. Worth*, c.1920, 10"H, 24"H with bottle. $185-275

A. **Grape Julep**; Syrup dispenser; ceramic, gold trim, c.1910, 14"H. $1200-1600

B. **Grape Julep**; Syrup dispenser; ceramic, c.1910, 14"H. $1200-1600

C. **Grape Smash**; Syrup dispenser; ceramic, c.1910, 15"H. $8000-10000

Note the three different pumps on these dispensers. As on most dispensers, a variety of pumps could be correct.

A. **Green's** Muscadine Punch; Syrup dispenser; ceramic, c.1910, 12"H. $800-1200

B. **Green River**; Syrup dispenser; ceramic, ceramic lid, c.1940, 13"H. $900-1100

C. **Green River**; Syrup dispenser; white milk glass, c.1910, 14"H. $900-1300

D. **Green River**; Syrup dispenser; frosted glass, c.1910, 14"H. $900-1300

E. **Green River**; Syrup dispenser; clear glass in metal base "trophy" shape, c.1930, 13"H. $300-400

F. **Green River**; Syrup dispenser; ceramic, holds bulk syrup bottle, c.1920, 9"H. $175-250

G. **Green River;** Syrup dispenser; for bulk syrup bottle, applied transfer, c.1930, 11"H, 19"H with bottle. $225-350

A. **Hires**; Syrup dispensers; blue, green and brown trim versions, Villeroy & Boch pottery, mfgr. by *Mettlach*, c.1890, 18-1/2"H. These three dispensers have commanded record prices for syrup dispensers. Condition has played an extremely important part in price volatility. Prices vary from $35000 to $60000+ for exceptional condition examples.

A. **Hires**; Syrup dispenser; "Munimaker" with clear glass globe and the version with the milk glass globe (D), marble with onyx handle, mfgr. by *Charles E. Hires, Philadelphia*, c.1905, 16"W x 16"D x 33"H.

The Hires Munimaker has seen considerable price volatility in the last three years. Current values could range from $8000-30000+

B. **Hires**; Syrup dispenser; stainless steel on black porcelain base, attaches to counter-top, c.1930, 6"W x 6-1/2"D x 21-1/2"H. $375-450

C. **Hires**; Syrup dispenser; same as B except blue porcelain base and logo variation.

E. **Hires**; Syrup dispenser; ceramic, hour-glass shape, c.1910, 14"H. $900-1200

A. **Howel's** Cherry Julep; Syrup dispenser; ceramic, c.1900, 15"H. $2000-2500

B. **Howel's** Orange Julep; Syrup dispenser; ceramic, c.1900. 15"H. $1500-2000

C. **Indian Rock** Ginger Ale; Syrup dispenser; ceramic, 15"H. $4000-5000

D. **Ironport**; Syrup dispenser; ceramic, c.1900, 14"H. $2800-3500

E. **Iron Port**; Syrup dispenser; ceramic, made in the same style as the Liquid Force dispenser (page 248), c.1900, 17"H. $7500+

A. **Jersey Cream**; Syrup dispenser; ceramic, c.1910, 14"H. $1800-2500

B. **Kel-Ola**; Syrup dispenser; ceramic, c.1910, 14"H. $2200-2800

C. **Lash's**; Syrup dispenser; green depression glass, black glass base, missing lid, c.1930, 11-1/2"H. $275-325

D. **Liquid Force**, The World's Greatest Health Drink; Syrup dispenser; ceramic, raised shapes of continents, bulbous top, rare, c.1900, 17-1/2"H. $8000+

E. **Lyons** Root Beer; Dispenser; barrel, wood with turn spigot, c.1950, 30"H. $325-500

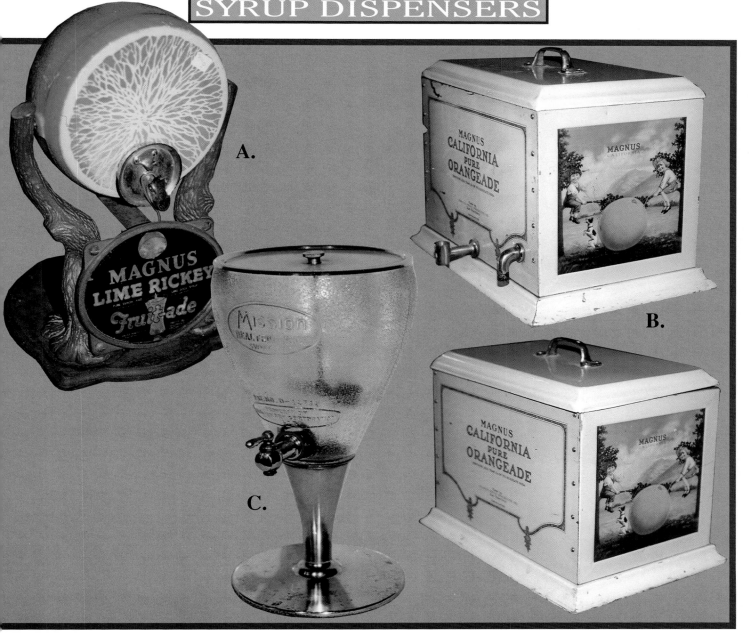

A.

B.

C.

A. **Magnus**; Syrup dispenser; cast-iron base with ceramic "Lime Rickey" syrup holder, 16"H. $2800-3800

B. **Magnus**; Syrup dispenser; wood base, enamel sides, unusual with multi-color "Parrish" like litho, c.1910-1920, 17-1/2"W x 12"D x 12-1/2"H. $2500-3000

C. **Mission**; Syrup dispenser; pink depression glass on metal base, stainless lid, c.1950, 12-1/2"H. $200-300

A. **Mo-Pep**; Syrup dispenser; ceramic, c.1920, 8"Dia. x 14-1/2"H. $1200-1600

B. **Moxie**; Syrup dispenser; clear glass on milk glass base, holds bulk bottle, c.1920, 18"H to top of bottle. $375-500

C. **Oak Street** Soda Fountain; Dispenser; marble with nickel over brass fountain heads, attached straw holder, c.1910, 24"W x 24"H. $850-1100

D. **Orange Crush**; Dispenser; stainless steel with enameled advertising on sides, has "Crush" finial on lid, 19"H to top of finial. $1000-1300

A. **Orange Crush**; Syrup dispenser; satin glass embossed bowl with black glass base, "Crush" decal on front, c.1920, 15"H. $375-500

B. **Orange Julep**; Bulk syrup dispenser; holds ice, bulk bottle sits in top, uses bulk syrup bottle, c.1915, 18"Dia. $275-400

C. **Orange Julep**; Syrup dispenser; ceramic, c.1910, 14"H. $1200-1600

D. **Orange Julep**; Syrup dispenser; ceramic, c.1910, 14"H. $1500-1800

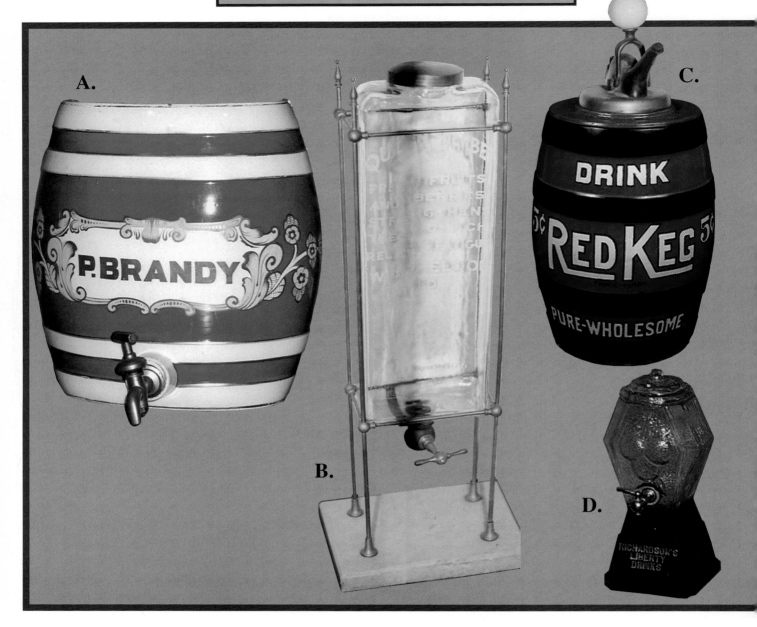

A. **P. Brandy**; Dispenser; ceramic, typical example of saloon-type bulk liquor dispensers, c.1900, 13"H. $400-650

B. **Queen Sherbet**; Syrup dispenser; clear glass on marble stand etched "Fresh Fruits & Berries Strengthens the Stomach Relieves Fatigue", c.1880, 10"W x 7-1/2"D x 27"H. $2600-3000

C. **Red Keg**; Syrup dispenser; ceramic, c.1910, 14"H. $1100-1500

D. **Richardson** Liberty Drinks; Syrup dispenser; clear glass on black bakelite base, c.1920, 13"H. $400-550

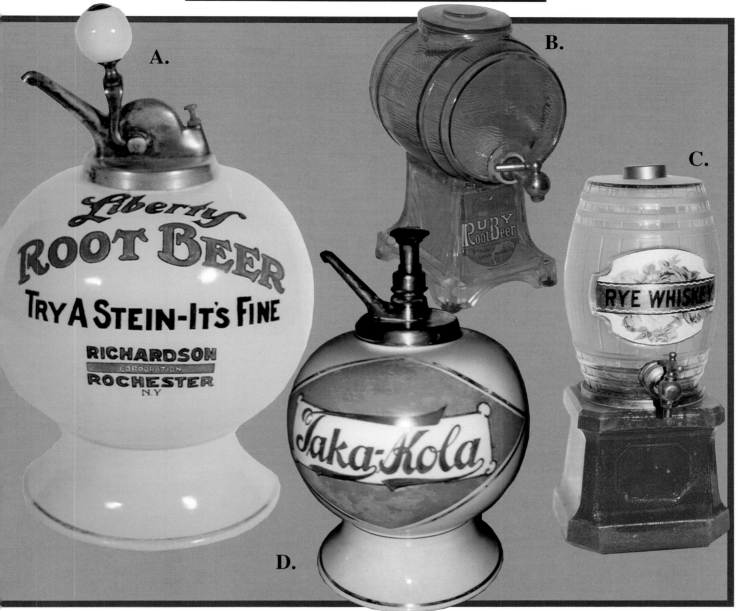

A. **Richardson** Liberty Root Beer; Syrup dispenser; ceramic, c.1920, 16"H. $4000-6000

B. **Ruby** Root Beer; Syrup dispenser; rare three-piece colored glass, c.1920, 13"H. $375-500

C. **Rye Whiskey**; Dispenser; although not a syrup dispenser, this is a unique example of other saloon dispenser types of the period, glass bowl with reverse painted glass label, sits on red reverse painted base (rare), c.1880, 14"H. $1600-2000

D. **Taka-Kola**; Syrup dispenser; ceramic, c.1900, 15"H. $2500-4000

A. **Ver-ba**; Syrup dispenser; ceramic, c.1910, 14"H. $1500-2000

B. **Viccola**; Syrup dispenser; ceramic, baseball figural, c.1900, 16"H. $8000+

C. **Vigoral**; Syrup dispenser with 13 cups; ceramic with transfer pattern on dispenser, lid and cups, cups marked "Vigoral", inside, c.1900, 12"Dia. x 18-1/2"H. Dispenser: $600-800, Cups: $25-40 ea.

D. **Vola**; Syrup dispenser; ceramic, manufactured by *Chicago Concentrating Co.*, c.1910, 16-1/2"H. $1600-2200

Ward's Lemon Crush; Syrup dispenser; figural ceramic in shape of lemon, c.1920, 13"H. $1500-2000

Ward's Orange Crush; Syrup dispenser; figural ceramic dispenser in shape of an orange, c.1920, 13"H. $800-1500

Ward's Lime Crush; Syrup dispenser; figural ceramic in shape of lime, c.1920, 13"H. $2200-2800

D. Ward's Orange Crush; Syrup dispenser; rarer larger version, figural ceramic dispenser in shape of orange, c.1920, 15-1/2"H. $2500-3500

Earlier versions of these dispensers say "Color Added".

A. **Wine Coca**; Syrup dispenser; early unusual footed ceramic dispenser, hole for spigot, c.1890, 16"H. 7000+

B. **Wool's** Cherry Cheer; Syrup dispenser; ceramic, c.1900, 15"H. $9000+

C. **Zipp's** Cherri O; Syrup dispenser; ceramic, c.1910, 14"H. $1100-1500

D. **Zipp's** Cherri-o; Syrup dispenser; ceramic, c.1910, 14"H. $1100-1500

E. Syrup dispenser fountain head; manufactured for Colin S. Few by *Chas. Lippincott & Co., American Soda Fountain Co., Phila.,* c.1890, 39-1/2"W x 24"D x 28"H. $5000-6500

Note; side mirrors and carved canopies can add substantial value to these early fountain heads, often times doubling the value.

A. **Afri-Kola**; Drink mix machine; c.1910, $325-450

B. **Baby Ruth**; Chocolate fudge dispenser; painted metal, aluminum lid, c.1930, 10"H. $225-300

C. **Bowey's** Hot Chocolate; Fudge dispenser; porcelain over enamel, aluminum lid, c.1930, 9-1/2"H. $350-450

D. **Bromo Seltzer**; Dispenser; metal base with plastic portion measure, c.1940, 16"H. $165-200

E. **Bromo Seltzer**; Dispenser; cobalt blue glass base with aluminum portion measure, cobalt drink glass and portioned "shot" glass, die-cut cardboard, two-sided jar-top "talker", c.1920, 24" to top of talker. $325-500

A. **Eskimo Pie**; Dispenser; blue and orange version, litho metal center section, aluminum lid and base with cast legs, c.1930, 8"D x 16"H. $800-1100

B. **Eskimo Pie**; Dispenser; orange and yellow, litho metal center section, aluminum lid and base with cast legs, c.1930, 16"H. $650-900

C. **Grape Smash**; Straw dispenser; glass, c.1910, 9-1/4"H. $2600-3000

D. **Heinz**; Baked Bean warmer; ceramic with ceramic insert and enameled metal lid, electric, *Helmco Inc, Chicago*, c.1950, 12"H. $185-250

A. **Hires**; Root Beer pitcher; ceramic, Mettlach, rare, c.1910, 10"H. $25000+

B. **Hires**; Bottom view of Hires pitcher; shows Mettlach markings.

C. **Horlicks**; Drink mixers; porcelain base, 14"H. $600-700 ea.

D. Hot Drinks heated dispenser; metal base with porcelain panels, *Mabey Electric &* *Mfg. Co., Manufacturer's Indianapolis, Ind.*, 7-3/4"W x 7-3/4"D x 15-1/2"H. $800-1100

E. Hot Soda dispenser; brass, original is nickel over brass, lower section boils water, steam pressure flips "Hot Soda" glass marquee, ruby glass, cut to clear, holds syrup bottles, c.1900, 36"H. $8500-11000

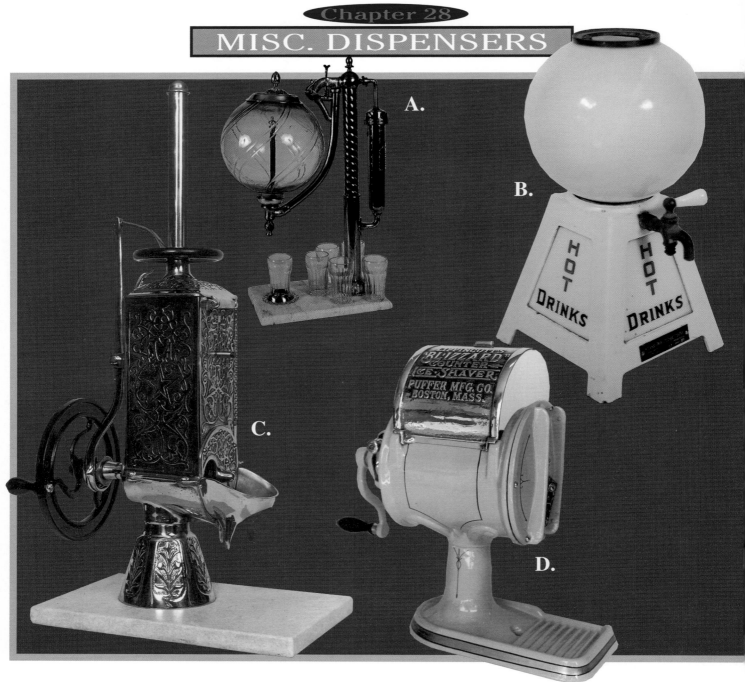

A. Dispenser; for purified water, pressed pattern in clear glass bowl, marble base, nickel over brass frame, c.1890, 16"H. $2000-2400

B. Hot Drinks heated dispenser; metal with porcelain base and panels, *Indianapolis Electric Co, Manufacturers, Indianapolis*, 7-1/2"W x 7-1/2"D x 15"H. $1100-1300

C. Shaved ice dispenser; marble base, nickel-plated brass and cast iron, c.1890, 18"H. $325-500

D. Shaved ice dispenser; restored, painted and nickel-plated cast iron and brass, *Lippincott's Blizzard Counter Ice Shaver, Puffer Mfg Co., Boston Mass.*, c.1920, 14"H. $250-400

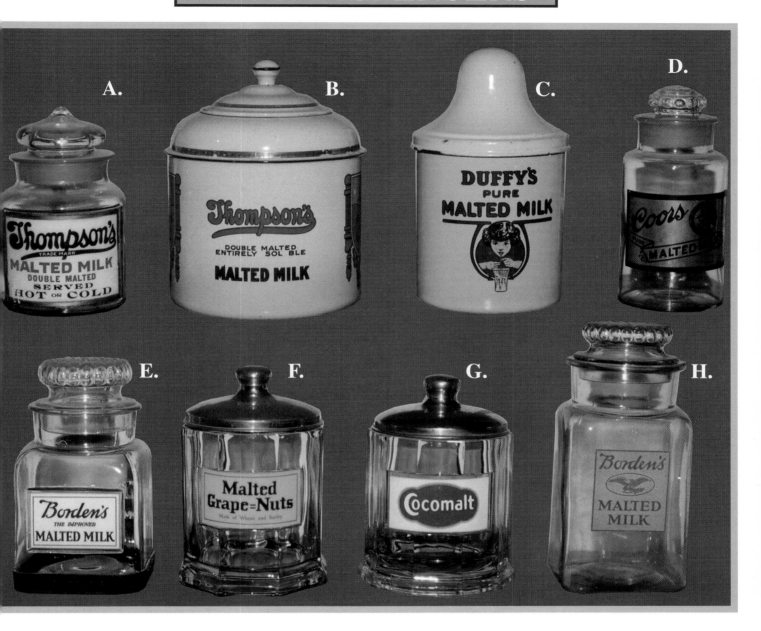

A. Malted milk jar; Thompson's, label under glass, 8"H. $550-650

B. Malted milk jar; Thompson's, enameled metal, 9-1/2"H. $550-650

C. Malted milk jar; Duffy's, enameled metal, 10"H. $550-650

D. Malted milk jar; Coors, painted label, 8-1/2"H. $350-450

E. Malted milk jar; Borden's, label under glass, 8-1/2"H. $450-550

F. Malted milk jar; Malted Grape Nuts, label under glass, 8-1/4"H. $450-550

G. Malted milk jar; Cocomalt, label under glass, 8"H. $450-550

H. Malted milk jar; Borden's, painted label, 10"H. $350-450

A. **Nesbitt's** Hot Fudge; Dispenser; painted aluminum with stoneware bowl, heated, c.1930, 9"Dia. x 11-1/2"H. $250-350

B. **Pure Ices**; Display piece; for ice cream or slush, c.1920, 20"W x 6"D x 15"H. $450-550

C. Steamed clams and clam broth dispenser; graniteware, two metal steaming containers, c.1920, 22"H. $425-550

D. Straw dispenser; pressed glass with lid and handles, c.1910, 11-1/2"H. $2000-3000

E. Straw dispenser; pressed glass tray, c.1910, 8-1/2"H. $400-500

F. Straw dispenser; Heisey "Colonial", pressed glass, c.1915, 10"W. $600-700

G. Straw dispenser; pressed glass tray, c.1915, 10"W. $400-500

These men are enjoying their coffee break at this c.1930 cafe. The trellis on the back wall holds a Coca-Cola festoon and a die-cut cardboard Squeeze Soda sign. A fried ham sandwich on toast is 15 cents.

The Annex offered its patrons cigars and hearty "Lager". These three c.1920 patrons enjoy tall glasses of dark ale. On the cigar counter, at left, is a cigar cutter. Notice the double dial regulator wall clock.

This photo, taken late in the day, shows a well-stocked Soda Fountain/Cafe. Notice the large display of Whistle soft drinks. On the back wall is a "Gallery" of 1940's advertising.

This Drug Store soda fountain not only offered sodas, it also sold books. This c.1920 fountain has a unique back bar with a draped, reverse lit, leaded glass panel. It complements the shade on the fountain head.

CONGLOMERATION

A. Single station barber back bar; beveled mirror, wash stand, movable towel storage stand, quartersawn oak, c.1910, $3000+

B. **Berninghause**; Barber chair; fancy carved oak, nickel-plated brass and iron trim, hydraulic lift, tilt back, in original condition, new upholstery, c.1910, $1800-2400

C. Barber pole; porcelain floor model, galvanized ball on top, c.1910, 90"H. $600-800

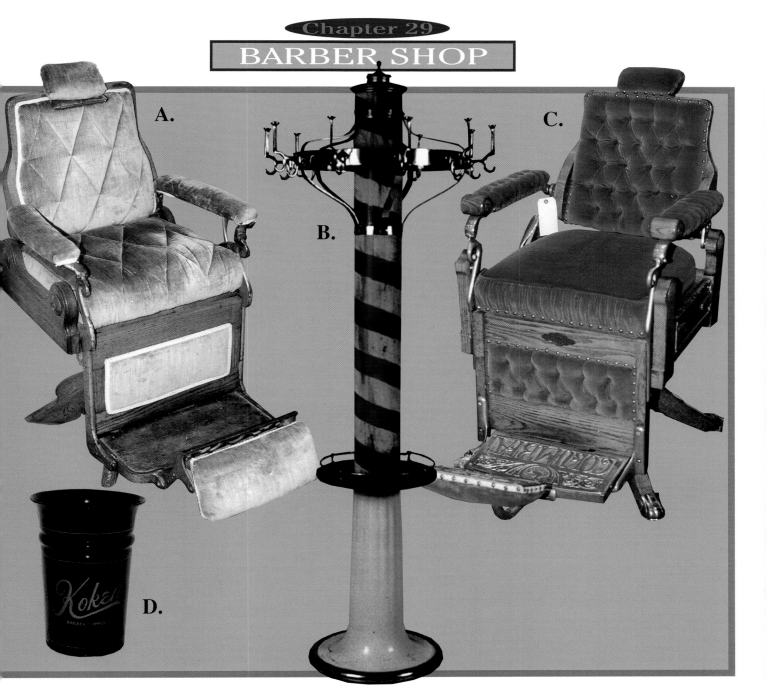

A.   Barber chair; oak with nickel-plated cast trim, hydraulic lift, tilt back, *Archer Mfg. Co., Rochester, N.Y.*, c.1910, $600-900

C.   Barber chair; oak with nickel-plated trim, hydraulic lift, tilt back, *Koch's Columbia*, c.1910, $900-1400

B.   Barber shop hat rack; porcelain base, painted wood column, with nickel-plated coat hooks, c.1910, 84"H. $900-1400

D.   **Koken**; Barber shop hot towel bucket; restored, metal with painted lettering, c.1910, 20"H. $125-200

A. **National**; Floor scale; penny coin operated, heavily embossed, cast iron, porcelain dial, c.1910, $1000-1600

B. **Sun**; Barber shop towel sterilizer; porcelain base with brass heater and towel reservoir, c.1920, 44"H. $1600-2000

C. Barber shop hat rack; oak, metal umbrella holders, with brass wash on iron hat hooks, c.1910, 78"H. $750-1000

D. Barber or dental cabinet; fancy early oak cabinet with tambour roll top, beveled mirror, porcelain pulls, c.1900, 60"H. $2400-3100

A.

B.

C.

D.

E.

F.

. **Abercrombie & Co's.** Royal Sandwich, Havana Cigars; Cigar cutter; cast iron, c.1910, 6"W x 9"D x 6-1/2"H. $700-900

. **Ambrosia**; Cigar cutter; cast iron, 3-1/2"W x 5-1/2"D x 3"H. $700-900

. **Bachelor** Cigars 5¢ Victor Thorsch; match plunger; cast iron, *J & M Co., Milwaukee, WI*, c.1900, 5-1/2"W x 4-1/2"D x 8"H. $600-800

D. Boat cigar cutter; cast iron, Hallmark on bottom, 8"W x 4"D x 2-3/4"H. $700-800

E. Bicycle; stand and match holder; (match holder says kilometer), brass, c.1910, 2"W x 5"H x 2"H. $2300-2800

F. Black Boy electric cigarette lighter; cast metal, c.1920, 3"Dia. x 5"H. $800-900

A. **Breslin & Campbell;** Cigar cutter; black boy cast iron, c.1910, 5"D x 2-3/4"W x 4"H. $1300-1500

B. **Celestino** Costelloy Ca Fine Cigars; Cigar cutter and lighter; cast iron and wood with brass reservoir, globe for lighter and revolving ad holder missing, c.1890, 6"W x 10-1/2"D x 13"H. $400-700

C. **Buffos** Tiny Spicy Havanas; Clipper only; cast iron on wood base, advertising on both sides of circle that flips over, *Erie Specialty Co.*, 4-1/2"W x 5-1/2"D x 6-1/2"H. $800-900

D. **George W. Childs**; Cigar cutter; cast iron with wind up cutter, c.1910, 10"W x 4-1/2"D x 10"H. $950-1100

E. **Concordia**; Cigar cutter; cast iron, glass panel with push bar, 8"W x 4-1/2"D x 4-1/2"H. $850-1000

A. **Country Gentleman** 5¢; Cigar cutter; cast iron, *The Brunhoff Mfg. Co.*, Pat'd. May 19, 1891, (re-cast contemporary version) 2-3/4"W x 4-1/2"D x 3-1/2"H. $125-200

B. **D & M** 5¢ Straight; Cigar cutter; Diem-McCormick Cigar Co., Buffalo, NY, *Carris*, 6-1/2"W x 8-1/4"D x 5"H. $500-800

C. **Della Casa** 5¢ Juniors Highest Quality; Cigar cutter with cigar box opener; cast iron with glass advertising panel, *Brunhoff*, c.1900, 4-1/2"W x 8-1/2"D x 5"H. $600-800

D. **Depose** (French); Match dispenser trade stimulator; cast iron, 8"W x 7"D x 15"H. $1100-1400

E. **Dolly Madison;** Cigar cutter; cast iron on wood base, with push bar and glass ad panel, paper applied on reverse side, *Brunhoff*, c.1900, 8"W x 6"D x 5"H. $600-800

A. **Paul Dudley**; Cigar cutter and match dispenser; cast iron, *Brunhoff*, c.1900, 6"W x 7"D x 8"H. $1400-1800

B. **Dutch Masters** 10¢ Havana; Cigar cutter; cast iron with glass advertising panel, maker unknown, 5-1/4"W x 7-1/2"D x 6-1/4"H. $600-800

C. **El Taymar**; Cigar cutter; cast iron and tin, cigar label fits under glass panel, *probably Brunhoff*, c.1902,

5-1/2"W x 6"D x 6"H. $375-475

D. **Frederick** 10¢; Cigar cutter with clock; cast iron, *Brunhoff*, c.1900, 7-1/2"W x 7-1/2"D x 13-1/2"H. $1200-1500

E. **Golden Wedding**; Cigar cutter; cast iron, Havana Cigar of Excellent Quality, O.C. Taylor & Co., Burlington, VT, *Brunhoff*, pat. applied for, c.1900, 9"W x 6-1/4"D x 8"H. $600-800

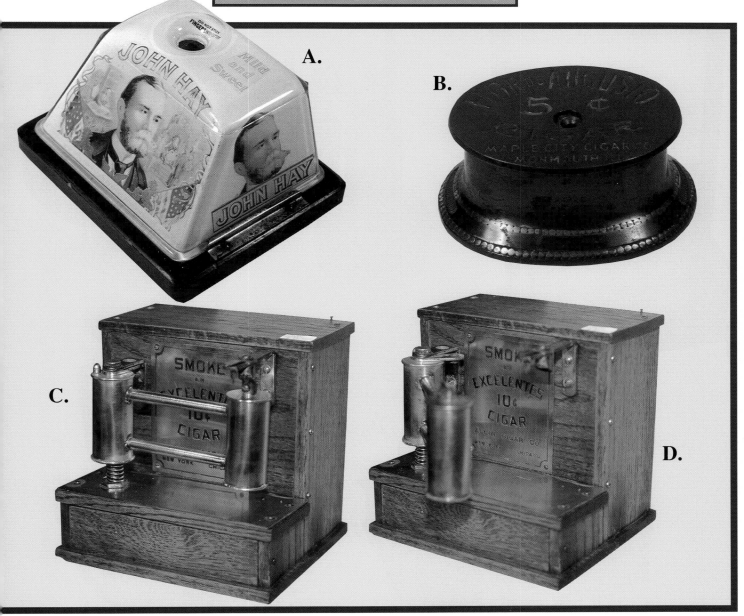

A. John Hay; Wind-up cutter; glass with paper applied inside glass, W.W. Stewart & Sons Reading Penna Makers, *Brunhoff*, patents 621185, 666074, c.1900, 8-1/2"W x 7"D x 4-1/2"H. $1200-1600

B. Hor De Augusto 5¢ Cigar; Cigar cutter; cast iron, Pat. #666074, Maple City Cigar Co., Monmouth, IL, *Brunhoff*, c.1910, 7"W x 5-1/2"D x 3"H. $600-800

C. Klein; Cigar cutter and lighter; wood and brass, insert cigar in trim hole on left, pull out tank on right, it cuts tip and lights flame, "Smoke Excellentes 10 cent Cigar", Klein Cigar Co., New York, Chicago, *Mfg. by Peerless Mfg., 12-14 Washington, Chicago, Il.*, c.1900, 7-1/2"W x 14-1/2"D x 8-1/4"H. $650-800

D. Klein; Cigar cutter with tank pulled out to light.

A. **Korisko Bros.**; Cigar lighter; oak case with advertising panel, "Undertaking and Embalming; For Ladies...", c.1910, 7-3/4"W x 4-1/2"D x 13"H. $800-1000

B. **Laminus Maxima**; Cigar lighter; cobalt blue glass plunger, c.1900, 3-1/2"Dia. x 8-1/2"D x 8-1/2"H. $600-800

C. **LaConfesion**; Cigar cutter; with paper applied inside glass, Cuban made cigars, Berito Rouira Co., Inc., c.1900, 8-1/2"Dia. x 4"H. $2300-2600

D. **Little Pea** Cigars; Cigar trade stimulator; wood, lead balls drop through pins, Standard Tobacco & Cigar Co., Cleveland, OH, *The Sun Mfg. Co., Greenfield, OH, USA,* $4700-6000

E. **Davis Londers**, "A Cigar of Merit 5¢ Straight"; Cigar cutter with lighter; cast iron, W.A. Davis, Syracuse, NY, *Brunhoff,* 9"W x 12"D x 12"H. $2500-2800

A. **John W. Merriam & Co.**; Cigar cutter; cast-iron dog house with bulldog, maker unknown, c.1910, 6"W x 4-1/2"D x 6-1/2"H. $1100-1300

B. **Midland** Jump Spark; Cigar lighter; maple with nickel-plated brass, panels for cigar advertising on sides, model "L", *Davenport Mfg. Co., Davenport, Iowa,* c.1920, 7"W x 7"D x 14-1/2"H. $800-1100

C. **Mogul** 5¢ Cigar; Cigar cutter; cast iron, Lagora Fee Co. Detroit, MI,

Northwestern, pat. July 13, 1909, 4"W x 6"D x 6"H. $600-800

D. **N.A.R.D.**; Cigar cutter; "Hand Made, 5¢ Straight", cast iron, Peter-Neat-Richardson Co., *Brunhoff Mfg. Co. #250,* c.1890, 6-1/2"W x 8"D x 8"H. $550-750

E. **Northwestern**; Robert Burns cigar cutter; with advertising, 1¢ coin operated match vendor, cast iron, c.1910, 10-1/4"W x 7"D x 16-1/2"H. $850-1200

A. **Old North State** Smoking Tobacco; Fabric pouch display; 9"W x 3"D x 13"H. $500-700

B. Get the **Ocho** Habit 10¢; Cutter with clock; wind up, *Brunhoff*, c.1900, 9-1/4"W x 6-1/2"D x 14"H. $2500-3000

C. **Omar** (Elephant); Cigar cutter with lighter; cast iron on wood base, c.1910, 12"W x 5-1/2"D x 13"H. $4000-5000

D. **Ongola** Clear Havana; Quick action cigar lighter; wood with cast-iron mechanism and glass panel in iron frame, *Knoblock Heideman Mfg. Co., South Bend, IN*, c.1910, 8-1/2"W x 7-1/2"D x 9"H. $800-1100

E. The Perfect Match Lighter by Diestler Co. oak case, push lever to clip cigar and match comes out and strikes on way out, *Hortonville, WI, R.E. Jack, Inventor* Pat. applied for, c.1910, 7"W x 8-1/2"D x 8-1/2"H. $1300-1500

A.   Phone cigar lighter; metal case with panel in front for Wisc. Advertising, c.1930, 10"W x 7-1/2"D x 11"H. $400-650

B.   **Piper Heidsieck** Cigars; Cutter; cast iron, in shape of champagne bottle, Rosenthal Bros., NY, *C.D. Woodworth, NY*, c.1910, 10-1/2"L x 3"W x 5"H. $600-800

C.   **Qua Placer** Habanas; Cutter; cast iron and brass, Louis B. Aronson, *Brunhoff*, c.1916, 5"W x 4-1/2"D x 7-1/2"H. $400-550

D.   **Rocky Ford** Cigars High Grade; Cigar cutter and match dispenser; cast iron, *Carris Novelty Co., Washington, LA*, May 31, 1904, 6-1/2"W x 8"D x 5"H. $500-800

E.   **Round Top** 5¢ Cigar; Cutter; wind up, cast iron, Dearstyne Bros. Albany, NY, *Erie Specialty Co.*, Pat'd. 1889, 4"W x 6"D x 3-1/2"H. $600-800

A. **Siegel's Musical Club**; Cigar cutter; *Brunhoff*, 8"W x 5-1/2"D x 8-1/2"H. $600-800

B. **Star Select Co.**; Cigar lighter; winged cupid on cast iron base, Waterloo, IN, c.1900, 8-1/2"W x 8"D x 21"H. $4000-5000

C. **Sun Cigar** Smoke the Sun 10 Cents; Cigar cutter and lighter; Syracuse, NY, c.1920, $1700-2200

D. Town Crier cigar cutter; cast iron, polychrome, put cigar in mouth and move arm down, unmarked, c.1900, 6-1/2"W x 3-1/2"D x 7"H. $900-1200

E. Town Crier cigar cutter; cast iron, *Carrey Brown & Co.* Manufacturers, Regulars - First Pick, c. 1900, 6-1/4"W x 4-1/4"D x 7-1/2"H. $1300-1500

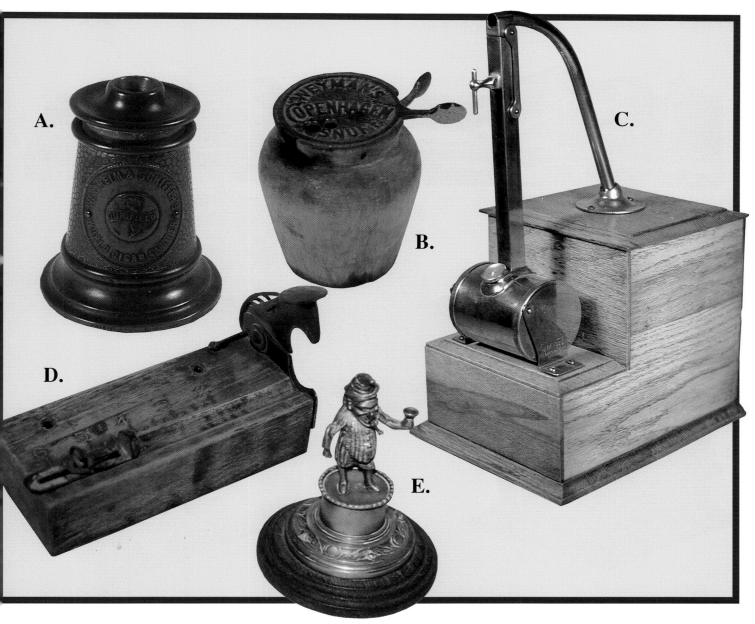

A. Werthern & Schiffer's Worth; Cigar cutter; "Our World", cast iron, pat. April '87, 5"H. $700-900

B. Weyman's Copenhagen Snuff; Cigar cutter; wood with cast iron top, unusual, c.1910, 3"Dia. x 4"H. $175-225

C. Wireless No 12; Cigar lighter; oak with nickel-plated brass, *Eldred Mfg., Co., Chicago*, c.1910, 7-3/4"W x 9-1/2"D x 15-1/4"H. $900-1100

D. Commercial cigar cutter; for trimming measured lengths, wood base, iron and steel, c.1900, 3"W x 8"D x 4-1/2"H. $175-225

E. Cigar lighter; "Punch", cast iron, 3"Dia. base x 7"H. $800-1100

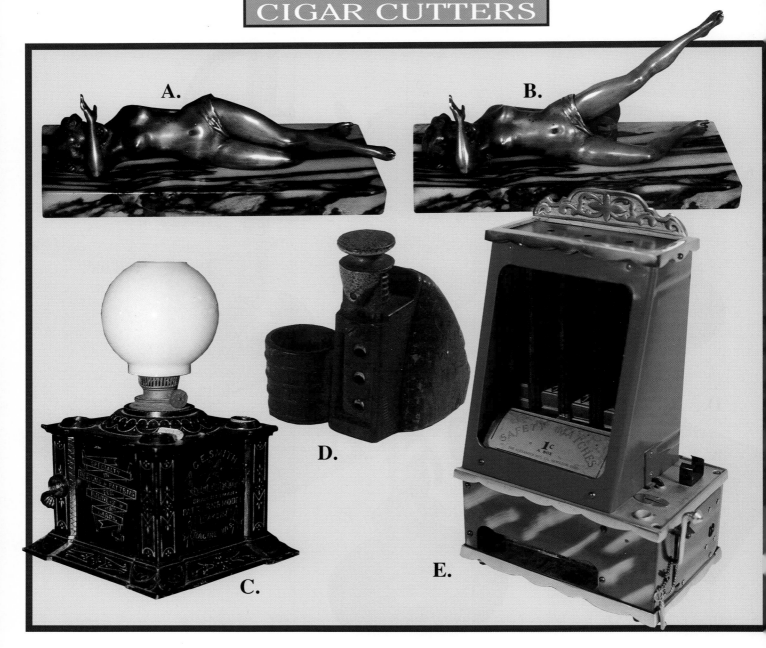

A.

B.

D.

C.

E.

A. Art Nouveau Woman; Novelty cigar cutter; bronze on gray marble base, (cutter closed) signed, "C. Kavba", (sculptor 1865-1923), c.1910, 9"L. $3500-4000

B. Cutter A open.

C. Cigar cutter and lighter; cast iron, opening to insert cigar, lever pulls down to cut tip, cast relief lettering on four sides, *C.E. Smith Designer, Draughtsman, pattern and model maker, Racine, WI.*, c.1885, 6"W x

6"D x 9-1/2"H. $825-1000

D. Cigar cutter; cast iron and wood, maker unknown, c.1890, 3-1/2"W x 3-1/2"D x 5"H. $500-700

E. Match vendor and cigar cutter; coin operated, cast iron and sheet metal, *Alexander Mfg Co., Hamilton, OH*, c.1910 10-1/2"W x 6-3/4"D x 17-1/2"H. $850-1000

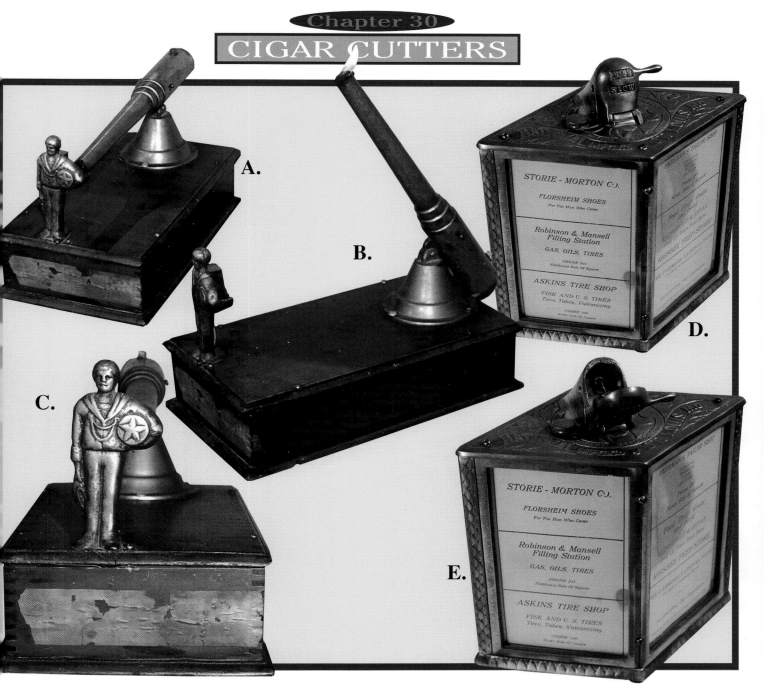

A. Cigar lighter; wood and nickel-plated cast iron, sailor with cannon, flip lever and cannon raises and lights, c.1905, 7-1/2"W x 14-1/2"D x 8-1/4"H. $4500-6000

B. Cannon raised with flame.

C. Front view of lighter A.

D. Cigar cutter; aluminum with advertising panels, *National Mfg. Co., St. Louis, MO*, c.1920, 12"W x 7"D x 12"H. $800-1100

E. With lighter open.

A.   **Boston** Garter; Countertop display case; oak with glass panel on top and in front, front panel hinged at bottom, tips out, reverse transfer on front glass, c.1915, 12"W x 11"D x 11"H. $300-350

B.   **Boye** Dress Fastener; Display case; wood and glass with advertising on three sides, c.1920, 10"W x 11-1/2"H. $150-200

C.   **Boye**; Patent spring curtain holder; multi-colored lithographed tin, *Boye Needle Co., Chicago, Il.*, c.1915, 9-1/2"W x 7-1/4"D x 7-3/4"H. $700-875

D.   **Brighton** Garter 25¢; Display case; painted soft wood with applied lettering, c.1910, 14"W x 10-1/2"D x 19"H. $350-475

E.   **Brighton** Garter; back of display case D.

A. **Richard Hudnut** Rouge; Display; mahogany stained wood, reverse painted glass front, holds eight samples, c.1920, 18-1/2"W x 12-1/4"D x 9-1/2"H. $275-350

B. **Hull** Umbrellas; Display; oak with paper label, leg swivels out to hold card display, c.1890, 15"W x 4-1/2"H. $85-125

C. **Ideal** Typewriter Ribbons; Display case; oak, applied lettering on three sides, c.1910, 22"W x 17"D x 17"H. $625-700

D. **Ideal**; back of typewriter ribbon case.

E. **Knickerchief**; Display; glass with glass shelves, reverse gold etching with over paint, c.1915, 6"W x 6-3/4"D x 14"H. $165-225

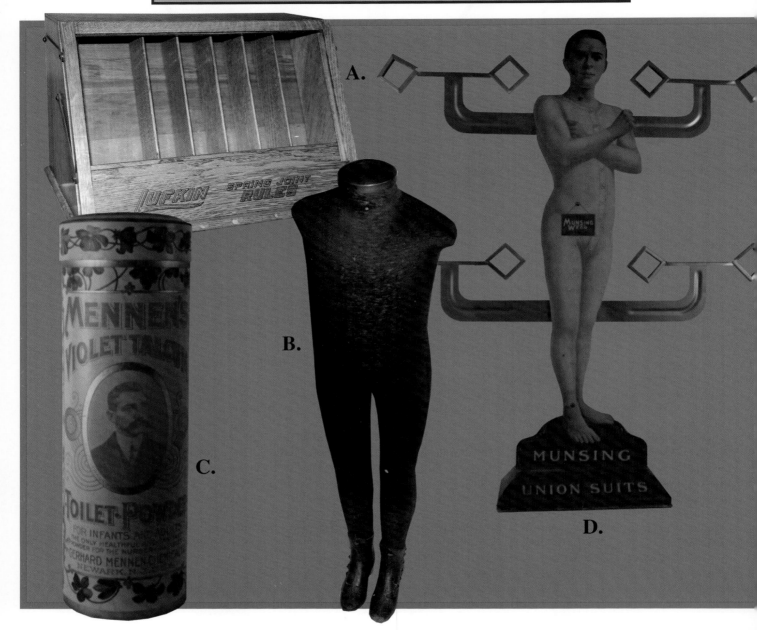

A. **Lufkin**; Ruler display case; "Spring Joint Rules", quartersawn oak with glass front, transfer lettering on front, c.1915, 15"W x 12"D x 13"H. $275-350

B. Mannequin; composition child's body with fabric covering and cast iron feet, c.1890, 40"H. $315-385

C. **Mennen's** Violet Talcum Powder; Display; cardboard, depicts trademark of Gerhard

Mennen, back reads what product relieves 10"Dia. x 30"H. $1500-2500

D. **Munsing** Union Suits; Display; two-sided die-cut tin display shows man wearing long johns on one side and shorter version on other side, four brackets hold product, c.1920, 35-1/2"W x 53"H. $1700-2500

A.   B.   C.   D.

A.   **Newport** Garters; Counter display; oak, applied transfer lettering, garters attach to metal bar, c.1910, 13"W x 7"D x 6"H. $275-350

B.   **Paris** Garters; Counter display; slant front, oak and glass, applied lettering, holds four boxes behind glass, c.1920, 8-1/4"W x 5-1/2"D x 8-1/2"H. $215-300

C.   **Phillipson** Clothing Company; Display cabinet; 3-drawer, wood, cast iron with brass flash plating drawer fronts, c.1900, 15"W x 10"D x 20"H. $450-500

D.   Postcard Ferris wheel; revolving display with ornately embossed metal, probably Columbian Expo display, c.1890, 17"W x 37"H. $2200-2800

A. **Rubberset** Shaving Brush; Display; die-cut countertop display with wood grained background, 15-1/2"W x 6"D x 13"H. $200-400

B. Sponge display case; oak with glass sides and curved glass top, four tip-down doors in rear, originally had wire shelves, c.1900, 21-1/4"W x 19-1/4"D x 60"H. $950-1300

C. **Julius Schmid Inc.**; Condom display cabinet; pine, stained walnut, brass knobs on pull-open doors with lift top showing prices, colorful artwork, c.1950, 13"W x 3-3/4"D x 18-1/2"H. $900-1200

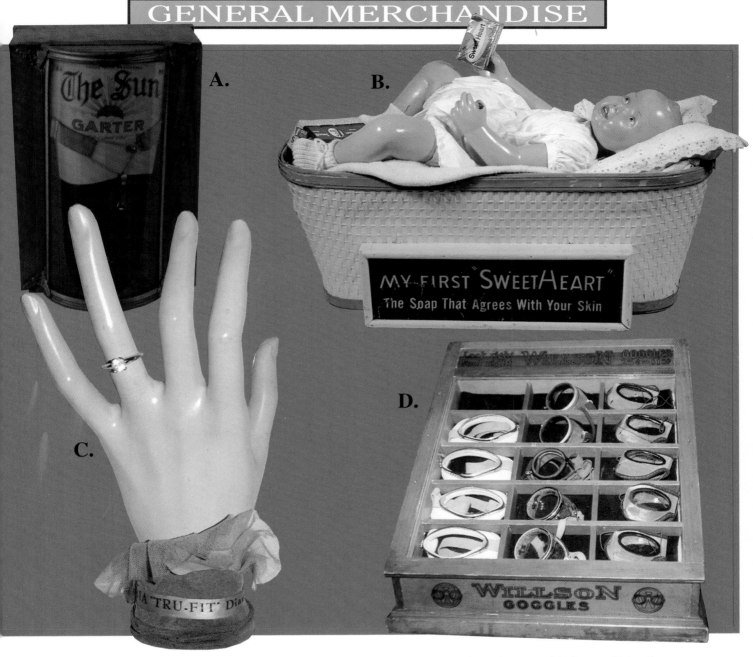

A.   **Sun** Garter; Display; wood, curved glass front with framed metallic filigree at four corners, glass in two side displays is stenciled with gold lettering, 11"H. $500-800

B.   **Sweetheart** Soap; Animated store display; life-size composition baby in basket, moves arm and leg, reverse lit panel below basket, c.1940, 29"W x 17"D x 20"H. $800-1100

C.   **True Fit** Diamond Rings; Display; composition bigger than life hand, adjustable ring slides on finger, hand holds display card, c.1950, 18-1/2"H. $135-215

D.   **Willson** Goggles; Counter display case; basswood with maple finish, applied transfer letters on front, reverse transfer on upper glass, holds 15 goggle sets with extra compartment behind, c.1920, 12"W x 14"D x 10"H. $225-275

A.   **Ace Combs**; Display case; by American Hard Rubber Co., c.1920, 6-1/2"W x 4-1/2"D x 13"H. $200-250

B.   **Bonnie B**; Hair net display; multi-color lithographed tin with mirrored panel, *The Bonnie B. Co., Inc., New York*, c.1921, 13-1/4"W x 11"D x 15-1/2"H. $1800-2200

C.   **Gainsborough**; Hair net display; slant front, wood, c.1920, 15"W x 17-1/2"D x 17-1/2"H. $200-300

D.   **Pinol**; Scalp treatment display; tapered wood, applied gold lettering, c.1930, 11-1/2"W x 11"H. $225-350

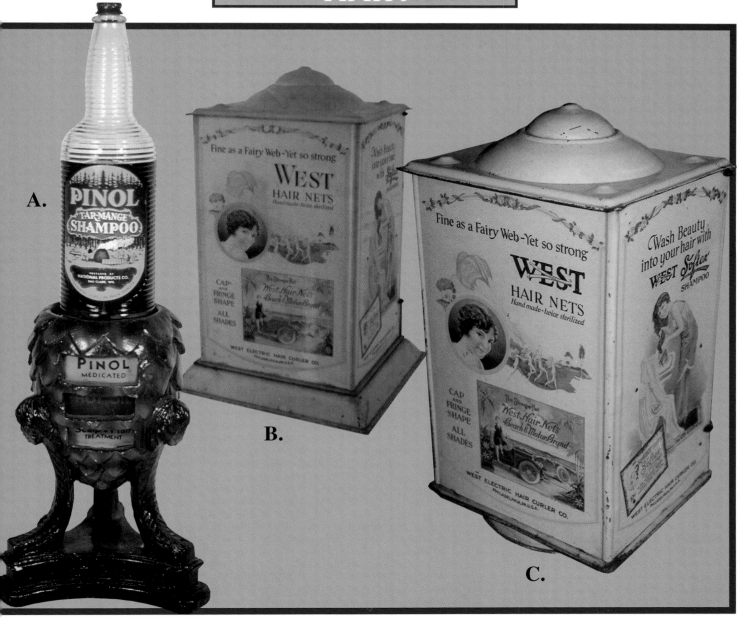

A.   **Pinol**; Shampoo display; painted plaster, back lit plastic panels, light bulb heats tonic that sits on glass panel above bulb, c.1940, 7"W x 7"D x 21"H. $300-425

B.   **West Hair Nets**; Counter display; multi-colored tin lithographed, also advertising West Electric Hair Curlers and Softex shampoo, c.1921, 13"W x 11"D x 19"H. $300-500

C.   **West** Hair Nets; Counter display; revolves, multi-colored tin lithographed, c.1921, 13"W x 9"D x 18"H. $850-950

A. **American Beauty** Electric Iron; Display case; oak with glass, litho under glass ad panel, reverse lit, original iron, c.1920, 12"W x 12"D x 24"H. $1300-1650

B. **Atlas Tack**; Display box; cardboard box shows trademark lady holding box of home tacks, c.1890, 9-1/2"W x 8"D x 2-1/2"H. $175-250

C. **Bissell Carpet Sweeper**; Display; die-cut wood floor display, stenciled lettering, 47"H. $550-700

D. **Bright Star**; Counter display; cast-iron and tin litho, revolves, six-sides, for batteries and flashlights, *Bright Star Battery Co., Hoboken, N.J., Chic., S. F.,* c.1920, 7-1/2"W x 19-1/2"H. $475-575

E. Buggy whip rack; cast-iron top with pine base and column, additional section goes in the top holding another bracket, c.1890, 24"Dia. x 33"H. $275-350

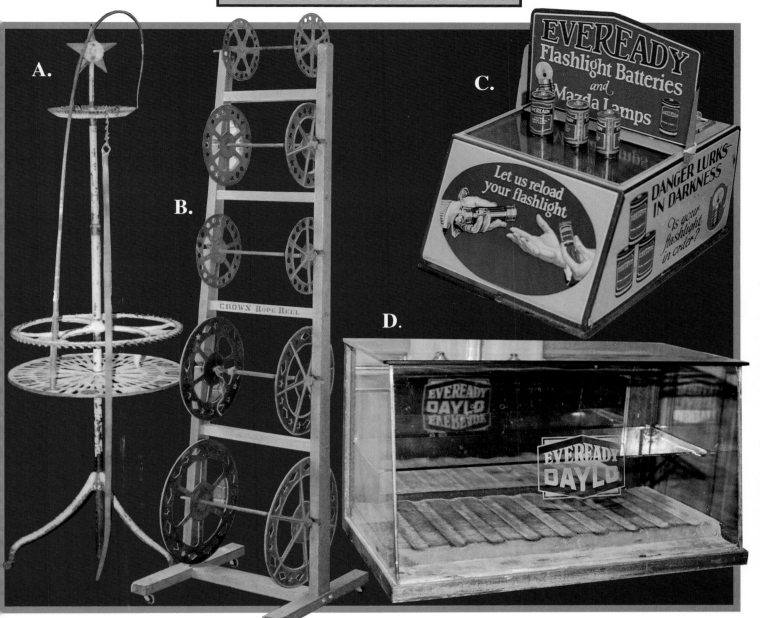

A. Buggy whip rack; cast iron, *John N. Best Galva, Il.*, Pat'd., Oct. 2, 1900, 30"Dia. x 84"H. $875-1100

B. **Crown**; Rope rack; oak frame on rollers, holds five sizes of rope on cast-iron reels, c.1890, 29"W x 29"D x 101"H. $1100-1600

C. **Eveready**; Flashlight batteries counter display; lithographed tin, c.1925, 8-3/4"W x 11-1/2"D x 11-1/2"H. $275-350

D. **Eveready Daylo**; Battery display case; oak with reverse etched glass front, shelf and molded tray hold batteries, c.1920, 21"W x 12"D x 12"H. $285-375

A. **Horse Shoe**; Wringer display rack; oak rack with hooks to hang wringers from, cast-iron legs, c.1910, 40-1/2"W x 21"D x 64"H. $425-600

B. **Icy-Hot Thermos**; Display; tin lithographed, c.1940, 32"H. $275-350

C. **Master "Quality" Padlock**; Display rack; holds 12 sizes of locks, deeply stamped figure of lion holding lock in mouth, c.1920, 11"W x 32-1/2"H. $275-350

D. **Ray-o-Lite**; Flashlight display cabinet; tin wood grain litho, back lit top, *Prop. of French Battery & Carbon Co., Madison, WI.*, c.1924, 17-1/2"W x 14"D x 29"H. $350-425

E. **Star Rite Heating Pads**; Counter display; tin with litho on stand-up marquee, 12-1/4"W x 7-1/2"D x 9-1/2"H. $200-275

A. **20th Century Wringer**; Display; two-sided wood display with metal sign on top "20th Century Wringers - Everyone Warranted - Simmons Hdwe. Co. Inc., - St. Louis, MO. USA", holds three wringers on each side, 72"H. $500-750

B. **U.S. Enamel Ware**; Display light; reverse lit bent glass on red/black wood base, 8"W x 4"D x 14"H. $375-500

C. **Varcon**; Piston ring display; tin with advertising panels on inside of doors, c.1920, 22"W x 8"D x 26"H. $225-300

D. **Varcon**; inside view of C.

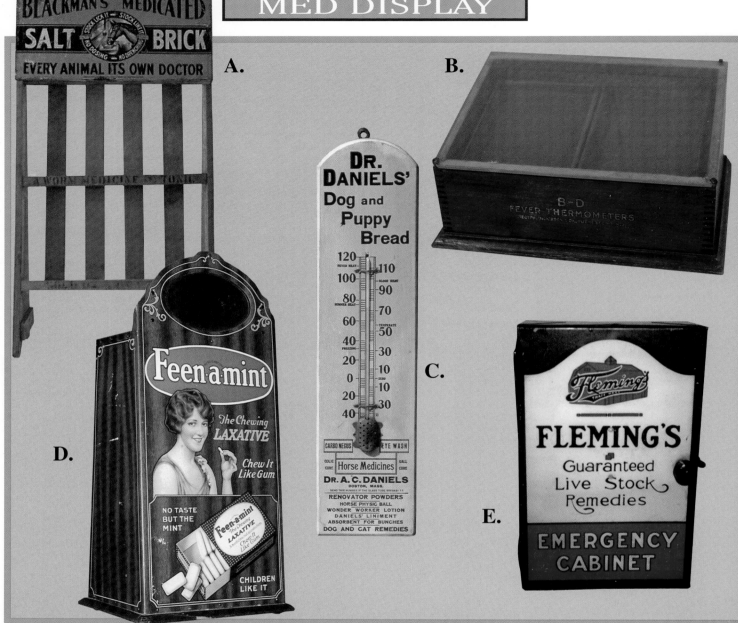

A. **Blackman's**; Wooden floor display; tin marquee shows horse licking "Salt Brick", *Blackman Stock Remedy Co. Chattanooga, Tenn.*, 16-1/2"W x 31-1/2"H. $200-400

B. **B-D** Fever Thermometers; Display case; *Becton, Dickerson & Co., Rutherford, NJ*, 14-1/2"W x 10-1/2"D x 7"H. $225-275

C. **Dr. Daniels'**; Thermometer; wood, c.1910, 6"W x 24"H. $600-800

D. **Feen-a-mint**; Laxative display; multi-colored lithographed tin, c.1920, 8"Dia. x 5"D x 16"H. $575-700

E. **Fleming's** Guaranteed Live Stock Remedies; Traveling case; metal, c.1920, 6-1/2"W x 2-1/2"D x 10"H. $600-800

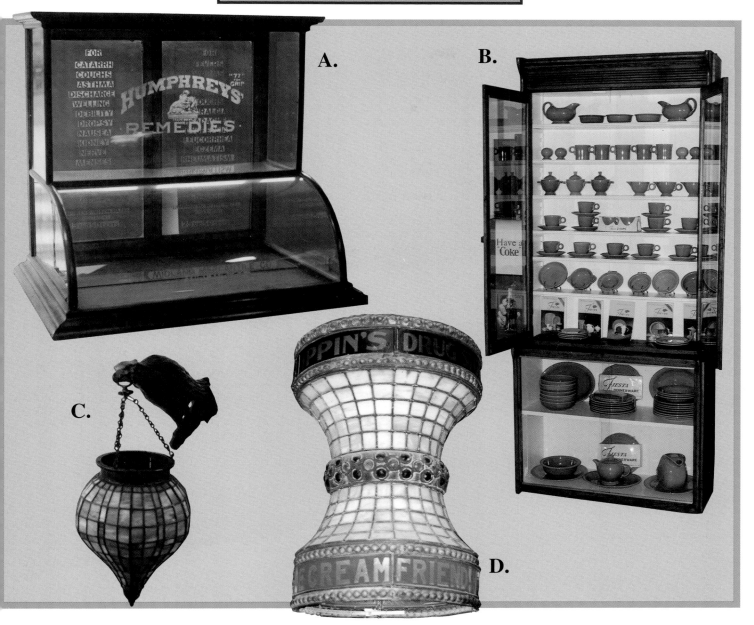

A. **Humphreys'** Remedies; Counter show-case; oak, curved glass, remedies etched on rear glass, logo and merchant name etched on front glass, *Midland Mercantile Co., Midland, GA, est. 1832*, c.1900, 36"W x 26"D x 33"H. $2200-2800

B. Oak drug store single section step back wall fixture; 40"W x 18"D x 7'-10"H. $1000-1200

C. Apothecary globe; cast iron eagle holds hanging stained glass globe, c.1900, eagle is 19"L, globe hangs 21"L. $1800-2200

D. Mortar sign; leaded glass light fixture in shape of mortar with jeweled center band, c.1900, 23"Dia. x 34"H. $3200-4000

A. Apothecary countertop partition; with bottom (not shown), butternut, gold leaf and reverse painted glass, Parke Davis, Prescriptions, Sundries, Candies, Kodaks - early c.1890, 73"W x 24"D x 49"H. $4000-5000

B. Apothecary countertop partition; (without lower counter section), gessoed faux grain painted pine, satin finish and engraved reverse painted glass panel, c.1890, 77"W x 23"D x 52"H. $2800-3500

C. Oak drug store three section step back wall display fixture; c.1900, 6'W x 24"D x 7'H. $3600-3800

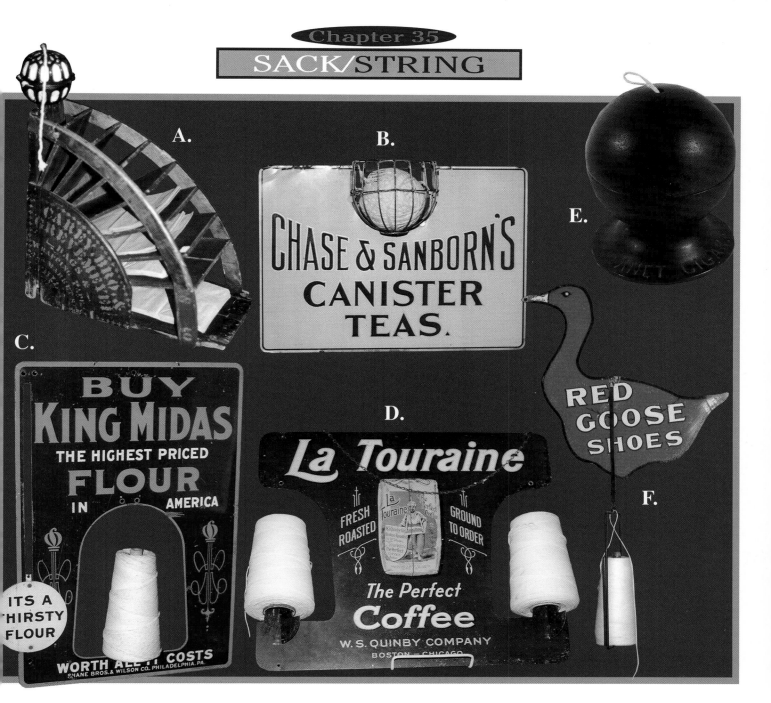

A.   **Carey Bro. & Grevemeyer**; Sack rack; stenciled wood with iron string holder and bag rack, 8"W x 16"D x 20"H. $350-425

B.   **Chase & Sanborn's**; String holder; tin, litho, two sides, 13"W x 10"H. $350-425

C.   **King Midas** Flour; String holder; metal die-cut, litho, *H.D. Beach Co., Coshocton, OH*, c.1910, 20"W x 13-1/2"H. $1400-1550

D.   **La Touraine** Coffee; String holder; metal die-cut, litho two sides, holds two string spools, unusual, c.1910, 20-1/4"W x 17"H. $3700-4000

E.   **Planet** Cigar; String holder; cast iron, c.1900, 6"Dia. x 6-1/2"H. $400-500

F.   **Red Goose**; String holder; die-cut metal, two-sided, c.1910, 29"H. $2200-3000

A. **Red Seal** White Lead; String holder; two-sided die-cut tin shows Dutch boy painting, three-dimensional pail holds string, 14-1/2"W x 27"H. $2500-4000

B. **Snow King** Baking Powder; Bag holder; die-cut tin signs in shape of can on both sides, 16-1/2"H. $1000-1500

C. **U.S. Hame Co.**; String holder; two-sided, shows T.M. buffalo on logo framed by two horse hames, lithographer *Chas. W. Shonk Co.*, 11-1/2"W x 26"H. $2500-4000

D. Sack rack and string holder; wire, c.1900, 10"W x 14"D x 40"H. $375-450

E. Sack rack; wire and wrought iron, each rack size held in place by spring-loaded "hold down", c.1910, 10"W x 15"D x 31"H. $325-425

F. Sack rack; wood and wire on revolving base, probably *Diefendorf Novelty, Alliance N.Y*, c.1910, 7"W x 7"D x 40"H. $250-325

A. **Cook's** Patent Safe; cast iron and steel, painted letters and trim, N.P. dial & handles, "Guaranteed Fire and Water Proof", c.1910, 9"W x 10"D x 14"H. $600-700

B. **The Hall's Safe Co.**; cast iron and steel, mtn. scene painted on door, N.P. hinge, dial & handle, "Montana Liquor Co., Butte, Mont." below door, Cin., Ohio, c.1900, 17"W x 18"D x 27"H. $575-600

C. **Hall's Safe & Lock Co.**; cast iron and steel, cast relief trim around door, N.P. hinge pins, dial & handle, door lettering and striping painted, Cin. & S.F, c.1910, 22"W x 24"D x 34"H. $575-625

D. **Meilink's** Home Deposit Vault; cast iron and steel with N.P. dial & trim, painted lettering and door trim, c.1910, 9"W x 10"D x 14"H. $675-775

E. Bank burglar alarm; cast iron, heavy relief of bulldog, "Always on the Job", *Bankers Elec. Prot. Co., Minn.*, c.1900, 6-1/2"W x 7-1/2"D x 21-1/2"H. $1400-2000

A. **Meilink's** Home Deposit Vault; cast iron and steel, mountain scene, c.1910, 9"W x 10"D x 14"H. $700-750

B. **Norris Safe & Lock Co.**; cast iron and steel on wheels, Seattle and Portland, c.1910, 19"W x 20"D x 30"H. $500-600

C. **Victor Safe & Lock Co.**; cast iron and steel on wheels, painted medallion on door, "Highest Award - Grand Prize Louisiana Purchase Expo, St. Louis, 1904", nickel-plated dial, handle and hinge pins, Cincinnati, Ohio, c.1905, 13"W x 15"D x 22"H. $575-650

D. **Ward's** Home Deposit Vault; cast iron and steel, painted trim and mountain fortress medallion on door, c.1910, 9"W x 13"D x 13"H. $575-675

E. Floor safe box; unmarked, cast iron and steel, nickel-plated dial and knob, c.1900, 12"W x 10"D x 8"H. $350-400

A. **Angldile**; Scale; front view, original condition, c.1910, 16"H. $450-600

B. **Angldile**; Scale; back view of A.

C. **Angldile**; Scale; restored, glass tray, base with cast legs, c.1910, 20"W x 10"Dia. tray, $800-1000

D. **Angldile**; Scale; original paint, glass tray, c.1910, 20"W x 10"Dia. tray, $700-850

E. Borden's Homo Milk; Penny scale; painted sheet metal body over Hamilton scale, c.1950, 48"H. $2800-3500

A. **Dayton**; Computing scale; painted cast iron with nickel-plated brass pan and trim, Dayton, OH, c.1900, 14"W x 8"D x 8"H. $550-700

B. **Dayton**; Grocery scale; restored with brass trim and tray, c.1910, 30"H. $800-1200

C. **Dayton**; Scale; original condition, green computing hardware scale with mirror and tin hardware bulk scoop, c.1910, 32"H. $225-350

D. **Dayton**; Scale; restored, beam with weights, c.1900, 16"W x 8"D x 10"H. $600-800

E. **Dayton**; Grocery scale; painted, brass trim, glass tray, c.1920, 17"H. $185-300

SCALES

A. **Dayton**; Scale; restored, grocery computing scale, glass tray and brass trim, mirror on top, c.1910, 32"H. $800-1100

B. **Dayton**; Scale; candy store scale with nickel-plated scoop, original condition, c.1910, 12"W x 4"D x 14"H. $275-400

C. **Dayton**; Scale; grocery computing scale, gold paint with marble tray and nickel-plated brass trim, mirror on top, original condition, c.1910, 32"H. $250-400

D. **Express**; Scale; restored, beam with weights, c.1900, 20"W x 8"H. $325-500

E. **Fairbanks**; Hardware scale; cast iron, beam with platform, tin scoop, original condition, c.1900, 24"H. $125-250

F. Grapette Grape Soda; Penny scale; plastic body over iron and steel Hamilton scale, c.1950, 45"H. $2300-2800

A. **National**; Candy scale; "Pennsylvania", #U-4, restored, nickel-plated trim and pan, c.1910, 9"W x 4"D x 10"H. $375-500

B. **National** Store Specialty Co.; Scale; restored, c.1910, 12"W x 4"D x 14"H. $325-450

C. **Dayton**; Planters scale; "fantasy" restoration, c.1920, 12"W x 4"D x 14"H. $375-500

D. Rocket penny scale; plastic body over iron and steel Jennings scale, c.1950, 52"H. $2900-3300

E. Royal Crown Cola; Penny scale; plastic body over iron and steel Hamilton scale, c.1950, 45"H. $2000-2500

F. Upper 10 Soda; Penny scale; plastic body over iron and steel Hamilton scale, c.1950, 45"H. $3000-3500

A. **Standard** Computing Scale Co.; Scale; restored, "Ice Cream Hand Packed", c.1920, 32"H. $475-800

B. **Standard** Computing Scale Co.; Scale; fantasy "Drink Coca-Cola" restoration, c.1920, 32"H. $675-900

C. **Standard** Computing Scale Co.; Hanging scale; restored, "Fresh Produce", c.1920, 30"H. $550-800

D. **Toledo**; Scale; restored, lights up, c.1930, 20"H. $275-400

E. **Toledo**; Butcher's scale; restored, ornate trim, beveled mirror above dial, plaque on back reads "Toledo Honest Weight and Values Guaranteed", c.1910, 33"H. $800-1200

F. **Trumbulls**; Novelty scale; restored, ornate cast iron and brass, c.1877, 14"H. $275-400

A. **Carruther's Figaro Shoes**; Shoe bench pair; ash and stained birch, 62"W. $675-775

B. **Crossett**; Shoe stand; wood with applied lettering, c.1900, 5"W x 5"D x 20"H. $150-200

C. **Hamilton Brown Shoe Co.**; Countertop shoe display; tin, die cut, shows Hamilton Brown logo, 9"H. $100-150

D. **Peters Shoes**; Shoe display; wood grained tin display for two shoes, directions on back, 10"H. $75-150

E. **Peters Shoes**; Shoe display; die-cut metal for "Diamond" brand shoes, two pieces, c.1915, 7-1/2"W x 4"D x 12"H. $185-250

A. **Red Goose Shoes**; Shoe bench; wood with cast-iron frame, three seats, "The Atlantic Shoe for Men, Red Goose School Shoes, The Pacific Shoe for Women" c.1920, 60-1/2"W x 35"H. $800-1200

B. **Star Brand Shoes**; Store bench; oak and ash, with pierced back panel, 59"W x 36"H. $550-700

C. **Victory Footwear**; Figural display; unusual painted figural fighting cock on composition display for boys, maids and children's shoes, c.1920, 10"W x 13"D x 24"H. $450-575

D. **Woodlawn Mills**; Shoe lace tin service station display, shows man driving shoe car while attendant services laces, c.1920, 11-1/2"W x 11-1/2"D x 11"H. $500-750

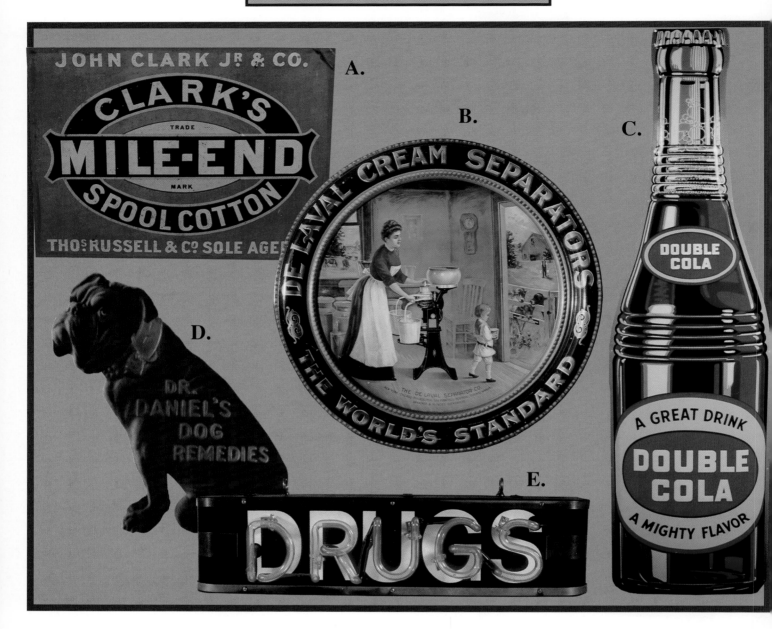

A. **Clark's** Mile-End Spool Cotton; Sign; 18-1/2"W x 14-1/2"H. $900-1200

B. **DeLaval** Cream Separators; Sign; embossed, multi-color tin litho, c.1907, 26"Dia. $4500-5500

C. **Double Cola**; Sign; tin, die cut, embossed, 65"H. $1800-2200

D. **Dr. Daniel's**; Sign; unique embossed die-cut cardboard sign of bull dog advertising Dr. Daniel's Dog Remedies, right front leg doubles as easel, 10"W x 15-1/2"H. $1300-1700

E. Drugs; neon sign; red neon, *Neon Products, Lima, OH*, c.1940, 22-1/2"W x 6-1/2"D x 6"H. $375-525

A. **Glover's** Dog Remedies; Sign; multi-colored litho on cardboard, c.1910, 28"W x 18"H. $400-600

B. **Grape Smash**; Sign; tin, c.1913, 11-1/2"W x 36"H. $3300-3600

C. Exterior sign; "Hands Cafe Pool Hall", two-sided metal with pierced letters and glass behind, reverse lit, c.1930, 41"W x 6"D x 28"H. $775-1000

D. Exterior sign; "Hardware", primitive wood back and frame with embossed zinc letters, c.1900, 86"W x 13-1/2"H. $650-800

A. Hat maker trade sign; copper and tin. c.1880, 42"W x 32"H. $6000-6700

B. Hat maker trade sign; cast-iron painted, c.1910, 7-1/2"H. $750-850

C. Horse head trade sign; wood with glass eyes, jewel in bridle, c.1890, 14"H. $3200-3700

D. Exterior sign; "International Harvester, McCormick Deering", wood frame metal panel with sand paint, c.1920, 120"W x 30"H. $1100-1500

E. **J. & P. Coats'**; Sign; tin, embossed "Crochet & Darning Cottons", c.1910, 24"W x 20"H. $1100-1300

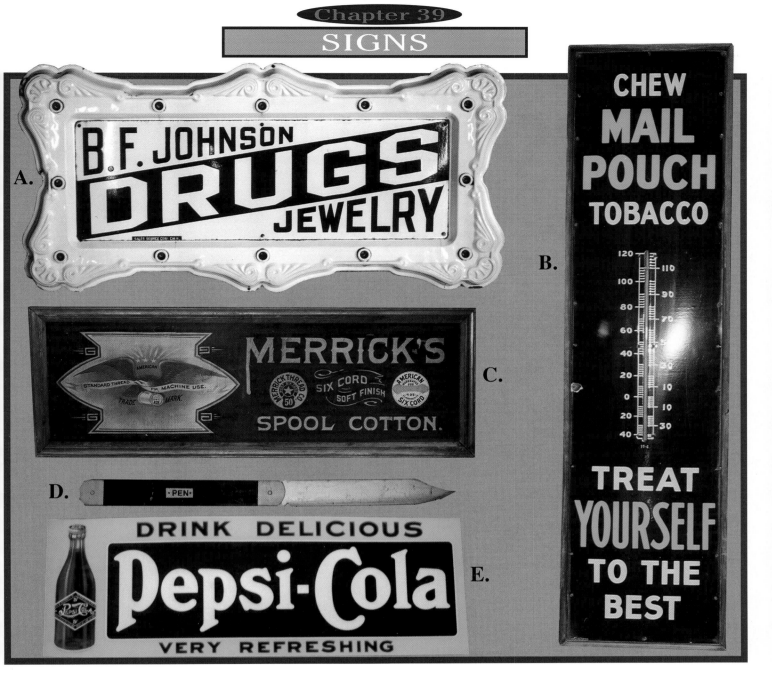

A. Exterior drug store sign; "B.F. Johnson", embossed porcelain, two-sided with porcelain panel, electrified to hold light bulbs, *Sales Service Corp., Chicago, IL*, c.1910, 72"W x 5"D x 34"H. $1500-2000

B. **Mail Pouch** Tobacco; Exterior thermometer; wood frame, porcelain advertising panel, c.1910, 19-1/2"W x 73-1/2"H. $750-900

C. **Merrick's**; Fabric banner; in wood frame, 64"W x 22"H. $1100-1500

D. **Pen** Pocket Knife; Trade sign; pine, c.1920, 48"W. $625-750

E. **Pepsi**; Sign; rare early tin, 39"W x 13-1/2"H. $4500-5200

A. Exterior sign; "Peter's Shoes", wood with sand paint, *Press Sign Co., St. Louis, MO*, c.1910, 94-1/2"W x 39-1/2"H. $850-1000

B. **Pratts** Food; Sign; "Greatest Animal Regulator" for Horses and Cattle, paper litho, c.1910, 28"W x 18"H. $150-250

C. Razor trade sign; pine with tin blade, razor closes like real one, c.1915, 14"W x 14"H. $275-350

D. **Royal Crown**; Sign; tin, die cut, bottle-shaped, embossed with pyramid logo, 59"H. $2700-3100

E. **RCA Victor**; Neon sign; red and blue neon, die-cast letters, reverse deep etched glass, *Neon Products, Lima, OH*, c.1940, 24"W x 6"D x 11"H. $950-1200

A.   Toilet Goods; Neon sign; blue neon, surrounds reverse deep etched glass, *Neon Products, Limo, OH*, c.1936, 27-1/4"W x 5-1/2"D x 7-1/2"H. $450-625

B.   Tru Art Diamonds; Neon sign; blue neon, surrounds reverse deep etched glass, *Neon Products Inc., Lima, OH*, c.1938, 22"W x 6"D x 12-1/2"H. $450-625

C.   Exterior sign; "Walkover Shoes", wood letters with wood frame on sand painted metal pierced panel, c.1910, 59"W x 28"H. $825-1000

D.   Watch trade sign; "E.L. Kneale Jeweler", cast iron and tin, two-sided, c.1900, 17-1/2"Dia. x 26"H. $575-700

E.   Watch trade sign; jewelers, cast iron and tin, two-sided, c.1900, 24"Dia. x 35"H. $625-725

A.   Watch trade sign; cast iron and tin, two-sided, c.1900, 34"W x 28"H. $2600-3000

B.   Watch trade sign; "F.S. Garrabrant Watchmaker", cast iron and tin, two-sided, c.1900, 21"Dia. x 29"H. $600-700

Bibliography

Auction Results;

Roy Arrington's Victorian Casino Auctions; May, 1998; Oct., 1997; May, 1997; Sept., 1996; May, 1994; May 1992.

Noel Barret Antiques and Auctions; April 1989

James D. Julia Inc., Nov., 1997; May, 1997; Nov.,1996; Nov.,1995; June, 1994; Nov., 1993; Oct./Nov., 1992.

Reno Oliver Auctions; March, 1991; Nov., 1989.

Richard Opfer Auctioneering; Oct., 1992; March, 1991; March, 1990.

Sotheby's; Sept., 1994.

Trade Catalogues;

Advertisement Display Mediums, Retail Management, International Textbook Company, (240 pages), 1909.

Barber Supplies Furniture, Kraut & Dohnal, Chicago, IL, Catalogue #2, (178 pages), 1910.

Hatch Barber Supply Co. Chairs & Furniture, Cedar Rapids, IA, (172 pages), 1911.

Meyer Bros. & Co. Illustrated Catalogue and Prices Current, St. Louis, MO, (631 pages), 1887.

Semi Frameless Show Cases, The Wadell Company, Inc., Greenfield, OH, (16 pages), 1927.

Showcases and Store Fixtures, H. Pauk & Sons Mgf. Co., St. Louis, MO, Catalogue No. 16, (103 pages), 1900.

Showcases and Store Fixtures, J.W. Storandt Mfg. Co., Rochester, NY, (104 pages), 1905.

Waddell Postal Fixture Co. Catalogue, Greenfield, OH, (60 pages), 1906.

Books;

Cravens, David W., Gerald E. Hills, and Robert B. Woodruff, *Marketing Decision Making: Concepts and Strategy* (Homewood, IL, Richard D. Irwin, Inc.) 1976.

Edwards, Charles M. Jr., and Russell A. Brown, *Retail Advertising and Sales Promotion* (Englewood Cliffs, NJ, Prentice-Hall, Inc.) 1959.

Engel, James E., Martin R. Warshaw and Thomas C. Kinnear, *Promotional Strategy Managing the Marketing Communications Process* (Homewood, IL, Richard D. Irwin, Inc.) 1979.

McCarthy, E. Jerome, PH.D., *Basic Marketing: A managerial approach sixth edition* (Homewood, IL, Richard D. Irwin, Inc.) 1978.

Petretti, Allan, *Petretti's Coca-Cola Collectibles Price Guide: 10th Edition* (Dubuque, IA, Antique Trader Books) 1997.

Individuals;

Cohen, Joseph C., Fort Lauderdale, FL; B.A. in Business Administration, collector, clock expert, national speaker for regional NAWCC meetings, author of "Evaluation, Research and Pricing of Antique Clocks", instructor at Florida Atlantic University, watch and clock consultant to ISA appraisers, local President of NAWCC Chapter.

Walker, Mildred D., Waco, TX; Curator of Collections, Dr. Pepper Museum, Waco, TX.

INDEX

318

INDEX

INDEX